Soldiers
of the
Strange Night

Soldiers
of the
Strange Night

Robert A. Newton

FREEDOM STREET PRESS
HILLSBORO, OREGON

Freedom Street Press
Hillsboro, Oregon
www.freedomstreetpress.com

Editor: Holly Franko, My Word! Editorial Services
Book Designer: Jennifer Omner, ALL Publications
Indexer: Sheila Ryan, Ryan Indexing

PUBLISHER'S CATALOGING-IN-PUBLICATION DATA
Newton, Robert A.,
    Soldiers of the Strange Night/Robert A. Newton
    Includes bibliographical references and index.
    LCCN: 2014918780
    ISBN: 978-0-9905036-0-6 (paperback)
    ISBN: 978-0-9905036-1-3 (ePub e-book)

To the memories of Robert J. Frie, MD,
and Joe Kienly,
the best friends any family ever had.

And to the iron soldiers of the First Armored Division, the
first American tank force to engage the German army in desert
combat and the only one of sixteen US armored divisions in
World War II not to receive any desert warfare training.

Most especially, to the noble *Famiglia Viozzi* and all
the courageous *contadini* who sacrificed everything
to help desperate men behind enemy lines.

Everything in this world had stopped except war
and we are all men of a new profession out in
a strange night caring for each other.
—Ernie Pyle, *Brave Men*

Contents

PART VI — BESIDE THE RIVER ASO

PART VII — RESCUE EFFORTS

PART VIII — LEGACY

Preface

From the balcony of my hotel room in Santa Vittoria in Matenano, I could faintly discern the modest skyline of the village of Servigliano, six miles in the distance. The emerald foothills seemed to roll in from the north like waves breaking on a towering shore. It was the summer of 1999, and many of the hills were checked with golden patches of harvested wheat fields broken by occasional outcrops of walnut or poplar trees rising from the scrub. On the rooftop, the air was still and I was alone with my thoughts.

I closed my eyes and tried to picture the night of September 14, 1943, when nearly 2,000 British and American prisoners of war escaped from Camp 59 in Servigliano and headed south into the unknown, most mistakenly believing that the Allied armies were only a matter of days away. The hilltop town of Santa Vittoria was on this southern passage to freedom, just about midway between the Adriatic Sea and the Sibylline Mountains. My arrival there was the culmination of a ten-year quest to discover the truth about the fate of my uncle and namesake, Robert Alvey Newton, known to family and friends as Alvey, an escaped American prisoner of war who was recaptured by persons unknown and executed on March 9, 1944, beside the nearby River Aso. Looking due north, I wondered if during the night of his escape, Alvey had taken the overland verdant route unfolding before me, or had chosen to stick to the road, which was easier, but also extremely dangerous.

Actually, my interest in learning the truth had developed long before my ten-year pursuit. While still a young boy, my father provided me with few details about his older brother who had been killed in World War II. Dad knew only that Alvey had been in the US First Armored Division, was captured by the Germans in North Africa and sent to a prisoner of war camp somewhere in Italy. As the basic story went, Alvey and a "Polish kid" were discovered hiding in a haystack in a barn by searchers who probed the hay with their bayonets. The two escaped soldiers were given cigarettes and then immediately executed by Italian Fascists. A letter from the US Army to my grandmother Susie had affirmed that Alvey was murdered by Italian Fascists.

Dad also mentioned that Alvey was both a scholar and an avid outdoorsman, who referred to Henry David Thoreau as "my tutelary god." It was also evident that my uncle had a strong appreciation for the irreverent, which seems to run in our family. Through the years, additional particulars regarding Alvey's fate surfaced, thanks to the extraordinary efforts of Joe Kienly and Robert J. "Doc" Frie, MD, my uncle's boyhood friends from their hometown of Logansport, Indiana.

At the dawn of World War II, Joe Kienly entered the United States Army as a private. He emerged as a major in 1955. Assigned to the quartermaster branch of the Eighty-second Airborne Division, he was engaged in some of the fiercest actions of the war in Holland, France, Belgium (including the Battle of the Bulge), and Germany and was awarded the Bronze Star, Purple Heart, and Combat Infantryman's Badge, among other decorations.

Subsequently, as the war wound down, Joe Kienly began to pursue the details about what had really befallen his friend both in North Africa and Italy. His search for the truth was impeded by the reticence of government agencies at that time to release any information pertaining to prisoners of war and American soldiers who had been killed in action. In fact, repatriated American prisoners were warned not to talk to anyone about their experiences behind the lines as that might jeopardize ongoing operations, or those still under enemy control, or evading capture.

Nevertheless, before he left the service, Joe Kienly was able to discover valuable pieces of the puzzle, which led to the revelation of an incredible story. In particular, he discovered that Alvey had been captured during the Kasserine, Tunisia, series of battles and killed near Santa Vittoria in Matenano, Italy, near a grain storehouse. In fact, Joe Kienly was somehow able to obtain a topographic map of the area and marked the exact spot with an "X" and the notation "Alvey Killed Here." The questions of who killed him and why remained mysteries for nearly a decade after that.

In letters home from the prisoner of war camp, Alvey provided scant details about the battle and the resulting burns to his hands and face. He did not want to worry his mother and father, so he just related these facts to his friends and asked them not to say anything. Nothing at all was heard from him after August 1943, and, consequently, nothing was known about the final months of his life after escaping from the camp in early September 1943.

But in the summer of 1964, Alvey's other childhood pal, Doc Frie, had an opportunity to travel to Italy with his friend, Tony Cruciani, in conjunction with a tour sponsored by the Sons of Italy fraternal organization. As it happened, the tour group itinerary included a stop in San Benedetto del Tronto, on the Adriatic Sea about twenty miles east of Santa Vittoria in Matenano.

Doc Frie and Tony Cruciani rented a car and drove west into the Apennine hill country, with Joe Kienly's topographic map as their only guide. About fifteen miles up the winding road to Santa Vittoria, Doc and Tony crossed a wooden bridge, probably over the River Aso. Doc told me that as they came to the other side he sensed in his spirit, "this is the place." He asked Tony to stop at a nearby restaurant beside the road to inquire if the local Italians knew anything about his friend.

Tony spoke Italian fluently, so Doc believed that they would be able to overcome any language barrier. They seated themselves at a table and a waitress appeared from the back of the room to take their order. As they studied their menus, Doc asked Tony to ask their waitress if she knew anything about a tall American soldier named Robert Newton, who had been killed near there twenty years before. The woman began to cry. Through her tears, she kept repeating the name "Roberto Newtoni. Roberto Newtoni." She had not only heard something about the American soldier, he had actually lived with her family after escaping from the prison camp at Servigliano.

The server, Maria, took them home to meet her family, who lived on a small farm just three miles from Santa Vittoria. There, as Tony translated, Doc learned that Alvey had stayed with Maria's family for many months after his escape from the camp. He had worked on the farm alongside her brothers to earn his keep. The family told Doc and Tony that Alvey spoke perfect Italian, had taught them to play pinochle, made wooden toys for the children and spoke of his plans to study to become a doctor after the war.

Finally, they told Doc and Tony that Alvey and another American soldier, "Martino," were hiding in a stable next to the house when they were surrounded by a German convoy that came swiftly down the road to the house. The two Americans were recaptured, then driven to a river and shot. The family said that the Germans who had murdered the Americans wore the black uniforms of the SS.

Before leaving the area, Doc took numerous photographs of the family and surrounding area and then immediately returned home due to his packed surgery schedule. Tony stayed in Italy with the tour group. Back home in California, Doc had the pictures developed but discovered that none of them had turned out. So he placed a call to Tony, who was still in Italy, and asked him to go back to the family and take replacement pictures. Tony did so, and Doc then had Tony's photos made into slides.

In the summer of 1965, my mom and dad and I went to Doc Frie's house for a party. My grandmother, Susie Newton; Doc's mother, Maggie Frie; and Joe Kienly and his wife, Nellie, were also there. While the women were visiting outside in the summer house, Doc called me, my father, and Joe Kienly into his living room and asked if we would like to see his slides from Italy. We all said we would, so he set up the projector.

Doc then asked my dad if he thought that my grandmother would like to see the slides as well. But my father told him that he believed that my grandmother was satisfied with what she already knew about her son's death. As Doc clicked through the slides, he provided a running narrative about what each depicted. The last slide in the series showed the spot where the Italians told Doc that Alvey had been killed.

In November 1978, I drove my parents to the wedding of Doc Frie's daughter Teresa. Joe and Nellie Kienly were also there. After the reception, we were all invited up to the Fries' home in Miraleste on the Palos Verde Peninsula. My dad, Doc, Joe, and I were all sitting around the kitchen table, enjoying stories about their lives growing up in Logansport, when Doc abruptly got up and went into an adjacent study. He returned cradling Alvey's Kaywoodie pipe in his hands. Doc pointed out the most celebrated inscription and a few others. Then he packed the pipe with tobacco and lit it. Joe Kienly, my dad, Doc, and I each took a puff.

After my dad's death a few years later, Doc asked me to come up to his house. After dinner, he and his wife, Edie, and I were sitting around the dining table. Just as he had done years earlier, Doc got up suddenly, left the room and returned with the Kaywoodie pipe. This time, with tears in his eyes, he handed it to me. I asked him if he was sure that was what he wanted to do, and he said it was.

Doc died about three years later. After his death, Edie gave me a picture of Alvey with his tank crew, Joe Kienly's topographic map, all of the Santa Vittoria negatives and slides, as well as a stack of letters Alvey had written to Doc during World War II from Fort Knox, Northern Ireland, North Africa, and then Italy while he was a prisoner of war. From my dad, I had also inherited Alvey's Purple Heart.

In 1989, I began researching this story in earnest. Two years later, I responded to an ad in my local newspaper announcing a meeting of the Northwest Chapter of the First Armored Division Association. It had been placed by Pete Fix, who had been in the Sixteenth Armored Engineer Battalion, a subunit of the First Armored Division in North Africa and Italy.

My wife, Shannon, and I were welcomed into the home of Pete and June Fix in Portland, Oregon, where we met some of the soldiers who had served in the same battalion with my uncle in North Africa and were captured with him at the Battle of Sidi Bou Zid, Tunisia, on February 15, 1943. They gave me numerous insights and additional leads, and suggested that I attend the upcoming national reunion of the First Armored Division later that year in Louisville, Kentucky.

I flew to Louisville in the summer of 1991, where the First Armored Division Association was celebrating the fiftieth anniversary of its formation. At Louisville, I met even more soldiers and ex-prisoners of war who told me their stories and gave me detailed information that led to the identification of Camp 59, in Servigliano, Italy, as the place where Alvey had been held and then escaped from. I also heard a great deal about the Battle of Sidi Bou Zid and how it unfolded and eventually debauched.

At subsequent reunions of the First Armored Division Association, I met some of the ex-prisoners of war who had been in Camp 59, then escaped and survived for months behind the lines. They in turn, led me to others whom I either met with personally, corresponded with or spoke with by telephone. The escapees provided me with crucial details and dates, as well as invaluable perspectives on what it was like to live on the run and forage for sustenance with the enemy more than likely to appear at any moment. Some even had details about the day my uncle and "Martino" were killed, having either witnessed their recapture from a distance or heard the shots that killed them.

Over the course of the next ten years, I contacted hundreds of ex-prisoners of war and veterans of the Battle of Sidi Bou Zid. Additionally, I read every pertinent book I could find, and combed the records of the National Archives in Washington, DC, and Suitland, Maryland, as well as the First Armored Division unit records maintained at Carlisle Barracks, Pennsylvania. I also obtained the directory of the American Ex-Prisoners of War organization and was able to cross-reference names and obtain current addresses of ex-prisoners through that invaluable resource.

But the most significant discovery of all until very recently was the war crimes files pertaining to my uncle's murder at the hands of German soldiers. The documents in those files included affidavits of Alvey's repatriated fellow ex-prisoners of war, who either had direct or indirect knowledge of the crime. Also to be found in the war crimes files were the names of local Italian witnesses. That was when I learned that Alvey had been sheltered and cared for by a family named Viozzi.

Along the way, everybody affiliated with the First Armored Division, the ex-prisoners of war, or their surviving family members went to extreme length to enlighten me and help me to fill in the blanks. They are all precious to me, and I will be eternally indebted to them for their grace.

My uncle touched many lives during his all-too-brief life. He indelibly impacted his immediate family, including my father, extended family, and loyal friends such as Doc Frie and Joe Kienly, to such an extent that none of them could speak about him without tears forming in their eyes.

Alvey's premature death was a signal event in the history of our family. It was one of those base tragedies that mark and change things forever. His murder underscores the terrible waste of war and the infinite sorrow attending the fact that some soldiers go off to war never to return.

But in uncovering the mysteries of his battle experiences, captivity, escape, and death, I gradually became aware of so many similar stories that a composite picture began to emerge. The collateral views of numerous witnesses to the same events, I believe, present a truer picture of the total ordeal and the overall human condition.

The former American soldiers and ex-prisoners of war did not just tell me their stories. Rather, they entrusted them to me. I am now the repository for an accumulation of battle accounts and behind-the-lines experiences that have never been related anywhere else in such quantity or detail. I have a solemn obligation to now share those stories with the public, since that was the implied reason that so many consigned them to me.

They all had fortuitous and timely help. The compassion and courage of the Italian *contadini* cannot be overemphasized. To the man, the escaped prisoners told me that were it not for the valorous intervention of the Italian people, they would have been immediately recaptured or killed. They conceded that foraging off the land could only have sustained them for a short while, particularly during the approach of winter in the Apennines.

The Allied prisoners fled into the Italian countryside in the middle of the night, with only a vague idea of the terrain, most not speaking the Italian language and not knowing what fate they would meet beyond the wire. Fortunately, they were saved by noble people who would not have been blamed if they turned away the *poveri figli* ("poor sons") out of fear of reprisals by the *fascisti* or Germans, or had succumbed to the lure of the 1,800-lira reward offered for each escapee.

Without exception, the Italian families who aided the escaped prisoners of war did so at the risk of their own lives and property. Many forfeited both. They should be celebrated for their heroic humanity as many times and in as many venues as possible.

My wife, Shannon, and I arrived at the Hotel Farfense in Santa Vittoria aboard the Mazzucca bus from Ascoli-Piceno. As we were getting situated, an elderly woman was sweeping the hallway just outside our hotel room. I asked her permission to show her some of the photographs of the Viozzi family that had been taken twenty-five years earlier. She stared at the group shots for a few moments, then pointed to one of the photos and murmured, *"in compagna,"* i.e., "in the countryside," and handed them back to me.

Later, while we were downstairs in the hotel restaurant communing with the locals and buying one another drinks, the owner of the hotel came to our table. He said that his mother had told him that we were looking for a family named Viozzi, then went on to say that he had located a woman by that name in Fermo. The owner had spoken to the woman by telephone and informed us that she and her husband would be coming to the hotel at 5:00 p.m. that evening to see us.

At about 5:00 p.m., there was a knock on our door. The manager told us that our visitors were downstairs in the hotel lobby. We were expecting two people, but as we descended the staircase, we saw ten members of the Viozzi family waiting for us below. We exchanged greetings, and I showed them Doc's photos, which they had never seen. We visited a while, and then they left. But the next morning, they returned, made us check out of our hotel and took us to their main house in Fermo, where we were treated like royalty and enjoyed a running feast for three days.

With this foundation, I now set out to relate the full scope of my uncle's story as well as the wartime adventures of his fellow soldiers and escapees as they struggled through a harrowing and fluid chain of events during the unfolding panorama of World War II.

Part I

BONDS

1

The Pirate Gang

The Victorian era township of Logansport, Indiana, rests at the confluence of the Eel and Wabash rivers. Until the middle of the twentieth century it was a premier rail crossroads with seven track lines radiating to all points of the compass. In 1901 alone, 216 trains passed through Logansport *daily* bound for Chicago, Cincinnati, Detroit, Indianapolis, Peoria, Pittsburgh, and St. Louis. Between 1880 and 1920, the population doubled from about 11,000 to 22,000, due primarily to the lure of employment in the rail industry, including the storied Panhandle Shops, where steam engines and freight cars were repaired.

It was the railroad that called my grandfather, Claude Lee "C. L." Newton, and his young bride, Susan (Alvey) Newton, from their family farmsteads in Clarkson, Kentucky, southwest of Louisville. The Newton and Alvey families were part of the emigration of Maryland Catholics to Kentucky beginning in 1785, when it was still a territory of Virginia. The emigrants were drawn by the availability of low-cost farmland and the promise of independent living in the backcountry.

C. L.'s first job as a railroader was with the Vandalia line, which ran from Logansport to South Bend. He worked his way up from general laborer, becoming a steam locomotive engineer, which in those days was viewed as an exotic and adventuresome vocation. In 1917, the Vandalia merged with the Pennsylvania Railroad, and my grandfather was employed as a steam engineer for the "Pennsy" during the remainder of his long career.

The Pennsy was an American Class 1 railroad, founded in 1846. For the first half of the twentieth century, it was the largest railroad in the United States based on traffic and revenue, and in its heyday controlled more than 10,000 miles of trackage. It was known by its motto, Standard Railroad of the World, which signified that it was the standard that all other railroads sought to emulate. There was also a solid foundation for the slogan, given that the Pennsy was an early proponent of standardization of rail equipment and had a corporate air of permanence.

C. L. and Susie were married in Kentucky in 1908. After moving to Logansport, C. L. and Susie had three sons. The first was James Glenial "Red" Newton, born in 1912. Then came Robert Alvey Newton in 1916, and my father, Joseph Norman Gray Newton, born in 1919. They also had a daughter, Mary Anderson Newton, born in 1910, who died at the age of two of spinal meningitis.

Logansport in the 1920s and 1930s was an idyllic world for young boys to roam, a "true" place with woods, rivers, lakes, hills, and gravel pits begging for exploration. Alvey's enthrallment with life in the outdoors began at a very early age. He often went into the woods alone, or with friends, traversing the banks of the rivers and streams while bearing a well-worn copy of *Walden* by Henry David Thoreau. He handwrote the following epigraph just inside the cover: "Thoreau: My tutelary god."

Alvey's express homage to Thoreau may be attributable to the first line from *Walden*.

> I went to the woods because I wished to live deliberately, to front only the essential facts of life, and see if I could not learn what it had to teach, and not, when I came to die, discover that I had not lived.

This call of the wild eventually led Alvey and his chums to form the infamous Pirate Gang. They also referred to themselves as the Floating Four. Robert Alvey Newton, Robert J. Frie, Joe Kienly, and Eugene Wormes were charter members. My dad, Joe Newton; and George Kienly, Joe Kienly's younger brother, frequently tagged along with the older boys. They had numerous adventures while exploring the local streams and fishing the rivers and at one point encountered two snakes busily devouring each other, forming a circle in the process.

On another occasion, Alvey, my dad, Robert Frie, and George and Joe Kienly were hiking in the woods "hunting" when they saw a small dog at the top of a rise. One of them shouted, "That's Boots Murray's dog." Boots Murray was a formidable town bully from the other side of the tracks who was a frequent antagonist. Without hesitation, Joe Kienly raised his .22 and fired. The bullet hit the dog in the leg and the animal bounced around yelping in pain before Robert Frie picked it up and carried it to Murray's house. Fortunately for him, Boots was not home at the time. Doc apparently explained to Mrs. Murray that it was an accident. But the awful truth can now be told.

In the winter, they looked for places to sled or glide on the ice. Once, while in the woods above a cliff, they took turns grabbing a vine and swinging out over the edge like Tarzan. But on the particular occasion in view, another boy missed the vine completely, slipped on the ice and crashed to the jagged rocks below. He was badly injured when one of the rock spines pierced his chin. The other boys then made a chair with their arms and carried him back to town for emergency treatment.

During another trip into the winter woods, the boys noticed bear tracks in the snow that paralleled their own and then quite abruptly disappeared. This caused some consternation, given the local legends that told of a monster in the Wabash River and the sounds of horses at the entrance to Mount Hope Cemetery, although there were no horses anywhere in the immediate vicinity.

Alvey and Doc joined the Boy Scouts and enjoyed summer camps with their local troop. In an essay written in the late 1930s at Indiana University, Alvey recalled the time-worn trick the older Scouts and their leaders used to play on the tenderfoot initiates. Essentially, the new boys were told around a campfire that they were going to be inducted into the Royal Order of Siam. They were blindfolded and required to recite the Scout oath and Scout laws. The candidates were twirled around several times and led into the dark woods. Depending on the troop, the route chosen could be easy or hard. Alvey's troop favored winding paths through thickets followed by radical hills. As the initiates stumbled back into the firelight and were forced to their knees, the Great Swami, or ostensible leader, then instructed them to repeat the magical words, "Owha Tanas Siam" ("O, what an ass I am.") Some of the hapless initiates had to keep repeating the phrase several times before they figured it out, initially puzzled by the uproarious laughter of their fellow Scouts.

Since any pirate gang needs a ship, after years on dry land Alvey and Robert Frie set about building a canoe from a roughly hewn log. They even persuaded Alvey's adventuresome cousin, Nell Loraine, to help them test its seaworthiness. Fortunately, the primitive transport actually floated, and Nell made it back safely to dry land. On yet another occasion, Alvey and Robert Frie and two friends made a canoe excursion to Lafayette. While they were asleep in camp, the river came up and carried away their canoes and paddles. Reflecting on the fact that they were stranded, Alvey simply said, "Well, let's just charge that up to experience. How about some breakfast?"

There were also diversions in the local parks. Since 1919, Logansport has been the home of an original Dentzel Carousel. Originally erected in Spencer Park, the attraction was moved to Riverside Park in 1949. It is one of just three original Dentzel Carousels in the entire country. The grand ride consisted of thirty-eight hand-carved wooden creatures, including lions, tigers, giraffes, goats, and even a reindeer. Significantly for the Pirate Gang, the center of the ride was supported by the mast from an old sailing ship. It does not take a great deal of imagination to envision the boys competing for who could grab the most brass rings with each revolution.

At that time and place in America, a kid might be walking down the street and suddenly spring into a handstand. There were numerous exploits and childhood "prize fights" in town as well. Boxing was then a popular sport, second only to baseball, and such amateur bouts were not uncommon. The gang's hero was Jack Sharkey, the heavyweight champion of the world after defeating Max Schmeling and the only man to face both Jack Dempsey and Joe Louis in championship prizefights. The boys had a chant about Sharkey's prowess, which has now been lost to history. Joe Kienly in particular was a dedicated boxing enthusiast. During one match in somebody's backyard, his brother, George, was fighting another kid, when Joe climbed up on a fence with a tire and urged George to maneuver his opponent a little closer so that he could drop the tire over the challenger's arms to pin them to his sides.

Life in "Logan" could also be tragically hard at times. Robert Frie's father, Joe Frie, also worked on the steam trains as a fireman. The primary job of a fireman, or stoker, on a steam locomotive was to shovel coal into the engine's firebox, making sure there was an adequate amount of fuel aboard. The fireman also helped by calling out signals for the engineer and raising or banking the fire depending on power needs during the rail journey. One such journey in 1927 ended tragically. Joe Frie was killed when his train wrecked and derailed. My grandparents had the unenviable task of bearing the news to Joe's wife, Margaret "Maggie" Frie. Maggie later said that she knew what had happened to her husband the instant she saw my grandfather's face. Joe left behind his wife and three children, Robert Frie, Joseph "Bud" Frie Jr., and Mary Louise "Sis" Frie.

In the days before antibiotics, child mortality was also a regular scourge. When friends or classmates died, they were put on view in their coffins at home behind parlor windows. The boys would walk up onto the porch or landing to pay their respects to the departed. They faced both life and death together.

Even members of the Pirate Gang had to attend school, as there were ever-vigilant truant officers on patrol. The boys went to both parochial and public schools, culminating in Logansport High School. Alvey, my father, and their brother Red all went to St. Bridget's Catholic elementary school, which was near their home. But they all became "Loganberries" at Logansport High School. According to his teachers, Alvey had the earliest promise as a scholar. He was extremely literary for his age and wrote home from Northern Ireland asking for his Latin and math books. Even on the eve of battle in North Africa, he wrote and asked for his copy of Giovanni Boccacio's *Decameron* and next asked for Montague's *Essays*. Still later, as a prisoner of war, he again included in his letter home a request for his copy of Darwin's *Origin of Species*.

It was said of him that the only thing that could keep him indoors was a good book. He was so focused on what he was reading that he did not hear and respond to people who tried to get his attention while he was intently reading something. Apart from the classics, Alvey also enjoyed math and science, particularly biology, and told several people of his plans to become a doctor someday. He and Robert Frie, in particular, enjoyed debating the relative merits of various authors and critiquing the latest movies.

This was during the height of the Great Depression. Jobs and opportunities were scarce, and the boys took whatever employment would provide them with spending money. Alvey worked in a hometown market, and my father sold magazines and worked as a movie house usher. Times were so hard that at least one of my grandfather C. L.'s brothers rode the rails as a hobo. It was not unusual for there to be a knock on the door in the middle of the night and in the morning to find an uncle asleep on the kitchen floor. But because my grandfather was a railroad engineer, he had steady work throughout the Depression in that essential industry. He was fond of saying, "Eight hours work. Eight hours play. Eight hours sleep. Eight dollars a day."

Riding the rails from hobo camp to hobo camp was fraught with danger. There were always the yard bulls who would throw them off the train. Many men were killed or injured simply trying to hop freights. There were even teenage hobos in those years. They were known as roving boys or boxcar boys. More than 250,000 young Americans left home to ride the rails to seek adventure, to look for work, or to escape from troubles at home, the Spartan regimen of orphanages, or the prospect of a long stretch in reform school.

It was also the era of bootleggers and gangsters. Al Capone's empire was just 100 miles away in Cicero, Illinois. The most notorious bank robber of all, John Dillinger, was from Indiana, and he did not spare the banks in his home state. At one holdup, he is reported to have told a bank customer trying to hand over his wallet, "We don't want your money mister, just the bank's."

Society was evolving on many fronts. Sally Rand was scandalizing the crowds with her famous bubble dance at the 1934 Chicago World's Fair. Big bands and jazz were becoming the rage. Musicals had people constantly humming show tunes. Families gathered around living-room radios to listen to their favorite programs, such as *Fibber McGee & Molly, Amos 'n' Andy, The Lone Ranger,* or *The Jack Benny Program.* People routinely sent telegrams, including singing telegrams, as well as radiograms. There were soda jerks, bellhops, and elevator operators. Men and young men would not think of coming to the dinner table without wearing a tie.

Nicknames were also popular, some without any regard for the overly sensitive. Kids called each other Sparky, Babe, Tootsie, Slim,

Beanpole, Four-eyes, and Gimpy. Understandably, Alvey was nicknamed Fig or Fig II, since his brother Red was Fig I. Robert Frie was often teased about his excess weight as a child, consequently Alvey gave him the nickname of Chubbins. Essence of Putrescence, Thing, Bobbie, and Robin were other favorite agnomens for him. Robert Frie was an excellent student but earned the reputation of always being late to class. In his 1935 yearbook, his senior classmates remembered him as follows: "When Bob enters class ten minutes late, everyone sighs, 'Better late than never.'" Therefore, it is probably no accident that he actually did become a doctor, with an official waiting room.

Joe Kienly was no stranger to the principal's office, and he quipped later in life that he enjoyed the eleventh grade so much that he was on the verge of repeating it three times. But Joe was the proverbial late bloomer. After his career in the army, he earned a master's degree and went on to become the only high school teacher in the state of California licensed to handle radioactive isotopes.

Alvey had a summer job in Colorado bucking barley on his cousins' farm. That basically involved throwing seventy-five-pound burlap bags filled with barley onto the back of a truck. This was in keeping with his ethos as an outdoorsman and abiding love for physical exertion. He reported back that the Colorado cousins were a rough crowd, as you could see the walls of their bunkhouse shake and bow out from the exterior while they fought with one another inside during their all-too-frequent bouts.

In the late 1930s, Alvey, Robert Frie, and Dick Walls made a road trip to the West Coast, driving an old jalopy with five spare tires hanging precariously from the body. They saw the ocean for the first time in their lives and enjoyed exploring Washington, Oregon, and Southern California. The desire to see the West was probably fueled by brother Red Newton's trip to the 1932 Olympics in Los Angeles, where Larry "Buster" Crabbe of Flash Gordon and Buck Rogers fame had won a gold medal in swimming the 400-meter freestyle.

Meanwhile, on the other side of the earth, ominous clouds were forming that would eventually envelope the whole world and impact the crew of the Pirate Gang forever.

2

The Farm

The Newton and Alvey clans have a long and storied history in the "holy lands" of West-Central Kentucky. Both families were part of the mass migrations of Catholics from St. Mary's County, Maryland, after the Revolutionary War. The colony of Maryland had started with noble promise in the New World. The Colonists left behind England and more than a century of war between Protestants and Catholics to found a settlement based on freedom of conscience, characterized by amiable tolerance of religious beliefs. For a time, Catholics and Protestants lived and worked side by side in a gentile harmony. But those days were short-lived.

After being invited in by the Catholics, Puritans took control of the government and then imposed a series of draconian laws targeting Catholics. The Papists were not allowed to hold office, they were excluded from voting and jury duty, their worship was restricted, intermarriage was forbidden, and Catholic lands were subjected to additional tax levies. In 1692, the Anglican Church was established as the ordained church of Maryland. Catholics suffered under these conditions of subjugation for nearly another hundred years before they sought virgin farmland and a renewed opportunity for freedom.

Religious persecution was not the only catalyst for the resettlement. The Revolutionary War had also taken its toll. For one thing, the British had consistently pillaged, plundered and ransacked Maryland, leaving many of the Catholic farmers in desperate condition. Those who could not pay their debts were compelled to forfeit their farms and lands. For another, the formerly verdant land in Maryland had gradually become depleted and fallow. But there was an unlimited supply of inexpensive, tillable soil to the west.

The year 1785 saw the formation of a Catholic League of Families, people who banded together to relocate to Kentucky and establish settlements there, primarily in what are now Washington, Nelson, Marion, and Hardin counties. In fact, at that time, Kentucky was simply regarded as an extended territory of Virginia. In 1785, about twenty Catholic families reached Kentucky. But that was just the beginning of a westward push. Between 1790 and 1810, approximately 3,000 pioneers left St. Mary's County alone, bound for Kentucky.

Both Newtons and Alveys are prominently featured in the histories of early Kentucky. They are also linked by generations of marriages to other eminent Catholic families in the migration, including the Spalding, Edelen, Gray, Carrico, Rhodes, Litsey, Clarke, Mudd, Mattingly, and Wilcox clans. My great-grandmother, Ida Ellen (Carrico) Newton was actually a fourth cousin of Daniel Boone, which is a claim also made by almost everyone in Kentucky and Missouri. Even after reaching Kentucky, both families continued to migrate within Kentucky itself, even as new counties were being formed.

Of necessity, the primary crops then were tobacco, wheat, corn, and flax. The ex-Marylanders had learned how to successfully grow tobacco as a cash crop while in Maryland. But they grew wheat to make bread, and corn as well for sustenance and animal feed. However, flax was grown on every spare plot of ground because it was needed to make clothes. Subsequently, cotton and hemp were also cultivated by the emigrants.

Members of both families eventually acquired farmland and came to rest outside the rural town of Clarkson, Kentucky, in Grayson County, about seventy miles southwest of Louisville. Others acquired or established farms near neighboring towns, counties, or states, while some offshoots left Kentucky completely for opportunities farther west, including in Colorado and California. Yet, they were all at heart a people of the land.

Newtons and Alveys, and their forebears, fought in the French and Indian War, the Revolutionary War, the War of 1812, the Civil War, and the Spanish-American War. Their descendants have contributed troops for every global conflict or police action thereafter. Although Kentucky was nominally a member of the Union during the Civil War, the truth is that it was probably the most divided and conflicted state as far as sentiments and allegiances during that dark period of US history. It was not uncommon for families to send sons to fight for the Confederacy as well as the Union. In fact, Kentuckians fought on both sides at the Battle of Pittsburgh Landing on the Tennessee River, which is known to history as Shiloh and named after the church at that site.

However, during the Civil War, the Newtons and Alveys or their immediate ancestors fought for the Union. My great-great-grandfather Anderson Gray married Mary Margaret "Polly" Litsey. Their daughter, Hannah Marie Gray, married John Alphonso "Jack" Alvey, and became the parents of my paternal grandmother, Susan (Alvey) Newton. Captain Anderson Gray is reported to have helped Judge Thomas R. McBeath recruit and organize in 1861 Company A, Twenty-seventh Kentucky Federal Infantry. Captain Gray fought at Shiloh in 1862, and was severely wounded by the explosions of cannon fire. The injury caused him excruciating ear pain for the few remaining years of his life. He died in 1867, at age forty-nine.

My uncle, Robert Alvey Newton, was not the first soldier in the family to be murdered in cold blood by vile and cowardly men. My great-great-grandfather was James Irvin Newton, who served as a private in C Company, Twelfth Regiment Kentucky Volunteer Cavalry during the Civil War. His unit initially fought in various skirmishes in Kentucky and Burnside's march into East Tennessee, before joining Sherman's campaign into Georgia and on to North Carolina and Virginia. Toward the end of the war, the Twelfth Cavalry trekked through the Blue Ridge Mountains back to Kentucky and was later involved in operations against "Sue" Mundy's guerrillas in the vicinity of Elizabethtown, Kentucky. The end of the war found the unit on duty in East Tennessee. James's involvement in the local operations against Confederate guerillas may have led to his untimely death.

The Civil War officially ended on April 9, 1865, with the signing of the surrender terms by Lee and Grant at Appomattox Courthouse. But some in the Confederacy were diehards, including John Wilkes Booth, who murdered Abraham Lincoln the following week. All organized Confederate troops were subdued by the end of May 1865, particularly after the capture of their president, Jefferson Davis, in Georgia on May 10, 1865. But in Kentucky, there were some who never surrendered, and the animosity between some families continues to this day.

James Irvin Newton had been wounded in battle and was discharged with a surgeon's certificate of disability on May 29, 1865. He returned to his home in Meadville, Meade County, Kentucky, and resumed his profession as the local blacksmith. The War Between the States was long over. But during the late afternoon of July 9, 1865, it returned to Meadville. The family was at the supper table when they heard the sound of horses in the front yard. James's wife, Elender, and the children saw James get up from the table and go toward the door. Some of the children accompanied their father to the door, including my great-grandfather, Benedict, who was eight years old at the time.

As James started to cross the front porch, he was greeted by one of the men, while the others remained mounted. The man shook hands with him with one hand and pulled a pistol and shot and killed James in cold blood with the other. Due to my great-grandfather's small stature, all Benedict could remember was the man's boots. James was murdered by Nightriders simply because he had been a Union soldier, or a Roman Catholic, or both. The attack was completely unprovoked. He was widely recognized in the community as an amicable person. In fact, on November 27, 1929, a neighbor of his named Albert Jacob Thompson provided an affidavit in support of some of James's children who were seeking compensation from the US government based upon his status as a Union Civil War veteran. Thompson was about 13 when James was murdered and 77 years of age when he made the following affirmation: "the murdered James Irvin Newton was a peaceable man, who got along with everybody peaceably and was not known to have an enemy." Thompson went on to state in the same affidavit that "I further solemnly swear that it is now and was at the time of the death of the aforesaid James Irvin Newton, my firm belief and conviction that he was killed on account of his service in the Union Army during the Civil War, and that it was the common opinion of the people of the neighborhood that his death was caused by his enlistment in the Union Army and service therein."

The family, perhaps with help from some sympathetic neighbors, buried James that night in a community cemetery in an unmarked grave on a low hill across the road from the town. He was buried at night because they were afraid that the Nightriders would come back. Although the Union Army sent patrols out from Brandenburg, Kentucky, to scour the countryside for the murderers, they were never caught. Yet, apart from the fact that feelings were running high in a community with divided sentiments, what kind of soulless monster would shoot down an unarmed man without any provocation in front of his children? My great-great-grandmother Elender was left a widow at age forty-four with nine children.

Most of James and Elender's sons became farmers. Benedict married Ida Ellen Carrico and they farmed a plot of land just outside Clarkson, Kentucky. The Alvey farm was nearby and by the 1920s was worked by Willard "Will" Conrad Alvey and his wife, Marguerite Belle Van Meter Alvey. Robert Alvey enjoyed staying at their farm as often as he possibly could to visit his three Alvey cousins, Dick, Nell Loraine, and Katharine. He would go down to the farm for extended visits as long as six weeks, to the point that his folks in Logansport were forced to often inquire as to when he might come home.

He and cousin Dick hunted hares, squirrels, and other small game in the vicinity and had other adventures fishing and swimming in local rivers and lakes. According to Dick, they were as close as brothers. On one occasion, Alvey accidentally shot a cardinal and was so remorseful that he did not pick up a gun for a long while. Alvey was very close to cousins Nell Loraine and Katharine as well. They all genuinely cherished one another's company. There were cold, bright moonlit nights when they would walk home from games. Sometimes they rode in an old Pontiac but had to push it home from town on more than one occasion. Alvey would push and jump on the running board while one of the women steered. One night the car's lights went out as they passed the Walls farm.

Katharine sent him pajamas for wear in the cooler climate of Northern Ireland. He wrote from the war front to Robert Frie, saying, "I'm telling you Bob, some men are damn fools when they don't grab onto a girl like Kathryn [sic]. She's tops." Cousin Nell Loraine, who was nicknamed "Blossom," or "Bloss," also frequently wrote to him. He sent her a five-franc note from North Africa, as well as a heart he had cut out of a crashed A-20 "Boston" bomber. Alvey wrote that he was homesick for the farm and looked forward to a time when he could again join Uncle Will smoking pipes and eating popcorn with their feet propped up on the fireplace — at least until they were scolded by Aunt Marguerite. She had also frequently chastised him for biting his fingernails. But his stays on the farm were not just about recreation. He also helped out with the crops and remarked in a letter home from Northern Ireland that he missed the cherry-picking season. Alvey claimed to be a whiz at that job but then had to concede that the bucket did not get full very fast.

Kentucky had suffered tremendous deprivation during the Great Depression. The vast majority of Kentuckians at that time were farmers. Farm incomes fell dramatically. Sharecroppers and tenant farmers were evicted from their land. Homes were abandoned. Sons left the farms to try to find work in the cities. However, because one-third of the populace was unemployed, they more often wound up in squatter communities known as Hoovervilles. Life for many was extremely dire. When President Franklin Delano Roosevelt addressed the nation in his second Fireside Chat, he said, "The country was dying by inches."

The economic disasters of the Great Depression were aggravated by adverse weather conditions. The first onslaught was the Dust Bowl, an extended drought that devastated the Great Plains and Midwest, including Kentucky. The second disaster with a local impact was the flood of the Ohio River beginning in January 1937, which lasted three months. Over seventy percent of Louisville was submerged for more than a week. Somehow the Alvey and Newton families were able to adapt and overcome the adversity of the sinking economy and weather to successfully farm their lands. But during that time in local history, survival was at a very primitive level. There was no electricity, light, heat, or indoor plumbing. Conditions really did not improve until rural electrification in the late 1930s.

In 1938, at the height of the Depression, Alvey enrolled at Indiana University and rented a house at 501 Fess Street in Bloomington. His intent was to ultimately become a doctor. But he did not shy away from courses in philosophy and literature, in addition to his science-laden curriculum. He even ventured into writing poetry and critiquing popular films of the day, such as *Dawn Patrol*. Alvey had worked at Keitzer's Grocery Store on Third Street in Logansport to earn enough money to attend, and he went whenever he could raise enough money to live in Bloomington. Sometimes he enrolled in Indiana University's extension programs.

While studying for college finals, he wrote the following legend in one of his textbooks: "Six more days, twelve more hours, egads, let's go smell the flowers." All remember him as highly intelligent, with a playful sense of humor. When his sister-in-law Carmen had her first baby, Sue Ann, he brought her a large box of candy. But when he found out that her doctor disallowed her from having any, he sat down and ate the entire box in front of her!

He was popular with girls, including girls from school named Rowena Pruitt, Monica, and Ruth, but was never in a serious relationship. He did refer to Eva Jane Blair as his "little cabbage from Oshkosh," writing home from the war. Alvey was also partial to a woman named Mary Jane, but according to Dick, Robert Alvey was not looking for a wife at that time.

Alvey continued his studies at Indiana University until late 1940. Just before he was drafted, he wrote to Eva Jane Blair and told her that he had not yet been so passionately eager to see his draft board as they soon would be to see him. He mentioned that his mother was somewhat worried about his going because she had lost a brother in the last war but now appeared to be resigned to the fact that he would be called up. Alvey also lamented that his dad was "still a belligerent pacifist." In closing, he told Eva Jane that the full realization had hit him that he was going to see her only once or twice more before going into the army, but allowed that even if army life was laborious and potentially dangerous, it would at least be exciting.

When he knew that the draft was imminent, Alvey asked his
aunt Marguerite if he could come down to the Alvey farm to
await his notice to report for induction. He was helping to roof the
barn when Marguerite went to the mailbox and found the official
envelope addressed to "Robert Alvey Newton." She immediately
knew what it was and dreaded giving it to him. Nevertheless,
he reported to his draft board and was transported to Fort Benjamin Harrison for induction into the United States Army on
September 13, 1941, less than three months before the sneak attack
on Pearl Harbor.

Part II

WARBOUND

3

Outbreak

War came to the world in escalating contractions. It is commonly perceived that World War II began on September 1, 1939, when Germany invaded Poland. But it probably began on September 19, 1931, when Japan invaded Manchuria and established the puppet state of Manchukuo. The next contraction was in October 1935, when Italy invaded Ethiopia (Abyssinia) in a colonial war and ravaged that country until it was completely conquered in May 1936. This victory over a vastly weaker nation substantially increased Benito Mussolini's popularity at home and emboldened him to become even more brazen in his aspirations for a revived Roman Empire.

The Spanish Civil War began on July 17, 1936, foreshadowing a new standard of total war. The Japanese next invaded China on December 13, 1937, and the six-week campaign known as the Rape of Nanking descended into absolute depravity. Austria was annexed into the Third Reich on March 12, 1938. That was followed by the infamous appeasement arrangement between British Prime Minister Neville Chamberlain and Adolf Hitler, signed in the early hours of September 30, 1938, which ceded the Sudetenland for absorption into Germany, without the consent or participation

of Czechoslovakia, which lost that entire territory with the stroke
of a misguided pen.

On April 1, 1939, the Spanish Civil War officially ended, and just
a week later, on April 7, 1939, Italy invaded Albania, conquering
that Balkan state in just five days. Since the world leaders appeared
to be reticent to challenge Hitler, Mussolini, or the Empire of
Japan militarily and were intent upon preserving the illusory peace,
it should not have been a surprise when Herr Hitler conjured up a
phony dispute and used that as a pretense to cross the border into
Poland on September 1, 1939. By the end of that month, Poland had
been abjectly defeated. Backed into a corner, Britain and France
were then forced to declare war on Germany just two days later.

Still, not much happened between the subjugation of Poland in
late October 1939 and April 1940, which is known to history as the
Phony War. Winston Churchill called it the Twilight War, while
the Germans alluded to the period as the *Sitzkrieg*, or Sitting War.
While German U-boats patrolled the Atlantic and sank British
shipping, England bombed German cities with millions of propaganda leaflets. For several months, the emphasis in Britain was
primarily upon homeland defense.

The Phony War ended on April 9, 1940, when Germany invaded
Denmark and Norway for the ostensible purpose of protecting
those countries from aggressive action by Britain and France. Subsequently, on May 10, 1940, Germany rolled through France and
swept into neutral Belgium, as well as the Netherlands and Lux-
emburg. The British and French were expecting another static
conflict as in World War I and were completely shocked and
routed by the new combined forces *Blitzkrieg*, or Lightning War,
introduced by the Germans. Within a matter of weeks, the British
were forced to evacuate their legions from the continent of Europe
at Dunkirk, between May 26, 1940, and June 3, 1940. The air campaign known as the Battle of Britain then began on June 10, 1940,
and ended on or about October 31, 1940.

On September 16, 1940, the United States began the first peace-time draft in its history. Registration commenced on October 16, 1940, and conscription started on October 30, 1940. America was finally preparing for an ever-widening war. It was a timely endeavor, because as of 1939, the United States had only the seventeenth-largest army in the world. That was not a credible force at all. Even tiny Romania had more troops under its flag.

Mussolini, witnessing the successes of his cohort and mentor Hitler, and perhaps because of pride or jealousy, on October 28, 1940, decided that it was an opportune time to invade Greece. His invasion eventually sputtered. By April 1941, it had become obvious that Mussolini's reach had exceeded his grasp, and Germany was compelled to ride to his rescue both in Greece and North Africa. In North Africa, German General Erwin Rommel, assisted by the Italian army, forced the British to retreat eastward through Libya and was poised to smash his way into Egypt. Meanwhile, the Germans set about conquering Greece, while simultaneously annihilating Yugoslavia in a four-pronged attack.

On March 11, 1941, President Roosevelt signed the Lend-Lease law, which provided for vast quantities of supplies and munitions to be shipped to Britain on favorable terms, since that country was rapidly running out of capital and its very existence was threatened by German U-boats. This was a barely disguised intervention by the United States, which was clearly choosing sides despite its regularly professed neutrality.

On June 22, 1941, Hitler abrogated his nonaggression pact with Josef Stalin and invaded Russia. Relations between the United States and Japan continued to rapidly deteriorate, resulting in the sneak attack on Pearl Harbor on December 7, 1941, and Hitler's ill-conceived declaration of war on the United States four days later on December 11, 1941. That same day, Mussolini chimed in with his own declaration of war, affirming that it was a pleasure to join with the Empire of Japan to bring rapid defeat to the Americans.

In the United States, by the summer of 1941, nearly one million civilians had been conscripted, augmenting the reservists and National Guardsmen. But the term of enlistment for initial draftees was only one year, which was set to expire in October 1941. Hence, the government was poised to lose two-thirds of its service personnel when the initial term expired. But after strong lobbying by the White House and Army Chief of Staff George C. Marshall, Congress passed the Service Extension Act by a single vote, whereby all military personnel were required to remain in the service for an additional six months after their original terms of service ended.

This caused an immediate fierce, irate reaction from the ranks, and the already fragile morale of the troops sank to a new low. The level of resentment rose to such an extreme that personnel vowed to join in mass desertions. They felt they had been deceived and betrayed by Franklin Delano Roosevelt and adopted the motto OHIO, which stood for "Over the Hill in October," and was often inscribed in their barracks' latrines or on artillery pieces.

The vow to go AWOL must be viewed through the lens and tenor of the times. Before Pearl Harbor, America was extremely isolationist in its outlook. Prominent America Firsters, such as Charles Lindbergh, tirelessly campaigned against US involvement in another war. There was mass resistance to helping to defend Britain at the expense of neutrality. Further, the inductees were tired of the boredom and routine of military life, as well as the nepotism that characterized many National Guard units. Some officers and noncommissioned officers gave extremely favored treatment and promotions to friends and family members at the expense of the newly inducted soldiers.

Everything changed at Pearl Harbor. A regular army of less than a million men and women increased to seven million by the end of the war, with every enlistee serving for the duration, plus six months.

4

Fort Knox

The notice that Aunt Marguerite pulled from her mailbox in the summer of 1941 directed Robert Alvey to appear at his local draft board in Cass County, Indiana. He was then transported to Fort Benjamin Harrison, near Indianapolis, for induction into the United States Army on September 13, 1941. After enduring the batteries of invasive physical examinations, injections and tests, he was sent to Fort Knox, Kentucky, for basic combat training (BCT), with Company C, Sixth Armored Replacement Battalion.

Fort Knox's Armored Force School and Armored Force Replacement Center had been established in October 1940. It was designed to address the growing threat on the horizon presented by German armor and the combined arms tactics that had only recently overpowered much of Europe, which was still enamored of static defense. In the replacement battalion, he was introduced to army protocol, discipline, and a training regimen that included armor tactics, gunnery, communications, and maintenance, over the span of twelve weeks. As the war dragged on, reversals were suffered and lessons were learned, which translated into an additional five weeks of basic training by the end of the war.

Alvey had expressed keen interest in training as a radio operator. However, the army, in its infinite wisdom, molded him into a tank gunner instead. At six foot three, it must have been a nearly insurmountable challenge for him to accommodate his lanky frame to the cramped confines of a tank. Nevertheless, he stoically accepted his lot, as so many others did in his generation. It must also be mentioned that he was initially flagged for the intelligence school. For reasons that only the army could fathom, he was not diverted from the tank corps. Although he was proud to be a tanker, he did at one time consider requesting a transfer to the Army Air Corps. But he was forced to concede that once he had acquired the specialized skills of a tank gunner, transfer to another branch of the service was extremely unlikely.

Reveille was at 4:00 a.m. and the training day ended at 4:00 p.m. The trainees would then race one another to the post exchange for a cold bottle of beer. Most private soldiers, including Alvey, frequently pulled KP (kitchen police) as well as guard duty. KP was extremely unpopular. Alvey wrote to Robert Frie, telling him about a particularly aggravating shift when those on duty were compelled to repeatedly clean the kitchen and floors. They had to scrub the mess hall from top to bottom three times a day. He claimed that he had gone through fourteen bars of GI soap washing dishes and was chewed out for using too much by the private in charge who was lobbying for a promotion to mess sergeant! Training for all must have necessarily involved many runs and marches up and down the infamous slopes of the dreaded Muldraugh Hill.

The First Armored Division had been organized on July 15, 1940, at Fort Knox. Its two light tank regiments, the First and Thirteenth, came from the Seventh Cavalry, George Armstrong Custer's storied brigade. Other army units comprising artillery, infantry, and cavalry contributed men and materiel as well. In fact, the division's triangular shoulder patch reflects its heritage by virtue of its yellow, red, and blue colors, representing the armor, infantry, and artillery branches. This pyramid of power was actually adopted in

1918 by then Lieutenant Colonel George S. Patton while he led the Tank Corps in France during World War I. Its nickname Old Ironsides was conferred by its first commander, Major General Bruce R. Magruder, after he saw a photograph of the frigate *USS Constitution,* the iconic stalwart of the War of 1812 when she captured numerous merchant ships and defeated five British warships, and is regarded as the world's first commissioned man-o'-war.

Fort Knox itself in the 1940s was a post in transition. It had been in existence since 1918, but at the dawn of World War II, the post was in the process of rapid expansion as America geared up for the emerging global conflict. It initially consisted of about 40,000 acres carved from three Kentucky counties, Hardin, Meade, and Bullitt, but by 1943 had expanded to more than 106,000 acres with 3,820 buildings. The fort's location south of the Ohio River was ideal for tank and half-track maneuvers and mock battles. On a daily basis, armored units moved out in attack formation from the steel lookout tower, OP Six, and advanced upon the "enemy" forces concentrated at various locations throughout the twenty-five-square mile wildlands of the base. In fact, the First Armored Division and Fort Knox starred in the 1941 US Army color docudrama *The Tanks Are Coming,* which featured a number of mock attacks.

In September 1941, the First Armored Division went south to Louisiana to join in three months of war games in Louisiana and Fort Jackson, South Carolina. Alvey was in the process of being drafted at that time and did not participate in the Louisiana or South Carolina maneuvers. The division did not return to Fort Knox until the day before Pearl Harbor. The very next day, the armored force suffered its first wartime casualty when Private Robert H. Brooks of D Company, 192nd Tank Battalion, was killed during the Japanese attack on Clark Field in the Philippines. That same month, the main parade ground at Fort Knox was named after him.

Except for the KP and guard duty, the fact that Alvey was stationed at Fort Knox for a time was ideal. He could go south to visit cousins in Clarkson, or go up to Indiana University in Bloomington, or Logansport to see friends and his mom and dad. His favorite haunt was the post library, although he frequently complained about the lack of engaging titles on the shelves. Once, he mentioned that he had gleaned five books, constituting a two-day supply. Alvey also frequented the post bowling alley, where in his own assessment, he was putrid.

While at Fort Knox, he wrote a number of letters to his folks, brothers, cousins, friends, and his steady, Eva Jane Blair. He lamented how there was too much time to kill after the training day was done. In one letter to Robert Frie, he recalled a friend named Riley who when asked if he would reenlist stated forthrightly, "Uncle Sam's nights are too long." Alvey affirmed that statement: "How true. Especially when there is no cash at hand."

Still he acknowledged that the hours there were much better than at Fort Benjamin Harrison. He said they could now get up at 6:15 a.m. and were off at 5:30 p.m. Their calisthenics alternated in hourly periods with lectures, mostly about what they could and could not do, and drill. But he told Frie that "the drill so far was not tough, and just like the first semester of ROTC."

The army administered both clerical and mechanical aptitude tests to him. He thought that he did well but later admitted that he was no mechanic. Alvey also commented on barracks life, and told Robert Frie that "the boys are daft on one subject — sex, and all its erotic variations." He observed that each man competed to be a bigger liar than the others.

In the same letter, he related another episode when they all had blood tests and the trooper behind him said, "I think I'm going to faint." Alvey and another soldier tried to catch the fainter as he fell into a gentle heap, knocking over racks and test tubes in the process.

The recruits practiced driving and went on motor marches, one of which was forty miles long. He said that "for sheer discomfort that was tops." They were forced to don field jackets and full field packs and rode in the back of an uncovered half-track through the pounding rain. The weather contributed to the misery as it was pouring and sleeting the entire trip.

They were also subjected to the obligatory gas-warfare training. That involved about ten men at a time entering and walking around inside of a building filled with tear gas. The first man had to wait until the last man was in before he put on his gas mask. Alvey told Robert Frie that, "Naturally, I was the first man in; tears come to my eyes now."

He chided Robert Frie to not write so big and admonished him that as a freshman (at Indiana University) he should take a writing course because his letters were so "un-collegiate." This was all good-natured ribbing, which is still common among young men in their early twenties.

As the year 1941 drew to a close, Alvey initially thought he would soon be leaving Fort Knox, but instead was transferred from the replacement unit to D Company, Second Battalion, First Armored Regiment, around New Year's Day 1942. He told his mom and dad in a letter that he had not been separated from all of his friends from the replacement center, as five of them had come to same company. He let them know that George Kienly was in the same division, but assigned to the Thirteenth Armored Regiment.

Alvey also commented to his mother and father that he had "not even seen a tank yet," but really enjoyed his training with automatic pistols, which he stated were "quite different from the revolvers we have been using." He had tried to buy the division's triangle uniform patches at the PX, but they had quickly run out of them.

As of January 1942, D Company was a light-tank company that was being transformed into a medium-tank company. The US

Army's light tank at that time was the M-3 Stuart, which sported a 37mm main gun, as well as five 30-06 Browning M1919A4 machine guns. This was the first American-crewed tank in World War II to engage in actions against enemy tanks. The medium tank at that time was also designated the M-3, but nicknamed General Grant. It featured a 75mm main gun mounted in a sponson that allowed for limited traverse, as well as a 37mm secondary gun. Alvey said that he expected to begin his training in the medium M-3 soon.

While at Fort Knox, he kept reminding his first sergeant of his interest in radio school. The first sergeant, named Sparky Keller-man, told him he expected there would be openings in the near future. About that time, the battalion commander confirmed "latrine rumors" telling the troops that they would probably be leaving Fort Knox within the month, but that only the War Department knew where or when. Alvey initially thought that their having just taken yellow fever shots in addition to many others was an ominous sign. That is, until he realized that yellow fever could be caught in all equatorial regions of the globe includ-ing Africa, South America, the Panama Canal, the Philippines, and points east of the Philippines. Still, the shot was mandatory for all personnel expected to serve in tropical regions.

Another red flag was that the army had converted to a seven-days-a-week schedule. The armored force troops were therefore only occasionally given Wednesday afternoons off. However, if they were not doing range firing, or on any special details, the troops were also off-duty on Sundays.

Still another caution was the chemical warfare lecture he and the others attended in January 1942. A staff sergeant advised them that in case of a gas attack, "the best thing to do is to grab a knife and cut it away." One of the more sensitive tankers in the crowd asked, "You mean to cut the gassed clothing away?" The sergeant fixed him with a stony stare and coldly replied, "I mean the flesh!" Alvey reported that every man in the room seemed to gulp a little.

He said another cheerful thing happened the same day. They all had to fill out cards stating the name of the person to notify in case they were killed in action. Everyone then increased their life insurance. Alvey told Robert Frie that he was now worth "five thousand bucks, though not on the hoof."

In his letters, he repeatedly urged Robert Frie to stay in school, become a doctor and enter the army as an officer to avoid the onerous burdens placed on enlisted men. In fact, he said that the army was "a foretaste of hell for me." He was speaking chiefly of the absence of time to be alone, study, and contemplate life. There was a total absence of privacy and never any opportunity to be alone. He said that if it were not for the library at Fort Knox, he would surely "go off a normal wavelength." To occupy his mind, he studied German. He observed that the United States was fighting the Germans and the German language was essential to fully understand scientific terminology. He even occupied his mind by trying to solve trigonometry problems, but concluded that like Ruth in the Bible, "I am standing amid alien corn."

His commanding officer told him in February 1942 that he would be going to intelligence school. Alvey liked that idea if only because it would get him out of KP and it represented a break from the monotony. There is no indication in the record that he ever did get to go to intelligence school. Rather, it appears that as a trained tank gunner, his immediate career had been decided by the powers that be. The downside of that was someone with native intelligence who could have fully used his mind in the service of his country was relegated to mundane tasks such as "cleaning up the tank for the umpteenth time." Still, he enjoyed working with "such a good bunch of fellows."

He went home to Logansport for the last time on a weekend pass in March 1942. In addition to his mom and dad, and brother Red, friends Rowena Pruitt, and Dick and Monica Walls stopped by to see him. They took a number of photographs. None of them knew that this would be the last time they would ever see him alive.

Alvey wrote home on April 1, 1942, to his folks to alert them to the fact that his unit would probably be leaving Fort Knox in the near future. He did not know where they would be going, but he guessed that it would be somewhere in the United States for some kind of maneuvers before leaving the country. He suggested that they come down to meet him in Louisville, Easter weekend. But he advised them that if they wanted to wait until after Easter to come down, that would be fine. A few days later, on Sunday, April 5, 1942, the First Armored Division began a mass movement by truck convoy and rail to Fort Dix, New Jersey, to await its deployment overseas.

5

Transit

Without any advance notice, the troopers were ordered to remove the triangular armored division patches from their uniforms as well as all other unit identification markings. The movement of the First Armored Division from Fort Knox to Fort Dix was supposed to be a secret. But somebody forgot to tell the citizenry of Washington Courthouse, Ohio, who waited four days for the division to roll in. The townspeople showered the war-bound troops with unabashed Midwestern hospitality. They invited "our boys" to movies, and provided them with "real" food, and hot water for shaving. Some of the local citizens hung a huge banner across main street that proclaimed in bold letters, "Welcome First Armored Division."

On April 6, the division proceeded to Washington, Pennsylvania; then Carlyle, Pennsylvania, on April 7, arriving at Fort Dix, New Jersey, on April 8. Two days later, on April 10, Alvey wrote to his mom and dad that the restriction on writing had been lifted and he advised them that he was at Fort Dix. He observed from the fact that they were housed in barracks instead of tents that it would not be a surprise if they stayed there awhile. His commanding officer told his men that "Even if we are somewhat crowded here, we're lucky to get warm barracks to sleep in."

Alvey reported that when they first came in, the rain was pouring down and they all got really wet. But after they put the tanks away, they were able to change into dry clothes. He closed his letter by telling his mother not to worry, although he said it was probably no use to do so.

While at Fort Dix, the division resumed training. There was extensive range firing and strenuous calisthenics as the men were hardened up. The administration prepared identification folders, and the men were subjected to even more immunizations. There were numerous personnel changes. They all took tank driving lessons.

He really enjoyed live firing the big tank gun. He was surprised that it did not make much noise with the tank hatch buttoned up. That was because most of the blast goes out the muzzle. But his initial impression was deceiving. He later made the mistake of sticking his head out the hatch when the big gun was fired and received the full effect of the muzzle blast, and said that it was a lulu. Yet, for him it was a genuine thrill to press the trigger and feel the backward surge of the gun. In a letter to Robert Frie he paraphrased Stuart Chase's *Men and Machines* and observed that "the machines of war are in the class of those which add to the egoism of man."

He made expert with the pistol. He found that when he held the revolver a certain way as proscribed, and squeezed off the rounds, there was a definite improvement in his performance. His hand was much steadier, and he had more confidence in his ability. He allowed that perhaps there was some method in the army's madness after all.

Alvey complained the he had been catching one guard duty after another. One time, he was in charge of six privates guarding the fort's water pumping station. It gave him quite a thrill, but the very thought of what would happen if someone tossed a bomb in the plant kept him from sleeping well. Nevertheless, he said "that didn't bother the boys any and I had a hard time keeping them from running around the country looking for women." In fact, one of the men did get together with a willing woman, but her mother caught up with her in a nick of time. As a corporal, Alvey was also in charge of quarters. He joked that he had to monitor the phones in case the president called. But he could write letters while keeping a wary eye out for the top sergeant. He said that he did not like Fort Dix much because it was commanded by an infantry general who had not endeared himself to them very much by insisting on cleanliness of barracks and lots of close order drill. He was referring to Major General Edmund L. Daley, who had the reputation of being a stickler for aggravating military routines, which the men regarded as "chickenshit."

When they were off duty, the men were given thirty-six-hour passes and went into New York City and Trenton as well as Philadelphia. On one occasion, Alvey went to the USO and read a book. Another time, forty of them went to a dance at the New Jersey College for Women in New Brunswick, New Jersey (now part of Rutgers). They had a good time dancing and flirting with the local ladies.

He remarked that he had seen the Atlantic Ocean for the first time and had been to Atlantic City, where he became rapidly broke again. For him, the dimmed lights were a little chilling. He said that although it was a large city, there was not half the sky glow there was above Logansport. The street lamps were blacked out on top and on the seaward side and the bright lights of the board-walk were all turned down. Of course, all of these measures were intended to counter the German U-boats lurking just offshore that had feasted on the easy targets presented by the silhouettes of ships backlit by the city lights. The wolf packs had exacted a heavy toll on Allied shipping until the government finally made the connection.

Alvey went into New York City several times and became an expert at getting lost. He said it was second nature for him.

He remarked that it was very exhilarating to come through the Holland Tunnel at fifty miles an hour in the back of an army truck. When they had three or four trucks, they were usually given a police escort that cleared the way. Once he drove a half-track into the city and stayed overnight in Manhattan at the Sloane House, a YMCA, on the twelfth story. He passed the time wandering around and looking at tall buildings.

He also visited Philadelphia, which reminded him of Louisville. He said, "the streets were narrow, the buildings old, and the women bold." To him, Independence Hall looked exactly like pictures he had seen, except that there were several buildings in the same small commons. He said that although Philly was full of soldiers, sailors, and airmen, there seemed to be some sort of truce in effect that bridled the usual animosity. He thought that maybe the branches fighting together in the Philippines had something to do with it.

Alvey liked the surrounding wild countryside very much. It was not quite what he expected when he had previously thought about New Jersey. Fort Dix was situated in a small pine forest with a sandy floor known as the pine barrens. He wished that he had time to really explore the area as he speculated there would probably be all kinds of fascinating snakes and bugs along the creeks. The place was surrounded by miles and miles of pine trees and cranberry bogs, where even deer skirted the boundaries of the fort.

On May 11, 1942, the bulk of the First Armored Division boarded the *Queen Mary* bound for Northern Ireland, arriving on May 16, 1942. His own outfit was not included in the first sailing, but its tanks and other equipment were. On May 28, 1942, Alvey warned his folks that he would probably be leaving the United States soon and said that they should not worry as the boat would be exceptionally well guarded. As of June 2, 1942, he was still at Fort Dix but mentioned that he had been to New York and seen his ship. He and some others took the Staten Island ferry and saw the Statue of Liberty.

His mom and dad received another letter dated June 6, 1942, in which he told them that he was marking time at Fort Dix and could not imagine what the army was waiting on. He said that he was not receiving any more letters from home because they were delivered to the main headquarters of the division that had already pulled out. Nevertheless, he urged them to keep writing and told them that he was bored hanging around Fort Dix. There was nothing for them to do now that their equipment was gone.

The next letter my grandparents received was on an undated USO letterhead. It started off by telling them that things had been moving fast, and he was finally on his way across the Atlantic. He bragged that he had not tossed his cookies yet, for which he was grateful. He then observed that the rolling of the ship was probably the same exact motion that his dad experienced on a locomotive deck. Alvey spoke of sleeping in hammocks in shifts. He said the food on board ship was better but that he did not feel like eating. He was not allowed to tell his folks about the convoy or its destination, but affirmed that they were well guarded.

He mentioned that they expected to be really busy if the ship ran into rough water, as the deck rails would be lined with men losing their latest meals. Even if not fatal, none of the troops were looking forward to that eventuality. Alvey promised that he would send them a radiogram once the ship had arrived.

On July 3, 1942, Alvey wrote to tell his parents that he had safely arrived in Ireland and was now located near Belfast and would confirm that by cablegram. He mentioned that he was glad to be sleeping indoors and asked for them to send him flints for his cigarette lighter, more candy, and some airmail stamps so that his letters would be transported on the clipper ship and be delivered to them much more quickly.

Alvey advised his folks that he could not tell them about the camp or the surrounding countryside. Still, he was able to let them know that because they were bivouacked so far north, it did not get dark until 12:30 a.m. and was light again at 3:30 a.m. Subsequently, in another letter dated July 18, 1942, he asked whether they had received the cablegram, and if not, he would create mayhem with Western Union as it had cost him nearly ten hard-earned shillings to send it. He closed the letter by asking his dad to keep the rifle and shotgun oiled up as they would need both someday.

6

Mount Panther — Northern Ireland

There is an uncomfortable reality attending the old army adage, "Hurry up and wait." It is closely akin to the truism, "There is a right way, a wrong way, and the army way." The lower enlisted ranks are never apprised of the big picture, much less the operational details. Consequently, to them nothing the army does makes any sense, hence the derivation of the timeless acronym SNAFU.

On May 11, 1942, the majority of the First Armored Division and its war materiel rolled out from Fort Dix, New Jersey, to the Brooklyn army terminal where they boarded the RMS *Queen Mary* and her support vessels, then set sail for Northern Ireland. Alvey's unit, the First Armored Regiment, and some collateral forces were inexplicably left behind at Fort Dix, without their equipment.

Due to the *Queen Mary's* renowned speed, even with a zigzag course, the first movement entered the Irish Sea just five days later and ended the passage off Gourock, where the men were then transported by ferry to Belfast. Meanwhile, back at Fort Dix, boredom set in. With their tanks and equipment gone, there was nothing for the men to do except make sporadic forays into New York City. However, if they left the fort, they had to tell the officer of the day where they were going and check back with him every two hours.

For weeks, Alvey kept writing to his folks advising him that he was "still here." His last letter written on American shores was dated June 6, 1942. He knew that a move was inevitable and told them not to worry yet as he was certain there would be transit time and extended training before he ever saw any real fighting. He told them that the men were more worried about seasickness than danger. Their anxiety was probably heightened by the fact that they had each been issued a parcel of "puke sacks," one for each day they would be on the water.

Nearly fifty years had passed before our family learned an important detail about his voyage to Ireland. It had been presumed that he had sailed on the *Queen Mary* with the rest of the First Armored Division. However, in 1990, I met Hubert "Herb" Olson, a veteran of the First Armored Regiment who was emphatic that his unit had sailed on a much slower ship named the *Thomas H. Barry*.

The *Thomas H. Barry* was a transformed steamer that had been originally christened as the *Oriente*. Throughout the Great Depression, the ship made the very popular New York to Havana runs. In June 1941, it had been purchased by the War Department and renamed in honor of an army general. The War Department quickly converted it to a troopship with accommodation for 3,600 passengers. The ship was very slow, but extremely durable and made seventy voyages as a troop carrier, including the very first and last of the war. *Thomas H. Barry* took about ten days to make the Atlantic crossing, about twice as long as the *Queen Mary*. Hammocks were stacked three deep in the holds, but there were still only enough for half the troops at any given time, which is why Alvey told his mom and dad that they had to sleep in shifts. In 1957, after more than one million miles of merchant voyages and half a million miles of War Department service, the *Thomas H. Barry* was sold for scrap.

During this time, other friends, and members of the Pirate

Gang had entered the military, or been transferred from place to place. Joe Kienly, having entered the service as a private, was rapidly promoted and undergoing quartermaster training as a lieutenant. Alvey's brother, Joe, had been drafted into the Army Air Corps. Cousin Richard Alvey was in the infantry and had qualified as an expert with the rifle. Sometime later, despite being warned by Alvey of a "serious ass-kicking" if he did so, Robert Frie dropped out of Indiana University's medical school, joined the army and became a medic.

In Northern Ireland, the First Armored Division was widely dispersed in and around Belfast. The division headquarters was at the palace of Castlewellan. Headquarters for the First Armored Regiment was at Seaforde House in County Down. But its men and tanks were bivouacked in Quonset huts at Mount Panther, a historic 170-acre estate.

The Mount Panther estate was set in rolling countryside, with views of the Mourne Mountains, Dundrum Bay, and the Irish Sea, and located off the main road between Newcastle and Belfast. The mansion on the property dated from the late 1700s and had hosted many dignitaries, including Jonathan Swift, the author of *Gulliver's Travels*. The surrounding lands were named after the Great Cat of Clough, a mythical predator said to have roamed the area in the distant past.

Training and tank maintenance had commenced immediately upon arrival in Northern Ireland. There were even joint exercises with British forces. In a letter to Robert Frie, Alvey marveled at the exorbitant speed of a hedge-hopping Spitfire, which, he said, "slid by and made the scenery fly backwards." The tank training primarily stressed gunnery, bore sighting, and direct fire on moving targets. Some of the training was conducted at night and included mock battles.

Still the men were generally impatient to leave the training behind and actually get into the war effort. Alvey wrote several letters to Robert Frie during his time in Ireland detailing the troops' never-ending quest for beer and women, and lamenting the fact that he and his buddies were nearly always broke.

With the bravado of an American youth unleashed on foreign shores, he spoke candidly about his lovemaking successes. He noted that one of the advantages of a blackout was the ability to find a nook or cranny on the street, which was quite cozy. But, he said, "You really need to do your loving on the run here! Either you're transferred, or they are; you're refused passes, or they are; you're broke, or they always are."

He mentioned one dark-eyed beauty in particular, named McAlister, who worked in an aircraft factory. He also met "a cute little blond ATS girl." She and two of her girlfriends were out with Alvey and two of his buddies when the ladies missed their 10:15 p.m. train. The women were assigned to the British Army Territorial Service (ATS) and stationed at Ballykinler. They had to be back before midnight, and some began to worry. He said that he and his blond were not that worried since she had previously been busted from sergeant-major, but she was just concerned for her fellow soldiers who were new recruits. He said it cost him a pound to get them a ride home from the friend of an Australian digger they had met.

The men were elated that an American Red Cross canteen had opened in Belfast, where they could purchase American Cokes — one per man. The place also had good beds and American women to flirt with.

For the first time, Alvey identified some of his fellow tankers. He mentioned Gregg, their sergeant, the only man in the barracks from California, with the admission, "and do we have arguments." Alvey noted that Gregg was "an excellent mechanic, with an uncanny ability for doing the right thing at the right time," and "undoubtedly one of the best tank men in the battalion." He spoke of Lee Kaser, "our radio tender, and a good one, who is from

Detroit, which is guaranteed to keep any argument going." Then too, he referenced the fact that they all kidded Phil Caldwell, the assistant tank driver from the hills of Tennessee, who bristled when they called him a razorback.

On August 21, 1942, Alvey sent home two pictures of his tank crew. He said they had just come in from a cold, wet day's run and had gassed up when they spied the cameraman roaming from group to group. Training was all too frequently conducted in summer downpours over boggy terrain. More than a few tanks sank in the mud up to their turrets and had to be excavated. One trooper suggested that the tankers should mine for them. Since it was a week after payday, Alvey's crew had a hard time scraping up the necessary six shillings. The tank's main driver, Alphonse E. Urbanovsky from Texas, was not in the first picture, "since a blackjack game was running." But he did make an appearance for a subsequent photo.

Although the men were almost always short of funds, nevertheless there were continuous blackjack games in the barracks. At one point, due to the deduction of his allotment and insurance, he had only about fifteen dollars left on payday. A trooper named Fuentes, from Texas with the nickname of Bloke, advised him to toss it all in the nearest blackjack game and "win a pile, or lose it."

On another occasion, he recalled, "The end of the month being at hand, the whole barracks couldn't buy the glue off a three-cent stamp. We are sitting around discussing ways and means of procuring a pint of Guinness — the favorite Irish beer. One of the boys having snowed under the local barmaid, our credit may be good, but I doubt it."

He spoke frequently about daily life in the barracks. "The place looks like washday in a tenement house." They had been working all day in the rain, and articles of wet clothing were hanging from the ceiling, lying on the floor and piled in heaps at the foot of each bed. He reported that "some of our amateur Boy Scouts are trying to build a fire with a match and no paper. Guess I'll have to take over."

The only thing the men liked better than the pay line was the chow line. Alvey expressed concern in one letter written late at night that he had forgotten to clean his mess kit. "When the first sergeant says 'Dismissed' tomorrow after reveille, I'll be handicapped in the rush to the chow line. Every morning, we have a rat race to see who'll be first. We of the HQ platoon are the most ardent chow hounds in the company. We nearly always manage to be in the front of the line."

They also had opportunities to counsel one another regarding their love lives. In his last letter from Ireland, dated November 26, 1942, he said, "A first class bullshit session is going on. One of the boys is having trouble with his woman and we're giving him some fatherly advice. Don't think it'll take though." Then a final observation, "Practically everyone's gone to town again tonight. I believe that this company drinks more than any other in the army. Somehow or other though, they're able to do duty the next day."

This was written two weeks after the Allied invasion of North Africa had begun. The men had spent a great deal of time waterproofing their tanks. But the vessels that had been retrofitted for beach landings were unable to carry the larger tanks. As a consequence, the initial invasion force consisted only of the light tanks of the First Battalion, First Armored Regiment, and the First Battalion, Thirteenth Armored Regiment. Alvey's friends George Kienly and Jack Hunter were in the Thirteenth Armored Regiment and part of the initial landing force. But Alvey and the Second Battalion of the First Armored Regiment with its newly delivered M-4 Sherman tanks did not arrive in North Africa until Christmastime 1942. This piecemeal commitment of the First Armored Division, coupled with the default to British command and the dearth of forward reconnaissance, proved to be catastrophic in the tankers' first encounter with Rommel's battle-hardened Afrika Korps.

Part III

THE MOUNTAINS OF THE MOON

7

Operation Torch

In the Dedication to this book, I alluded to the fact that the First
Armored Division was the only American tank division to see
desert combat in World War II and the only one to get *no* desert
warfare training. The revelator of that ironic, fateful circumstance
was General Hamilton H. Howze (Ret.). On the threshold of
Operation Torch, the Allied invasion of North Africa, then Lieutenant Colonel Howze was the G-3 of the First Armored Division,
the staff officer responsible for movement, training, and combat
operations.

After graduating from West Point, Howze commenced his
career as a cavalryman and transitioned to the armored force at the
outbreak of World War II. General Howze went on to command
a tank regiment in the First Armored Division, and after commanding US Forces in Korea, served as Commanding General of
the Eighth Army, retiring as a four star general in 1965. In his
memoir, *A Cavalryman's Story*, he makes a number of other astute
observations regarding the First Armored Division's preparation
for its baptism of blood in North Africa.

> The 1st Armored Division (IAD) spent March of 1942
> turning in peacetime gear and packing the rest for

departure from Fort Knox; almost a month moving to
Fort Dix; a month at Dix, waiting, without equipment
to train with; a month getting to and settling in Ireland,
with totally inadequate terrain on which to do no more
than very limited gunnery practice — the maneuvering
of tank and armored infantry battalions being out of the
question; two months getting to and waiting around in
England, without equipment or training area; and some
weeks in preparation and movement, as we shall see, to
North Africa. Our sharpness, our cutting edge, was
about that of a broom handle.

As the G-3 for the division, he was in a unique position to
know and honestly evaluate its readiness for combat at that time
in history. In fact, he later lamented, "None of the division was
worth a damn." But ready or not, Allied planners were targeting
North Africa, intent upon sending a hastily assembled hodge-
podge of disparate forces into the fray. Thus, the invasion force
bound for the deserts of North Africa consisted primarily of units
that had most recently been training in the rain, mud, and bogs
of Northern Ireland. Meanwhile, the US Army's intensive desert
warfare training was now well under way — in the Mojave Desert
of California.

The code name for the invasion of North Africa was Operation
Torch. That designation was coined by Winston Churchill, who
reportedly adopted it from a phrase in Act I, Scene I of Shakespeare's *Measure for Measure:* "Heaven doth with us as we with
torches do." Much of the impetus for Torch was attributable to
Churchill's obsession with the Desert Fox, Erwin Rommel. He
kept repeating within earshot of others, "Rommel, Rommel,
Rommel, Rommel, what else matters but beating him?" Thoughts
of Rommel and his martial genius dominated the planning by
Allied politicians as well as commanders.

Rommel was regarded as an ominous specter. He could not be allowed to threaten the Suez Canal or rampage though the rich oil fields of Persia and Arabia, perhaps culminating in his linking up with the German army in the Caucasus. Then too, apart from the British interests in the Middle East, and the fact that the Eighth Army was daily growing in strength and had effectively forestalled Rommel's juggernaut through the eastern desert into Egypt at the Battle of First Alamein, there was a compelling need to open a second front to relieve the German pressure on Russia. Churchill sought and obtained an agreement with the United States to defer the invasion of northwest Europe in favor of concentrated landings in Morocco and Algeria.

The Allied intent was to exert extreme pressure on the German and Italians from the west, even while Montgomery's Eighth Army doggedly pressed Rommel and the Italians from the east. The Americans were designated to spearhead the invasion of North Africa because of the French animosity toward the British, due to competing colonial interests and the fact that the British had on July 3, 1940, sunk the bulk of France's Mediterranean fleet in the Port of Mers El Kebir, Algeria, in order to deny those assets to the Germans, resulting in the deaths of 1,200 French sailors.

Planning for the invasion occupied the Allied commanders and their staffs for about six weeks and was completed by September 5, 1942. The Allies were intent upon landing troops and war materiel in advance of the onset of winter. The planners were mindful of other salient concerns, including the prospect of Vichy French resistance and the opportunity to close Erwin Rommel's Afrika Korps in a vice.

The massive invasion consisted of three separate armadas: the Western Naval Task Force sailing across the Atlantic from the United States to Morocco, and the Center and Eastern task forces making the sea voyage from the United Kingdom to Oran and Algiers. Even Herr Hitler was somewhat awestruck by the combined assault. He later remarked, "This is the largest landing operation that has ever taken place in the history of the world."

Approximately one-third of the First Armored Division was detached and joined the Center Task Force, which consisted primarily of the First Infantry Division. The combined detachment was named Combat Command B and included the First Battalion of the First Armored Regiment, the Second Battalion of the Thirteenth Armored Regiment, and the Sixth Armored Infantry Regiment as well as support units. These elements of the Center Task Force were ordered to land east and west of Oran, Algeria, about fifty miles apart, in a classic pincer movement.

The armada sailed from British ports on October 26 and November 1, arriving off the coast of Algeria just before midnight on November 7. The main objectives for the green troops of the designated battalions of the First and Thirteenth Armored Regiment were to assist in the capture of two airfields south of the city at Tafaroui and La Senia in two "flying columns" of light and medium M-3 tanks.

At this time, the US Army's light M-3 tank, also known as the "Stuart" to Americans and "Honey" to the British, was armed with a 37mm main gun and several .30 caliber machine guns, while the medium M-3 ("Grant") sported a 75mm cannon mounted in a sponson, as well as .50 caliber and .30 caliber machine guns.

The plan had called for the medium M-3 tanks to be off-loaded by cranes onto docks, while the light M-3 tanks would drive out of the bows of landing ships on their own power. But the landings did not go as smoothly as planned. Much has been written about the mishaps and disasters attending the invasion. One such incident was reported by Alvey in a letter written months later. He had linked up with family friend Jack Hunter in January 1943. At that time, Hunter told him that a ramp was lowered too soon, and that as Hunter's own tank was being driven off the wharf, it abruptly sank in thirty feet of blue Mediterranean. Hunter did not know anything was amiss until the water started pouring in on his shoulders. He said that the poor driver had drowned. Nearly fifty years later, Jack Hunter confirmed his tragic initiation into combat in a letter to me.

While someone has pejoratively referred to Operation Torch as "an orgy of disorder," it was actually an overall success. Once the initial objectives were subdued and the Vichy French forces joined the Allied cause, the bulk of the invasion force turned east toward Tunisia. In my view, the most conspicuous shortcoming of the invasion was the failure to exploit the element of surprise and take Tunis before the Germans were able to reinforce North Africa and link up with Rommel's retreating army. Had elements of the invading armies been landed farther east at the outset, the war in North Africa most likely would have been shortened by months. There would have been no battles of Sidi Bou Zid or Kasserine Pass, and Rommel would have been trapped with little or no means of escape.

Back in England, the majority of the First Armored Division, including its commanding general, Orlando Ward, and Alvey's unit, the First Armored Regiment (less First Battalion) occupied abandoned military billets and a country estate at Chester, adjacent to Wales. While the bulk of the division in England prepared for transit and engaged in minimal training, it was equipped with new M-4 "Sherman" tanks, which were vastly improved weapons platforms compared to either of the M-3 tanks then in service in North Africa. In particular, the M-4 featured a full-traverse turret, a longer 75mm gun, and the more reliable FM radios.

Alvey and the Second Battalion of the First Armored Regiment with its newly delivered M-4 Sherman tanks did not completely land in Algiers and Oran until around Christmastime 1942. There was never to be a reunion of the entire First Armored Division in North Africa, which proved to be strategic blunder. One would expect that the combat-tested and "blooded" units should have been joined with the newly arrived elements. That would have constituted a force multiplier if the division had simply been allowed to fight as a whole. In hindsight, it appears that the men of Old Ironsides were destined to learn a hard lesson from the German army about the superior firepower of a wholly integrated armored force. Indeed, the commander of the US Army II Corps, Major General Lloyd Fredendall, repeatedly referred to the Desert Fox as Professor Rommel.

8

Algeria — The Mountain of the Lions

The Allied invasion of Algeria and Rommel's fighting retreat westward spanning the Libyan coast turned into a feverish race to Tunisia. Adolph Hitler was on a train bound for East Prussia when he learned of the Allied encroachment. He realized immediately that he would need to placate Mussolini and Italy's African colonial interests. Il Duce was doubly disappointed as he had made preparations to ride triumphantly into Cairo on a white stallion when it seemed that Rommel would sweep through Egypt. Now, he had to face the hard reality that Libya and all of Africa could be completely lost to him. There would be no triumphal parade for the Caesar wannabe.

In order to appease Mussolini, Hitler immediately had his staff initiate the reinforcement of Tunisia, and redirected troops, tanks, and resources originally intended for Rommel. The field marshal had long regarded Africa as a lost cause. He had to endure the incredulity and false optimism of Hitler and Commando Supremo, who refused all of his pleas for permission to evacuate the Afrika Korps. While Rommel had repeatedly been promised sufficient quantities of fuel and war materiel, they had either been sunk in the Mediterranean Sea or diverted to the Russian front. On the other hand, the British and the Americans had enormous stockpiles of supplies already ashore with more on the way.

More than 15,000 German troops flown from Italy landed in Tunisia in November 1942 alone. That number was increased by 17,000 more German and Italian fighters by the beginning of December. Even more Italian ranks traveled from southern Libya into the eastern Tunisian salient. At their peak, the reinforcements totaled more than 100,000 men, with an additional 70,000 under Rommel's command.

The Germans won the race and repulsed initial Allied thrusts toward Tunis and Bizerte in late November and December 1942, outnumbering the Americans and British by a margin of two to one. Elements of the First Armored Division linked with British units in attacks on Tunis. The Allies endured heavy losses at Chouigui Pass, Longstop Hill, and Bald and Green Hills before abandoning the quest for a speedy victory.

Rommel was initially tasked with holding Libya, while German commanders Albert Kesselring and Hans-Juergen Von Arnim dealt with the Allies pouring into Tunisia from Algeria. But it was eventually concluded by the Axis leadership that Libya would have to be relinquished and the Allies defeated in Tunisia, then in Algeria and farther west, where the Germans held out hope that Franco's Spain would join them. But it never did. Panzerarmee Afrika was established under the command of Von Armin in early December 1942.

It must be mentioned that the decision to reinforce Tunisia was undoubtedly influenced by the unfolding debacle of the Battle of Stalingrad, among the bloodiest battles in the history of warfare and arguably the pivotal strategic event of World War II. The German army lost momentum there that it never regained, and at this time the potential prospect of setbacks in both Russia and North Africa weighed heavily and caused the Axis to forestall that outcome.

The bulk of the First Armored Regiment sailed into the harbors adjacent to the ancient Moorish city of Oran, Algeria, on December 21, 1942. By Christmas Eve, the unit was already twenty miles southeast of Oran. Alvey wrote his first letters from North Africa on December 23, 1942. He told Robert Frie and his folks that he was in North Africa, and could not tell them where he was, but that he had been to Oran. The name "Oran" derives from the Berber word *wahran,* meaning lions. As the local legend goes, in 900 BC ferocious lions inhabited the area. The last two were killed on a mountain just outside the city proper, which is still known as *La Montagne des Lions,* the Mountain of the Lions.

In his first letters from North Africa, Alvey described his initial impressions of Algeria. He took particular note of the people and that they spoke French, Spanish, and Arabic. As far as their clothing, he mentioned that the French people dressed like Europeans, while the Arabs were arrayed in tribal dress that resembled bedclothes. He was particularly pleased that he could barter for oranges and tangerines that were in abundance, but he said it was difficult converting values in American dollars, English shillings, and French francs. The troopers walked down a road until they met an Arab with his donkey loaded down with oranges, tangerines, dates, and olives. Then they pulled out their money and pointed to what they wanted. But the Arab traders had the uncanny ability to read their eyes for what the Americans wanted even before they began to point.

Alvey said he wished he had taken French instead of Latin in school. He was enthused to be learning a few French words, like *"Combien?"* meaning "How much?" But he observed that the traders quickly grasped his meaning. The fruit peddler would then name a price about twice the going rate, and the dithering really began. He said that *"Allez! Allez!"* was the first phrase they had picked up, and it had become quickly overworked. He translated it as French for "Scram!" He also noted that the Spanish speakers in his unit had adopted a mongrel form of French-Spanish in order to communicate with the locals who spoke each language.

He genuinely enjoyed the oranges and tangerines that had been in such short supply in Northern Ireland and the stormy ocean voyage from Liverpool. In fact, as he wrote in the dim winter light, many of his letters were stained with fruit juice. The tankers also liked the local wine, which was good but cheap at about seventy-five cents to a dollar a quart.

They did not have any opportunity to interact with Muslim women. In fact, they were strictly forbidden any contact. Each US soldier was given a "Pocket Guide to North Africa" that included the following severe admonition:

> These few rules are to be strictly observed in relation to
> Moslem women:
> Never stare at one.
> Never jostle her in a crowd.
> Never speak to her in public.
> Never try to remove her veil.
> This is most important. Serious injury, if not death at
> the hands of Moslem men may result if these few rules
> are not followed.

Yet, that did not stop lonely troopers from wishing that the government would ship over a few WAVES (Women Accepted for Voluntary Emergency Service) and WACs (Women's Army Corps). Alvey said that he and (Everett) Gregg were going to put in a requisition for two medium-sized brunettes. But as the paraphrase of the adage goes, "If the army wanted you to have a woman, it would have issued you one."

9

Tunisia — Prelude

In early January 1943, the elements of the First Armored Division southeast of Oran began the long trek to Tunisia. The division had since come under the command of the US Army II Corps, headed by Major General Lloyd Fredendall. Under a power-sharing agreement between the Allies, Fredendall's commander was British First Army General Kenneth Arthur Noel Anderson. At that time, it had not been determined how the First Armored would be deployed in Tunisia, except that the II Corps planners had been working on a proposal to seize the eastern coastal town of Sfax, which would operate to cut off Rommel from the Axis elements to the north. If snared, the Desert Fox would be crushed between the British and American forces. However, Eisenhower intervened and wanted the First Armored to consolidate near Tebessa to dissuade Rommel from forays to the west once the Desert Fox arrived in Tunisia. Further, the Allies were forced into defensive positions in the Ousseltia Valley on January 18, 1943, due to enemy incursions designed to envelop the French outposts and clear a path to the coastal plain. Hence, Operation Satin, the plan to seize Sfax, was initially tabled and then abandoned.

Rommel's well-executed 1,400-mile-long retreat ended in Tunisia in late January 1943. Of his 96,000 German and Italian troops, roughly 59,000 had been killed, wounded or taken prisoner. The field marshal had lost more than 400 tanks, many of them abandoned due to fuel and parts shortages. But once he reached Tunisia, the situation changed when he was able to link up with the reinforcing units and war material rushed in from Italy.

Alvey's next letter to Robert Frie is dated January 19, 1943, written as the sun was going down. He said that the days had been for the most part clear, cool, and moonlit, and observed "this African moon is really the nuts." He said that they were sleeping in the field and living in the open, but that he had always liked camping out. It had been quiet except for the occasional "moan of an airplane engine or the roar of a tank engine." He did comment that it was occasionally chilly and that "a tank turret is the coldest thing this side of Admiral Byrd's headquarters."

He said that after dry-running on his 75mm cannon for nearly a year, he should be able to hit something, and quoted his tank commander Everett Gregg as having said, "I've been chicken-shitting around in this damn army for two years, now I'd like to get even with those so-and-sos for putting me to all this trouble."

Because they were in the captain's tank, they always got their news directly and were grateful that they had a clearer idea of what they were doing or supposed to do. Then too, he appreciated the fact that they always parked near the chow wagon, which was a decided advantage.

He told Frie that he had just received a Christmas present consisting of a box of candy three weeks late. Candy was highly prized. He confessed that he and Lee (Kaser) had burgled several boxes of candy that Captain Winkler had purchased in England and that Winkler also had a quart of sloe gin in the tank left over from New Year's. Winkler told Kaser, "You all can have all the candy you want, but keep away from the gin." Alvey told Frie, "We only drank about one-third of it," even though Winkler had it thumb-marked. When I first heard from Winkler in 1991, he did not remember the incident with the gin and said he actually favored whiskey. But that was nearly fifty years after the fact and the gin may have been all that was available for a New Year's celebration in the war zone.

Alvey again wrote to Robert Frie on January 29, 1943, congratulating him on being accepted into the medical school at Indiana University, but kidded him with the comment, "Lo, the poor patient." He mentioned that he was acting as sergeant of the guard. He did not have to walk any post, but had to check on the guards frequently, which was something of a chore at night. Alvey then related another episode he had experienced two nights before. He told Frie that he had been up to the kitchen to get some water and was returning to his tent, which was pitched about 400 yards from the company. The moon wasn't up yet, and he wandered off course. After climbing around the rocks for half an hour, he fell into a slit trench. His canteen went one way and his helmet another. He cursed his way out but was grateful that the slit trench was not of the type dug for sanitary purposes. He said that if he ever fell into one of those, "I'll merely roll over, draw my gun and translate myself immediately."

Alvey spoke at length about the life of a tanker in North Africa. He said it was far from a bed of roses but had its compensations. He began by mentioning certain drawbacks, including that the tradition of the cavalry from which the armored force had evolved was still with them. No matter how tired, hungry, sleepy, cold, or wringing wet you were when you pulled into bivouac, you took care of your mount first. The tank had to be serviced to fulfill the ironclad rule of the Tank Corps: "Thou shalt be ready to pull out at any time."

He said the tanks were "cold in the winter and hot in the summer; wet when it rains; dusty when its dry; as delicate as a newborn babe and as rugged as any man-made piece of machinery." But one compensation was the pride in being a tanker that only a tanker knows: "To draw up alongside a column of mere infantry and look down on them as disinterestedly as one would look on a column of ants gives a distinct feeling of satisfaction."

On one occasion he related how he had ridden the turret while they tried to catch up with the company that had gone ahead. A brilliant moon lit up the road like daylight. The "driver floorboarded her and we really took off." There wasn't a sound except for them and nothing moving anywhere. He said that the countryside looked about as hospitable as the moon and that he could "see why the mountains along the North African coast are called the mountains of the moon."

Actually, the so-called mountains of the moon are in Uganda near the source of the Nile. He may have confused the Atlas Mountains bordering Algeria and Tunisia, where he presumably was, with the mountains of the moon of legend. Nevertheless, that eastern segment of the Atlas Mountains does resemble an eerie moonscape.

He was eagerly anticipating the receipt of more reading material, including a copy of Boccacio's *Decameron* that Frie had sent in addition to a copy of Thoreau's *Walden*. Things to read were necessary to fight boredom while they were resting. There was really nothing much to do except keep their eyes peeled for Messerschmitts and Stukas. Then Alvey told Frie that his first encounter with the German planes had occurred quite some time ago. They had been on the go all night and were plenty tired, cold, and hungry. He was in the turret relieving Gregg, who was driving. They were on the tail end of the column, which was unusual because they usually led the company with the captain. Suddenly, he saw a jeep coming toward them at breakneck speed, with the driver swerving in and out of the row of tanks. The driver yelled, "Watch her, they're strafing the head of the column."

Lee Kaser jumped for more ammunition while Alvey grabbed the .50 caliber machine gun and swung it around the sky trying to lock on a target. He said his head was "on a swivel." He could hear other machine guns hammering the sky, but they did not see any planes. But after they had pulled into bivouac, the planes returned with reinforcements. They were ME 109s carrying 250-pound bombs.

He said that everyone enjoyed themselves after dry-running so much, except Kaser, who "got caught in the middle of a badly needed shit." Gregg was lying under the tank and laughing "like a damn fool" while Kaser finished his business and scrambled for cover. Alvey was up in the turret firing the .50 caliber. But they had pulled in between two trees and every time he started to fire, the machine gun barrel would catch on a branch. Still, it pleased him to finally get some combat firing in. No one in their outfit was hurt, and an after-action report claimed they shot down two of the German planes. However, more than one officer has observed that in North Africa they probably shot down more of our own planes than Germans.

Alvey said that the next time the planes came around, they stayed high enough to be out of range. One thing they all took away from the encounter with the ME 109s was the resolution to dig their slit trenches a little deeper. But Alvey quoted Jack Hunter as saying, "When they bomb, we just jump in the tank, close the doors and let 'em bomb."

There were other humorous incidents in bivouac. Alvey said that he had just come in from chow when he heard a raucous cross between a cough and a grunt magnified ten times. A young camel had wandered unattended into their area and "naturally someone was trying to ride him." But the would-be jockey didn't stay on long because "those darn things can buck."

On another occasion, Alvey and Gregg tied Kaser into his bedroll while he was asleep. Kaser awoke cursing and writhing around to free himself. Alvey then wondered how his own bedroll would look the following morning.

He said that they were located near a French encampment and had a good time "parley-vouying" with them. They all really liked the hard-looking French soldiers, who he said really hated the Germans, and he noted that each of them had the "wickedest-looking bayonet and looked as if they knew how to use it."

While in Africa, he observed that the tank crew had become completely "communistic." Everything literally belonged to everyone in the tank. They had by then eaten all of Captain Winkler's candy, and he had smoked their cigarettes. Alvey went on to summarize his experience of the martial life, saying that,

> Women are not missed unless you stay too long in one place; that it was better to take half an hour to fix your bedroll than to freeze all night; that slit trenches should be six inches longer and several inches wider than the body, otherwise ground waves will break bones; that a camouflage net is an instrument of the Devil and the damndest thing you ever fussed with on a dark night; that a wise soldier stacks his belongings in one place so as to facilitate packing in inky blackness; that sentries should be approached with discretion on dark nights; that four thousand miles of water makes everyone a potential homebody; and that mess kits must be washed clean or you'll fall through the rim of your own ass!

Looking forward to the end of the war, he said that when he got home, the one thing he and Frie were going to do was to build a bigger and better canoe, launch it in the Wabash and pull it out in the Gulf of Mexico!

On February 8, 1943, he wrote to Frie and thanked him for sending *The Decameron* and told him that there was already a long waiting list to read it. He next wrote to his folks on February 10 telling them about the weather and other routine observations.

Most significantly, he thanked his mother for the Kaywoodie pipe she sent him, which was destined to be an artifact of heartrending mystery.

His last letter from North Africa was written to his cousin Nell Loraine on February 13, 1943. He told her the same story he had related to Frie about being bombed by ME 109s and his excitement about the chance to fire at something besides a target. Then he said that they had just been paid and he had a pocketful of francs and nowhere to spend them. He enclosed a five franc note for her, as well as a little heart he had cut out of the plastic front window of a crashed bomber. He apologized, saying that "until we get to some large town there's not much in the way of souvenirs I can get."

As this letter was written, Alvey was with the Second Battalion of the First Armored Regiment bivouacked somewhere between Maktar and the Ousseltia Valley, about fifty miles north of Sidi Bou Zid. That very night, Eisenhower, who had just been made a full general, accompanied by his entourage of junior commanders and planners, arrived at the First Armored Division command post west of Sbeitla. The Allies had advance knowledge that an attack would come the next day, they just did not know where it would develop. Ike was briefed by officers in Combat Command A regarding the precarious disposition of Allied troops and of the enemy's advantages in the event of an attack. After the briefing, the group moved east, to yet another briefing. Then Ike and his team entered and surveyed the village of Sidi Bou Zid. Its white houses shimmered in the moonlight as Eisenhower surveyed the shadows cast by the distant opposing Djebels Lessouda and Ksaira and weighed the gravamen of his briefings.

At the moment of Eisenhower's visit to Sidi Bou Zid, the Germans were massing just outside the entrance to the Faid Pass about ten miles away. However, General Anderson had thoroughly convinced himself that any attack launched by Rommel would come much farther north at Fondouk, not through Faid Pass or Gafsa. It is unfortunate that Eisenhower accepted Anderson's short-sighted appraisal and concluded that the dispositions near Sidi Bou Zid were "as good as could be made, pending the development of an actual attack and in view of holding the forward regions if it could possibly be done."

Eisenhower left the Sidi Bou Zid area at about 2:00 a.m. on February 14, 1943. Shortly thereafter, a fierce wind began to blow up from the Sahara that muffled the sounds of German engines and tracked vehicles drifting in from the east.

Part IV

THE CHARGE OF THE LIGHT BRIGADE WITH TANKS

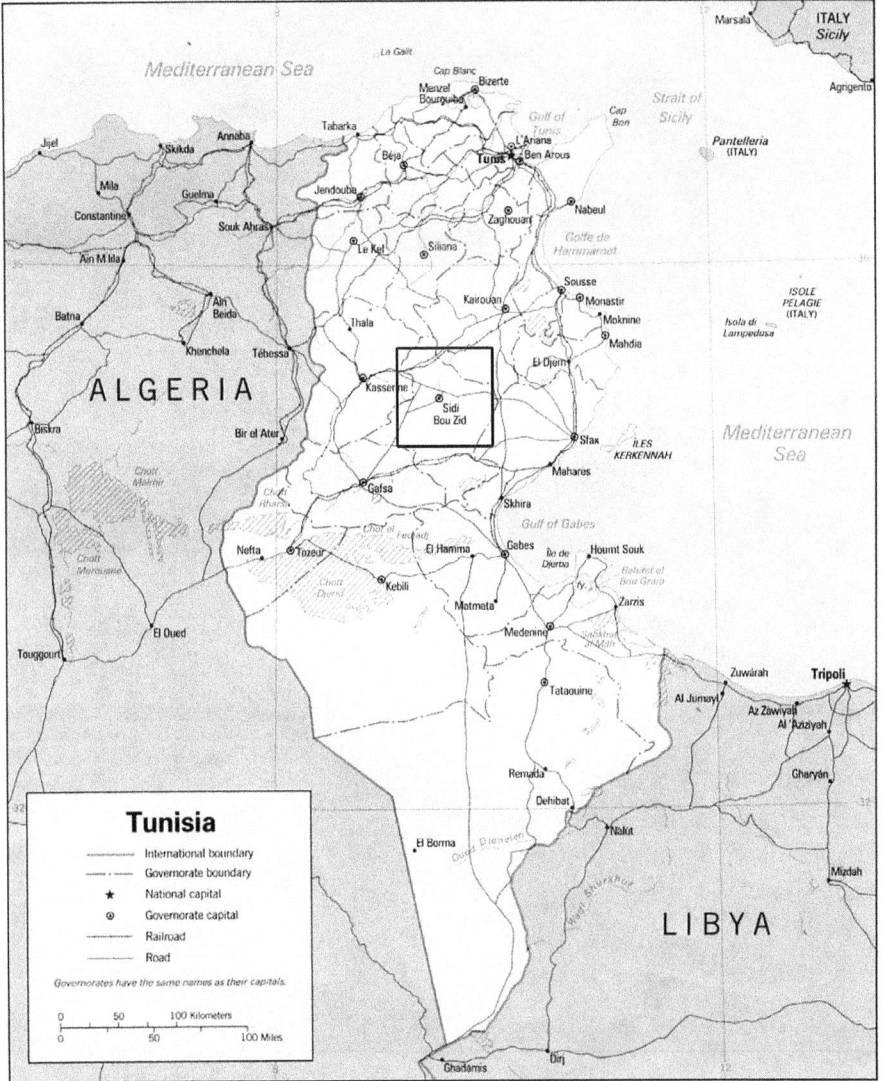

Tunisia. (Courtesy of U.S. Central Intelligence Agency)

10

Sidi Bou Zid — The Killing Zone

If Eisenhower had any reservations about the command's tactical readiness, he did not make any changes, but abruptly climbed into his armored Cadillac command car, left Sidi Bou Zid, and headed west, back to Fredendall's II Corps headquarters. It is shocking that he did not order or even ask Fredendall to accompany him on his survey of the dispositions in the vicinity of Sidi Bou Zid. Equally staggering is the dearth of accurate intelligence that should have disclosed the German buildup beyond the Eastern Dorsale. The Allies had already obtained a German Enigma code machine and cracked the cipher, enabling them to read secret enemy communications from the battlefields. They had even intercepted a German communiqué advising that there would be an attack on February 14, 1943. How and why they did not derive actionable information from such intelligence coups remains a mystery.

The return trip was delayed by sporadic gunfire near Sbeitla. Eisenhower and his group deployed to defensive positions, but the random shots were later attributed to nervous sentries. Another delay befell the group when Eisenhower's driver fell asleep at the wheel and careened into a ditch.

Upon reaching Fredendall's compound, Eisenhower shivering and dog tired, rolled into his sleeping bag fully clothed in the

tent beside his usual driver, Kay Summersby. On his first visit to
Fredendall's command post, the day before, Eisenhower had been
taken aback by the frenzied construction activity at the remote
site. Engineers wielding pneumatic drills were burrowing into the
walls of the ravine, busily constructing reinforced bunkers. Evidently, Fredendall had heard that the enemy was targeting leaders
and did not want to be susceptible to any attack, even more than
sixty miles behind the front lines. Fredendall was hunkering down,
ready for World War I style trench warfare! Eisenhower asked a
staffer whether they had taken care to first construct defenses for
the troops on the eastern front, and the terse reply was, "The divisions have their own engineers for that!"

American General Lucian Truscott provided the most apt
assessment of Fredendall as a commander.

> Small in stature, loud and rough in speech, he was
> outspoken in his opinions and critical of superiors and
> subordinates alike. He was inclined to jump to conclu-
> sions which were not always well founded. Fredendall
> rarely left his command post for personal visits and
> reconnaissance, yet he was impatient with the recom-
> mendations of subordinates more familiar with the
> terrain and other conditions than he.

During the North African landings at the commencement
of Operation Torch, Fredendall had remained aboard the ship,
rather than command troops on the ground. True to form, he was
cloistered in his secure bunker while Eisenhower was assessing
conditions at the front. A bona fide dugout commander, Fredendall had never personally visited Sidi Bou Zid or reconnoitered
the area east of the town where 1,700 American soldiers with the
168th Infantry were isolated on the hills known as Djebel Lessouda, Djebel Ksaira, and Garet Hadid. These promontories lay

astride the road leading west from Faid Pass, but were too far apart to allow for mutual reinforcement. Fredendall placed too much reliance on maps and should have at least walked the ground. Fredendall had initially gained the full confidence of Chief of Staff General George Marshal. Eisenhower had also given him the benefit of the doubt, and despite the warning signs kept him in command until his catastrophic failure.

Eisenhower was seemingly not alarmed by the advice previously given on January 25, 1943, by Colonel Benjamin Abbott "Monk" Dickson that "Rommel can be expected to act offensively in Southern Tunisia as soon as rested and rearmed." Dickson also stated his belief that any attack by Rommel would debauch through Gafsa or Faid Pass and not Fondouk in the north as expected by the British First Army planners and its leader General Anderson.

It is now known that Anderson was so convinced of his own view that an attack would come in the center of the Allied line that he refused to even discuss any suggestion that a German thrust might come from the south. That, coupled with Fredendall's remote, centralized command and the fact that reinforcements were too far away from the front, resulted in an epic disaster. Both men thought they knew best and rejected out of hand valuable input offered by subordinates. Anderson and Fredendall despised each other, and Fredendall did not like or trust Orlando Ward, the Commander of the First Armored Division whom he viewed as incompetent. As a consequence, the top commanders did not communicate well with one another and Fredendall actually undermined Ward's control by dictating a flawed battle plan instead of allowing Ward to fight his own division. In fact, Fredendall actually dictated battle orders down to the company level.

On the other hand, the Germans were battle hardened after years of desert warfare and seasoned experts at fire and maneuver. There is now no doubt that they had technical weapons superiority. They were also adept at creeping up on an enemy force and at Sidi

Bou Zid were ably assisted by windstorms and haze that obscured their furtive forward movements.

Although Ike had listened attentively to briefings given by Colonel Paul Robinett, Commander of the Thirteenth Armored Regiment, and Colonel Peter Hains, Commander of the First Armored Regiment, the night of February 13, he did not take their admonitions to heart. Robinett was the most battle-hardened tank commander in North Africa and told Eisenhower, whom he greatly respected, that he had personally reconnoitered Fondouk and determined that an enemy attack there was highly unlikely. He also emphasized that the troops on the hills around Faid Pass could not offer mutual support. He flatly told Eisenhower that the troops there were more important than the prestige of the position and that the Allied situation was "impossible" given German capabilities. Hains reinforced the vulnerability of the soldiers stationed on the hills around Faid Pass and also reported that hundreds of German vehicles had recently been spotted near the pass and were strafed by Allied pilots. However, Eisenhower was most alarmed that mines had not been placed around Sidi Bou Zid and ordered his commanders to get their mine fields out first thing in the morning.

Erwin Rommel was not disposed as Fredendall was to secrete himself in a bunker far behind the lines. Rather, Rommel was always leading up front with his troops, roaming the battle area and reconnoitering on the ground and in the air above the fray in his Storch observation plane. He repeatedly adapted his battle plans as dictated by the ever-changing conditions. Many have acknowledged that Rommel also had *Fingerspitzengefuhl,* a rough translation of which means "fingertips feeling." In other words, Rommel had an intuitive flair or instinct for combat and the ability to keep his finger on the pulse despite the dynamic ebb and flow of a battle. He was always hands on and the fate that befell the First Armored Regiment between February 14–15, 1943, bore the classic fingerprints of Rommel.

Still, the field marshal was hamstrung by the myopia of Commando Supremo, and a rivalry with the aristocratic Colonel-General Hans Juergen Von Arnim, who was by then a rising star, and completely dismissive of an ill Rommel and his middle-class origins. Nevertheless, despite such obstacles, Rommel was still a deadly foe whose tactics should have been anticipated by the Allies, particularly the British who had been contending with the Desert Fox for two years.

By that time, there were about 250,000 German and Italian troops braced to confront the Allies in Tunisia. The Axis commanders were very concerned about the threat the Allied forces posed to the mountain passes of the Eastern Dorsale. The Germans in particular wanted to preclude attacks by the Allies through the passes, which could cut their lines of communication and capture the all-important Mediterranean seaports, including Sfax, which was seventy-five miles northeast of Sidi Bou Zid.

At dawn on Valentine's Day 1943, Rommel sent the Allies a Valentine they would rue forever. Much has been written about the Battle of Sidi Bou Zid, including by me in an article featured in *World War II* magazine published in September 2002 under the title *Ambushed by the Afrika Korps.* The first day of that fight, highly experienced German tank crews of the Tenth and Twenty-first Panzer Divisions debauched through Faid Pass in Operation *Fruehlingswind* ("Spring Wind") and annihilated the Third Battalion of the First Armored Regiment. The Germans employed Rommel's tactic of armor swarming in from all directions. Companies G, H, and I of the First Armored Regiment were wiped out. At least forty Sherman tanks were destroyed or captured, together with miscellaneous equipment. Their crews were killed or went into captivity. The 168th Infantry troops on Lessouda, Ksaira, and Garet Hadid were completely cut off and surrounded by German forces. The Germans took control of Sidi Bou Zid but ceased to exploit the attack. Nevertheless, the Allies were forced to withdraw from the area. A counterattack was cobbled together for the next day, February 15, 1943, to rescue the trapped American troops and drive the Germans back through Faid Pass.

Despite the mauling suffered by three companies of the First Armored Regiment, Anderson continued to believe that the attack through Faid Pass was merely a feint and that the major Axis demonstration would take place farther north. Therefore, he did not react by throwing all of his reinforcements into the fray. Rather, the First Armored Division was condemned to piecemeal disbursement throughout the theater and was never able to fight as an entire division in North Arica as the Germans so ably did.

Anderson and his command cohorts were fixated on the misconception that the German thrust on February 14 was merely a diversion. General Orlando "Pinky" Ward wanted his scattered division to be reunited, but he had been stripped of a great deal of tactical authority by Fredendall, who was submissive to Anderson's flawed approach. The sad reality was that Ward had his beloved division taken away from him. However, at the behest of his superiors, Ward authorized a counterattack for the next day by Lieutenant Colonel James D. ("Gentleman Jim") Alger's Second Battalion of the First Armored Regiment, consisting of fifty-four M-4 Sherman tanks, flanked by tank destroyers and supporting units of artillery and infantry.

Alger's battalion had most recently been engaged in reconnaissance sorties throughout the Ousseltia Valley, and was bivouacked near Maktar when its radios crackled with reports from the engagement at Sidi Bou Zid. It had not yet been tested in tank-to-tank combat with the Germans. Now, its baptism of fire would come without the benefit of any forward reconnaissance, familiarity with the terrain, or the precise numbers and disposition of the enemy units they would be facing.

At 1500 hours on February 14, Alger received a coded radio message stating: "Move immediately to Hadjeb el Aioun. Report to Stack. Further details there. Signed-Russell." By 1530, the battalion started to roll out from its bivouac. The convoy was bombed by Stuka dive bombers en route, but they were driven off by the .50 caliber machine guns, with two of the planes trailing smoke. The Stukas returned a short while later and dropped additional bombs along the line of march.

Around midnight, Alger was briefed at a farmhouse by Colonel Robert Stack on the day's events, which were extremely sketchy. Certain officers reported to him regarding some details of the terrain around Sidi Bou Zid, but they had no terrain maps of the area. They gave him only rough estimates of the strength of the enemy forces in the area. The consensus of conjecture ranged from fifty-five to sixty German tanks observed near Lessouda and Sidi Bou Zid. Actually, there were more than 200, including the fearsome Tiger tanks.

At 0400 Alger was given the following order:

> This force will move south and by fire and maneuver destroy the enemy forces which have threatened our hold on the SBEITLA area. It will so conduct its maneuvers as to aid in the withdrawal of our forces in the vicinity of DJEBEL KSAIRA eventually withdrawing to the area north of DJEBEL HAMRA for further action.

The rear echelon of Alger's battalion left Maktar by 0700 on February 15, headed into the unknown. Some of the veterans of their first encounter with the Germans have mentioned to me how cocky they were at the time. They genuinely believed that the American army would quickly whip the German army and be home in no time at all. Churning through the ambient dust, the tankers endured three more German bombing runs before arriving at the launch point about 1100 hours.

Colonel Peter C. Hains, the Commander of the First Armored

Regiment, and Lieutenant Colonel Louis V. Hightower, Commander of the Third Battalion, First Armored Regiment, decimated the day before, then provided a supplemental briefing to Alger. Again, there were no terrain maps to review, but they did tell the young commander to be wary of the wadis (gulches or arroyos) and irrigation ditches combing the front.

At 1330, Alger's force moved out in an inverted wedge formation bound for Sidi Bou Zid. The attack was led by Captain Winkler's D Company. Immediately behind him was Alger's command tank, flanked by reconnaissance platoons, followed by Captain John L. Peyton's F Company, and the battalion artillery, then Captain Harris O. Machus's E Company, followed by two tank destroyer platoons. Visibility was good, even if slightly hazy, as the white houses of Sidi Bou Zid shimmered in a distant mirage.

As the formation rolled forward, the strains of that familiar anthem, "The Stars and Stripes Forever," reverberated from a loudspeaker mounted on a jeep. The attack was held up by the need to cross three steep-sided wadis at the only available points, which "canalized" forward progress. Additionally, Alger was told by a radio message from a Major Sweeney to delay the attack because American planes were on the way to bomb the German positions. The message was: "Our birds will visit first objective soon. Delay attack until they have completed mission." Our birds never did show up, but two Stukas did. The battalion tanks turned donuts in the sand and maneuvered to avoid the bomb blasts as the screams of the Stukas' sirens echoed across the desert. In Sidi Bou Zid, the waiting Germans held primary fire until the initial units had crossed the wadis. A little after 1400, Company D received artillery air bursts from German gun emplacements deftly concealed in and around the town, as the units to the rear were still struggling through the numerous ravines.

Because Captain Winkler was riding the turret in the command tank, Sergeant Gregg, the usual tank commander, was driving.

Alphonse Urbanovsky was the assistant driver/gunner that day. Lee C. Kaser was the radio operator/gun loader, and Alvey was the 75mm gunner. The usual assistant driver, Philip Caldwell, followed behind with one of the tank destroyer units. He told me that he survived the battle and was not hurt or captured, but was later seriously wounded when he was bombed by our own planes.

I believe that the Battle of Sidi Bou Zid should actually be called the Battle of Sidi Salem, a hamlet about two miles west of the objective. Sidi Bou Zid had already been occupied by the Germans the day before. Based on government records and survivors' accounts, the attacking force never got far beyond Sidi Salem. D Company entered Sidi Salem about 1500 and was somewhat shielded from artillery fire by the houses. Some German machine gun nests were wiped out together with a few enemy tanks, but shortly thereafter the trap was sprung. Dust sprays were seen coming from the north as well as the south. The Tenth Panzer Division was rolling on the northern flank even while the Twenty-first Panzer Division came at the Americans from the southern wing. Meanwhile, Alger's battalion was pounded by artillery fire from the center, including the deadly, high velocity 88mm anti-aircraft cannons set for a flat antitank trajectory. The 88mm gun could punch a hole in an American tank at a range of 2,000 yards, while the Sherman 75mm gun suffered reduced effectiveness after only 1,000 yards.

The Germans thus executed one of Rommel's favorite martial tactics. That is, pounding the enemy with an artillery barrage from the center of the line, coupled with a simultaneous pincer attack from both northern and southern flanks. The dust trails from the encroaching Panzer tanks were noticed and engaged by Alger's battalion, but it was soon overwhelmed by superior firepower. There were between forty and fifty German tanks on each flank. The hapless battalion was effectively ambushed by the Afrika Korps. The gunners of D Company, F Company, and E Company initially acquitted themselves well by knocking out thirteen Mark IV German tanks, a few machine gun nests, and miscellaneous artillery pieces. However, they were hit by an angry swarm of German armor from every direction of the compass.

It is undisputed that the Germans had newly activated Tiger tanks in the area mounting 88mm main guns. However, there is disagreement among the experts as to whether any of them were actually engaged in combat at Sidi Bou Zid. Nevertheless, given the number of Mark IV German tanks on the field that day, with their seasoned crews, they would have been sufficient in and of themselves to wipe out the hapless American unit. The American counterattack was doomed because of poor planning, the lack of

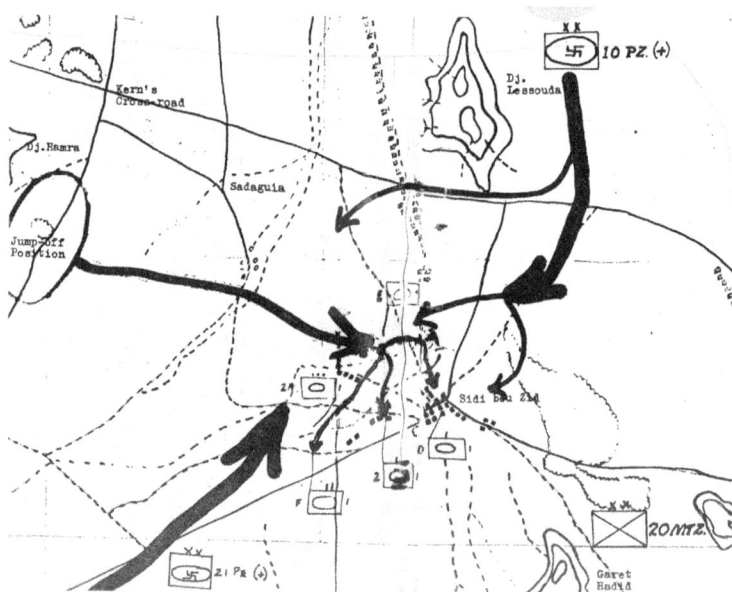

A swarm of hornets. Elements of the German 10th and 21st Panzer Divisions ambush and destroy James D. Alger's Second Battalion, First Armored Regiment, near Sidi Bou Zid, Tunisia on February 15, 1943. (U.S. Army, First Armored Division Archives)

any forward reconnaissance or air support, and a serious under-estimation of the German strength and dispositions. Even while the situation for Alger's battalion worsened, Anderson still continued to hold units in reserve for the expected "real" attack upon Fondouk.

By 1615, the situation had seriously deteriorated. Alger completely lost contact with Winkler's tank. I believe that the D Company command tank was hit by one or more high explosive antitank shells striking the left side of the tank from a German tank to the north. This conclusion is due to Alvey's subsequent letter as a prisoner of war written to Robert Frie explaining that "poor Lee was instantly killed by the same explosions which burned me." Alvey was burned on the face and hands. About that time on the other side of the earth, my grandfather C. L. awoke from a nightmare saying, "that boy's been burned on his face."

As the radio operator/loader, Kaser would have been sitting on the left side of the tank, with Captain Winkler in the middle and Alvey as the gunner on the right side. Hence, it is most probable that poor Lee Kaser took the full force of the high explosive blast screaming in from the northern flank.

Also, Winkler told me in 1991 that he had his own head down in the turret when the tank was hit by a large explosion. The skin and hair from his neck up were burned. His eyes were seared shut and he could not see. When they got out of the tank and on the ground, one of the crew told him that everyone was out except Kaser. The interior of the tank was on fire. Their captain asked them to help Kaser out and someone returned and said it was no use. Winkler then asked someone to lead him to the nearest officer's tank so he could check in with Alger by radio. He believed that it was Gregg who suggested that he (Winkler) should start walking out and they would pick him up if they got the fire out in the tank.

In 1992, I located Al Urbanovsky in Waco, Texas, and spoke with him by telephone. His only observation about the battle was, "We never had a chance. It was five to one against us."

The Sherman was a durable tank produced in large quantities during World War II. On later fronts in Europe, it simply flooded the battlefields with overwhelming numbers, like hordes of insects that had to be picked off one by one. But the M-4 Sherman was clearly inferior in many respects to the German tanks of the era. In particular, it had a high profile, while the German Mark IV warhorse had a much lower silhouette so it was harder to hit. It did not help in the Battle of Sidi Bou Zid that the Shermans had bright yellow stars on the turrets for the German gunners to aim at. Also, the Mark IV was more agile, had better gun sights, and its cannon had a greater velocity.

However, the Sherman's worst drawback was that it had a tendency to catch fire, or "brew up" as the British commonly said. In fact, the tank was nicknamed the Ronson after the popular cigarette lighter of the day, simply because "it lights every time."

However, the Americans learned some hard lessons as a result of the Sidi Bou Zid annihilation of two tank battalions in two days. By the time they invaded Italy, crews welded additional armor plate around the turrets, while the top decks of the tanks were festooned with sandbags. Then too, the engineers designed a wet storage system for the 75mm ammunition in the tank turret that helped to protect the crews somewhat from the penetrating high explosive rounds. Sights were eventually improved, and a faster 76mm gun was added to the arsenal. Yet, on this grave occasion, all of those retrofits remained in the unreachable future.

The sun was rapidly setting. Winkler recalled that it was sometime between 1615 and 1630 when he started walking west to the American lines. His only guide at that point was the warmth of the descending sun on his burned face. He did not know how far he walked before he heard an American voice. That voice belonged to a member of D Company whose tank gun had been hit by an aerial bomb. The crew did not know where to go to reach American lines. Winkler told them to follow the sun. At the time, he thought this was the only tank to come out of the fight. He and the others made it back to the American lines by dark. After his burns healed, his eyes opened, and although he had sight in his left eye, he completely lost his right eye.

For nearly fifty years, Lee Kaser's family did not know what had happened to him. The War Department told the family he was missing in action and provided very few details. This was despite the fact that Captain Winkler made it back to the lines, and Gregg, as well as Urbanovsky, were taken prisoner and could have been asked about Kaser after the war. Also, Alvey had disclosed in a letter from the prison camp to Doc Frie that "poor Lee was instantly killed." Therefore, the army's failure to tell Kaser's family the truth is probably attributable to the fact that everyone was mustering out once the war was over and easing back into civilian life. The initial need for secrecy was replaced by benign indifference.

Lee Kaser was declared dead a few years later. But the family never had any details. Although my grandmother Susan had corresponded with Mary Kaser, Lee's mother, my own grandmother never told her that Lee had been instantly killed. I believe that this is because my uncle told a white lie to his parents as a prisoner of war by saying that he had not been wounded. He did not want them to worry. Consequently, he told only Frie the truth and asked him not to say anything to them about his own wounds. When I established contact with Lee Kaser's brother in 1992, he said they thought that Lee had been hurt and simply wandered into the desert where he had died. I told him what I knew, and then I heard from Lee's mother, Mary, who was still alive. She told me that Lee was one of nine children and "was a gentle boy." Mary Kaser continued to send me Christmas cards every year and lived to be 100. I gave her Winkler's address and she wrote to him as well. It is my profound regret that I was unable to obtain any more definitive information about the whereabouts of Lee's remains before his dear mother died. However, I have since that time deduced a plausible explanation for what I believe happened to him.

After the battle, the Germans roamed among the destroyed tanks and began salvaging equipment. Captain Machus, who was wounded, witnessed them burying our dead. His own tank was struck by an armor-piercing shell on its left side near the mosque in Sidi Salem. He had a severe wound to his neck and was captured and taken to a German aid station. He, like so many others, was told by his German captors that, "for you, the war is over."

It is probable that the Germans buried Lee's remains too, without his dog tags or other identification, which may have been burned in the tank, or otherwise separated from his body. When the Germans relinquished control of the area weeks later, the US Graves Registration teams entered the battlefield and disinterred the buried Americans. They may have missed Lee's body, in which case it is still somewhere near Sidi Salem, or he was found and later reburied in the area marked for unknowns at the American Cemetery at Carthage, Tunisia. His name is actually carved on a memorial there as among the missing. One would hope that if he was buried as an "unknown," that some US government entity would have seen fit to have kept a record of where particular remains were found. It may then be possible to cross-reference the disinterred remains with the locations of the burned-out tanks, which were all marked by the army in a battlefield survey conducted in April 1943.

There is some dispute as to the content of Alger's last report to headquarters as he headed north toward Sidi Bou Zid to link with D Company. Near 1650, some accounts state that Alger radioed the reply to Colonel Stack, "Still pretty busy. Situation is hard."

Other reports relate that he said, "Still pretty busy. Situation in hand." Based on the developments and Alger's own observations, it is extremely doubtful that he reported that the situation was "in hand." Maybe that was true from the German perspective, but certainly not his own.

Not long after this, Alger's command tank was rocked by a quick succession of German shells. His own radio operator, Warrant Officer Frank D. Leger, was struck by the final blast and died instantly. Again, this indicates to me that Alger's tank was facing east as it was struck on the left side killing Leger, the radio operator, instantly. Alger and two of his crewman bailed out of the burning tank as he counted thirteen holes in the armor plate. The dismounted tankers headed for the concealment of a wadi, but by 1730 were surrounded by German tanks and infantry and quickly captured.

Although an order to withdraw was given, it was never received by the Second Battalion due to Frank Leger's death and the destruction of Alger's radio and command tank. Alger had operational control of the entire attack, even though he did not have visibility of all of the units, particularly those that were well behind him. Because of that salient fact, once communication between the upper echelon commanders and Alger was severed, the entire battalion was cut off and remained in the killing zone.

The rout was complete. Only four tanks made it back to the American lines. Fifteen officers and 298 enlisted men from the Second Battalion and affiliated units were reported as missing in action at that time. Most of the American wounded were loaded into trucks and transported to Sfax on the coast. The officers and enlisted men were separated. From there, the prisoners of war were sent to Italy by plane and boat. Ultimately, a number of the officers were sent on to prison camps in Germany and then Poland, including Captain Machus and Lieutenant Colonel Alger.

The First Armored Regiment ceased to exist as a fighting force that day. However, it was later reconstituted in the Italian campaign as the First Tank Battalion. The conclusion made by British General W. G. E. Jackson provided the best summation of the February 15 counterattack to come out of the war.

> If ever there was a repetition of the Charge of the Light Brigade at Balaclava this was it. How it was thought that this small force could rescue two infantry battalions over 13 miles away with one, let alone two panzer divisions ready to dispute its passage is hard to imagine.

Alger fully concurred with this assessment. He later commented, "Unfortunately, General Jackson was not the Allied Commander in Central Tunisia." Jackson's comment motivated Alger to pen a paraphrase of the poet Alfred Lord Tennyson's classic "Charge of the Light Brigade." Alger also later lamented that "there was little or no foresight in planning or execution of the operations."

The ground" or "map bound" attack formation certainly contributed to the decimation of the 2nd Battalion. They should have employed "battle ground" tactics like the veteran German armored forces did. After the war, the officers of the 2nd Battalion also had this to say about the doomed formation which was essentially forced upon them by Colonel Stack:

> CC "C" Stack, with whom the 2nd. Bn. had never worked before, prescribed the formation for the counter-attack as "column of companies" and rationalized this by saying this would give depth to the attack. Had we known of the 10th. Panzer Div. and the Mark IV Bn. in the vicinity of Lessouda and the 21st. Panzer Div. near Ksaira, we would have spread our attack formation out with at least two companies on line in the attack echelon. This would have uncovered

the Germans north of the Sebeitla-Sidi-Bou-Zid road as well as the 21st. Panzer in the vicinity of Ksaira and Hadid. But regardless of what formation we took we were faced with a staggering task.

The Germans grilled the prisoners and were mystified as to why the assault was so under strength and wondered where the rest of the attacking force was. They remained on alert all night waiting for the expected echelons of American armor. Meanwhile, they exploited their tactical advantage in the series of skirmishes known to history as the Battle of Kasserine Pass. During the apex of that campaign, Fredendall, by then ensconced in his new villa far behind the lines, turned to his chief of staff and chortled, "Dabney, open up the bottle. Let's have a drink."

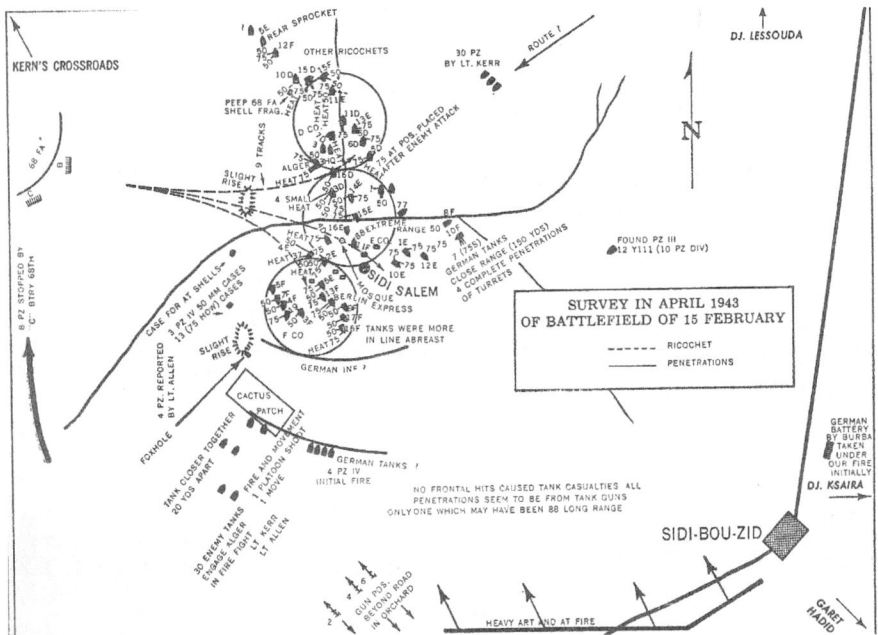

Aftermath of the Battle of Sidi Bou Zid, February 15, 1943,
showing the locations of the destroyed American tanks around
the village of Sidi Salem. (U.S. Army Survey, April 1943)

11

The Aftermath

Negative deconstructions of the Battle of Sidi Bou Zid may be labeled as "hindsight." But as LTC Alger later observed, "there was little or no foresight in the planning and execution of the operations." It is interesting that Erwin Rommel did not say very much about the Battle of Sidi Bou Zid, except to criticize Commando Supremo for not exploiting the victory. However, it is clear that the entire scheme of defense for Sidi Bou Zid had failed miserably. The forward American positions were not mutually supportive. Hence, the tankers were completely surrounded by the Germans who came at them like a host of angry hornets. Burnt out hulls of American tanks were huddled abreast in tight clusters, their turrets with gaping holes bored by high explosive antitank rounds. In a battlefield survey conducted by the US Army in April 1943, the investigators concluded as follows:

> NO FRONTAL HITS CAUSED TANK CASU-
> ALTIES. ALL PENETRATIONS SEEM TO BE
> FROM TANK GUNS ONLY ONE WHICH MAY
> HAVE BEEN 88 LONG RANGE.

Because of the propensity for the Sherman tank to catch fire, the Germans called it the "Tommy Cooker," referring to the fate of British tankers who were inside tanks hit by armor penetrating shells. This defect was mainly attributable to the dry storage of ammunition surrounding the three crew members in the turret, coupled with an inadequate layer of protective armor. When a high explosive antitank round hit the turret, it was like a welder's torch suddenly burning through steel. Penetration was preceded by a bright red glow of molten metal, followed by a splash of liquefied steel fragments, known as spall. Whatever was caught in the spray of scorching splatter was immediately engulfed in superheated flames.

Thus, a number of crew members suffered horrific burns, resulting in death, or months of agonizing suffering. Kaser was killed in the initial blast from the high explosive antitank round. Captain Winkler was burned, and his eyes were melted shut. Alvey suffered severe burns to his face and hands. Zulah Ray, who was a tank gunner with G Company, Third Battalion, First Armored Regiment, was captured on February 14 and also suffered excruciating burns to his face and hands.

The injured Americans were picked up by German searchers and at first taken to an aid station and attended by German doctors. All reports from survivors indicate that they were treated well by the Germans who generally abided by the Geneva convention. The Germans were somewhat condescending and seemed to feel sorry for the Yanks who had just received a vicious beating. They expressed wonderment as to why the Americans were even there, because in their view America had no business in the fight since Adolph Hitler seemingly had no designs on the United States of America.

A number of American medics had been captured and were allowed to keep their medical kits and help treat the US soldiers who had been taken captive. However, there was a general shortage of painkillers. Many of the captives died from the severity of their burns and because they had inhaled flames and superheated smoke.

During the morning of February 17, 1943, the American wounded were loaded onto personnel carriers and driven about seventy-five miles to an Italian-German field hospital near Sfax on the east coast of Tunisia. Wounds were cleaned and fresh bandages applied. About twenty Allied prisoners were lodged in each tent. As their conditions improved, they were moved to camps on the Italian mainland by Italian hospital ships and planes. The Red Cross logo on the side of each ship was brightly lit by a floodlight to be certain that planes could make no mistake in identification and strafe or bomb the ship.

Many were suffering from the pain of their wounds, became seasick and did not eat for three days. The slow journey across the Mediterranean ended at the port of Bari on the heel of the Italian boot. In Bari, they were fed with a roll of dark bread and sour red wine. Many of the wounded Americans were then loaded onto trains and transported to an electric tram that wound uphill to Camp 204 in the village of Altamura, which was a convent school converted into a hospital. There, the GIs were meticulously cared for by the Italian *sorellas,* (sisters) who acted as nurses. But by the time the wounded arrived it was late in the afternoon, and they had missed the main meal and had to wait until breakfast for a ration of hard bread and chicory coffee.

Alvey was in this hospital together with other members of the First Armored Regiment, including Zulah Ray, Charlie Lum, J.B. Tackett, and Kenneth Robertson, all of whom would be together until the mass escape from Camp 59 in Servigliano the night of September 14, 1943. Robertson and Lum were from Bakersfield, California, and in E Company, Second Battalion, First Armored Regiment. They were also friends of Everett Gregg, who made his home in Bakersfield.

While Ray and Alvey and about a third of the troops had

suffered from the same type of turret burns, Robertson had been shot in left shoulder and had a chunk of flesh ripped from his left buttock. Hence, he was the "butt" of many jokes and puns. Most claimed he was "half-assed." His friends also told him that nobody in the American army was entitled to have two of anything. But Zulah Ray told me that Robertson had one particular method of getting even with them. His upper arm and shoulder were in a cast, which over time developed an extremely putrid odor. Hence, Robertson would walk by their beds and wave his arm until the full force of putrescence assaulted their nostrils until they kicked him away.

The hospital had bars on the windows, and although the guards at the doors were lackadaisical, the GIs were in no condition to escape. For weeks and in some cases months, the nuns served the prisoners from wheeled carts. They had some pasta and a weak rice stew, black chicory coffee, bread, cheese, peppers, and what the nuns referred to as thistle. But there was never any salad or fruit available.

The wounded prisoners in Italy were treated well by the Italian and German medical personnel, but there were chronic shortages of drugs and medical supplies throughout Italy. Other able-bodied captives did not have the same experience, particularly captured infantrymen. Some ground soldiers reported to me that they were dragged in parades through Italian cities, villages, and towns while the local populace spit at them and jeered. They were also subjected to verbal, emotional, and physical abuse by Italian soldiers and the *carabinieri*. This sordid treatment was in direct abrogation of the Geneva convention. Evidently, it was part of the Fascist doctrine to oppress, abuse and intimidate any opposition. However, as the tide of war turned against the Axis, this type of abuse rapidly diminished, particularly after the Allied landings on the Italian mainland.

A telegram arrived at the home of Susan and Claude Newton on

March 11, 1943, informing them that Alvey was missing in action. By that time, news of the catastrophes in North Africa, generally encompassed by the series of fights commonly known as the Battle of Kasserine Pass, had received a great deal of press in the American papers as well and was the subject of an article in Time magazine. Even Ernie Pyle had written about the doomed counterattack, having witnessed it from the summit of Djebel Hamra, accompanied by Alger's senior commanders. There was a strong sense of foreboding among all of the mothers, fathers, and families of American troops known to be in that general area.

Meanwhile, Alvey had written the following brief message to his mother on a postcard provided by the Italian government. It bears a censor's postmark of February 28, 1943:

UNINJURED PRISONER. SENDING ADDRESS LATER. CAN SEND THREE POUND PACKAGE WEEKLY THROUGH RED CROSS. SUGGEST SOCKS, CIGARETTES, SWEATER, STATIONERY, CANDY, UNDERWEAR, TOILET ARTICLES. LOVE.

He was then a *severely* wounded prisoner, but he did not want to alarm his mother and cause her any more worry. This was a common ploy used by the prisoners of war writing home. Some had legs and arms blown off and told their folks they were not injured. One unfortunate aspect of this was that the US armed forces then reviewed this correspondence as it entered the United States and created records erroneously reporting these brave men as uninjured. They should have all been immediately awarded Purple Hearts instead, and one can only hope that this error was eventually corrected.

The most compelling example of this I can give concerns Stanley Macieiski, a tanker with F Company at the Battle of Sidi Bou Zid.

Stanley was captured with the others and wrote the following letter to his mother from a prisoner of war camp in Italy:

> Am a P.O.W. slightly wounded. Nothing serious. Don't worry. See you after the war. Will send my address as soon as possible. Your son.

In truth, Stanley and a lieutenant were on top of their burning tank trying to help others get out. The lieutenant was killed by a shell blast, and the next round sheared off both of Stanley's legs. He was eventually exchanged for a German prisoner of war in Spain and repatriated. After the war, Macieiski served as the warden of the Vienna correctional facility in Illinois and as mayor of the city of Chester, Illinois, for eight years. He died in 2001 at the age of 85.

Alvey sent an Italian form postcard to his mother dated March 4, 1943, showing the return address of PG Campo No. 204. In Italy, the prisoner of war camps were designated PG which was short for *Prigione di Guerra* ("War Prison"). In that first post card home from the hospital he simply said the following:

> AM WELL. TAKE PACKAGE MONEY FROM ALLOTMENT. SEND WARM CLOTHING, GLOVES, STOCKING CAP AS PACKAGE WILL TAKE SIX MONTHS TO ARRIVE. ADDRESS ABOVE. LOVE ALVEY.

That was followed by another postcard home dated March 24, 1943, in which he reiterated that "I am alright. I have not been wounded."

While at PG 204, he also wrote to Robert Frie telling only him the sad truth:

Please don't tell mother of this. Poor Kaser was instantly killed by the same explosions that burned me. All the rest escaped with minor burns and cuts.

He was obviously unaware at the time of the true extent of Captain Winkler's eye damage, probably because he was dealing with his own injuries and pain immediately after the tank was hit, and Winkler told me it was Gregg who took his arm, led him away and advised him to walk back to American lines.

His next letter home does not bear a visible postmark, but he mentions that he has been a prisoner for over two months. It shows an address of PG 75, a transit camp outside Bari. Consequently, it appears that he was undergoing medical treatment for two months and then moved to Camp 75 to await transfer to a permanent prisoner of war camp. He told his mom and dad that he was getting along well and studying German and Italian. He said that he was sending the letter via airmail to speed things up and that he did not know when he would hear from them. He asked them to write as often as they could and to tell his friends to write also.

Alvey also wrote to Frie from PG 75, telling him that they were playing soccer with the South African and English prisoners, while debating the relative merits of their respective armies. He said that naturally, he was learning Italian. But he was also working on German. In fact, a South African friend named Hans Pretorius from the Transvaal had loaned him his German-English dictionary. Alvey mentioned that he was on a detail that morning helping to fix their new soccer court. He closed with the report that they were having a lot of fun teaching the other boys baseball, basketball, and American slang.

It is likely that his next letter to his parents in mid-April 1943 was written from PG 75 because he mentions that he has decent barracks to sleep in and is getting enough to eat. Still, he could not have been at PG 75 for more than a few weeks because the next letter was from him to Robert Frie and is dated May 14, 1943, with a return address of Camp 59, his last prisoner of war camp, in Servigliano, Italy.

Part V

CAPTIVITY AND ESCAPE

Italy. (Courtesy of U.S. Central Intelligence Agency)

12

Servigliano — Camp 59

The town of Servigliano, Italy, is located in the rolling verdant foothills of the Apennine Mountains forming the extended spine of the Italian peninsula. It rests beside the Tenna River in the province of Le Marche, about ninety miles northeast of Rome and twenty miles inland from Porto San Giorgio on the Adriatic Coast. While World War I was raging, a prison camp was constructed just outside the town in proximity to a rail spur. During that conflict, the camp housed Austrian prisoners of war. It was closed in 1935, then reactivated in 1940 at the outbreak of World War II and redesignated as Prigione di Guerra Campo 59.

Camp 59 initially held Greek prisoners, but after February 1942, it was occupied primarily by British and American prisoners of war. The camp contained brick and wood structures on stone foundations, with tile roofs. It was surrounded by a stone wall about twelve feet high, with glass shards imbedded in the concrete cap. Each of the sixteen barracks had 144 beds in two tiers. The barracks were all unheated. Heating was only available in the infirmary. However, the troops were given two dark gray wool blankets to ward off the cold. Commanding the camp was a Colonel Bacci, who was an ardent Fascist. The "man of confidence," (the prisoners' personal representative and go-between) was a British Sergeant-Major named Hegarty.

The prisoners slept on wooden beds with slats and straw mattresses that were restuffed every four months. Instead of a real pillow, there was a slanting board beneath their heads. For some reason, the Italian General Staff ordered that the prisoners' sheets be taken away. However, some have reported that the Americans were given sheets after most of the British were assigned to other camps. There was one shower house that could handle 180 men per day. As a result, the captives could have one shower every ten days. There was one latrine with running water that could accommodate thirty men at a time. The toilets were of the hole in the floor squatting type favored by Europeans at the time.

Once a week, each man was provided with one postcard and a letter form for correspondence. The American prisoners complained about the slowness of their mail. Many did not receive any responses for six months after first writing to their families as prisoners of war. Charlie Smith reported that he did not receive the very first care package from his folks until 1945! Over the course of six months, Alvey mentioned several times in his letters from Camp 59 that he had not heard from anyone.

Initially, the Americans were provided once a week with British Red Cross parcels. It took a long time for the American Red Cross parcels to get through to them, which was the subject of another complaint. As of April 7, 1943, only sixteen American Red Cross parcels had arrived at the camp. Still, those Red Cross parcels were a godsend. Many repatriated soldiers have since acknowledged that they would have starved to death without them. The Americans really liked the Canadian parcels due to their large size. Other Yanks preferred their own because they contained American cigarettes and real coffee, while the British favored their own due to the can of condensed milk provided for their tea. The

Italians punched holes in all of the tins so that they had to be consumed immediately and could not be hoarded for an escape.

The men were given one lira per week with which to purchase fresh vegetables. They were also credited with seven lire per day for general expenses and given internal coupons to make purchases. Those working within the camp were provided with supplemental rations. They could also buy toilet articles, wine, and fruit from the canteen within the camp and received a ration of about thirty-five cigarettes per week, in addition to those provided in Red Cross parcels.

There was an infirmary staffed by two British doctors, which consisted of three dormitories with eight beds. The camp also had a British dentist who provided free care to the prisoners. Artificial teeth were even provided, once approved by the Red Cross. If major medical care was required, the prisoners were sent to hospitals in Teramo, Ascoli-Piceno, Bergamo, and Besceglie. However, the ambulance was unreliable and the conditions were primitive. One ex-prisoner told me that he suffered from extremely painful constipation and had to be transported by oxcart to a hospital. For his treatment he was handed a wooden spoon to help "break things loose." A number of the Americans suffered from influenza, and one of them died from some non-descript illness while in captivity.

Twice a week, they were allowed to use a sport field adjacent to the camp. Additionally, 300 prisoners per week were allowed to join escorted walks outside the camp. They could read books at the camp library, and play cards and games provided by the Red Cross. They did whatever they could to fight the boredom.

For the most part, the ex-prisoners of war report that they were not abused at Camp 59. However, one has claimed that the Italian guards would eat oranges and squirt the juices in the prisoners' faces. Yet, humorous incidents also prevailed. Francis Cecil "Dick" George of the Royal Navy reported that the captives taught an obscene English word to a local priest visiting the camp. They told him that it meant good-bye. As the padre left the camp, he turned to bless the troops, raised his arm and uttered the expletive. The men collapsed in hysterical laughter, to the puzzlement of the cleric.

The Swiss Legation at Rome visited Camp 59 at various times, and at the behest of the Red Cross and US State Department reported on the conditions there. The conclusion was "the impression given by camp No. 59 is good. Its organization is now in order and the relations between the man of confidence and the Italian authorities are correct and based on mutual understanding."

A number of American prisoners would beg to differ. More than one has described it as "a pest-hole." Although the Swiss Legation described the camp as free of vermin and lice, the prisoners had daily encounters with bedbugs as well as body lice. There was no spray available, so they had to take their bed clothes outside in the bright sun to pick the bugs out one by one. Sometimes, the "thistle" soup they were served was infested with bugs. Most just picked them off, but some of the men did not mind the added protein.

Keith Argraves reported that Dan Cole said he caught several bedbugs trying to move a Red Cross parcel. Also, Argraves related that Tony Cole said that when he heard about the Italian capitulation, "I saw four bedbugs moving about on the top of my bed. All were waving sheets. They had given in too."

The Swiss Legation reported that no escape attempts had been made. However, there was ongoing tunneling activity. But the consequences of escape were severe, resulting in weeks of solitary confinement in a dungeon, or stooping chambers, with only bread and water.

As of March 17, 1943, there were 1,337 Englishmen in Camp 59, as well as 445 Americans newly arrived from the fighting in Tunisia. There was 1 South African in the camp, and 6 Poles,

22 Irishmen, 15 Canadians, 46 Cyprians, 11 Australians, and 19 soldiers of various other nationalities. At that time, a number of British soldiers had already been transferred to make room for the Americans then arriving from Tunisia.

By June 12, 1943, the number of Americans in Camp 59 had increased to 913, while the British numbers declined to 313. The numbers of troops of other nationalities remained about the same.

Alvey wrote a postcard to his parents on May 14, 1943, the same day as a longer letter to Robert Frie. He told his mother that the Kaywoodie pipe had really come in handy. In his letter to Robert Frie, Alvey asked if he had been getting any of his letters or post-cards. Alvey told Frie that he was studying German, which would help him get that one big part of his medical education out of the way. By this time, Frie was himself an Army medic, having tem-porarily dropped out of medical school. Alvey said that he could actually study five languages in the camp and that he had plenty of time to learn them.

Then, he told Frie that he was long-healed of his burns, but had a few scars and said that he was very fortunate "after seeing what happened to poor Lee." He closed by relating that they were start-ing to receive American Red Cross parcels, with his first American cigarettes in three months, "and were they welcome!"

He followed with a letter to his folks dated May 21, 1943, saying that he was sending it by airmail in the hope that they would get it sooner than the letters he had sent in the past month. Alvey also told them that they were getting Red Cross parcels and the only thing he really wanted were some Lucky Strikes, pipe tobacco, and a copy of Montaigne's *Essays*.

On June 23, 1943, he wrote home and said that he was beginning to look hard for a letter. Alvey said that some of the boys that were taken at the same time had already received letters from home. He asked them not to send any heavy clothes as the British Red Cross had fixed them up pretty good. Significantly, he asked them to write to Mrs. Glacile Skinner in Galena, Kansas, and tell her that her son Ray was there with him and was well. Ray was also in D Company, Second Battalion and was captured at Sidi Bou Zid. Alvey said Ray was doing the same for him and that they would have a better chance of getting a letter through.

Alvey wrote to his mom and dad in July and said he had still not heard from them, but that it looked as if mail should be coming in then. He said to tell George Kienly that Tex Rowland was there with him. Alvey also mentioned that he knew about Bart Dempsey, another soldier from Logansport, as they had been captured at the same time. He could have been referring to either Dempsey's capture or death. The National Archives simply states that Dempsey "died of wounds."

Alvey sent his mother a postcard dated July 28, 1943, advising that he had just heard from her for the first time and needed nothing except cigarettes. He had earlier that day sent her a letter again lamenting his nonreceipt of any mail. On August 4, 1943, he sent another postcard to his mom and dad saying that he had finally received their radiogram dated April 6. He mentioned the same radiogram in a postcard to them on August 18 and said it had come through the Vatican. In nearly every letter home from the prison camp he had also asked about the welfare of friends and family members.

It is unknown whether he or any of the other prisoners knew that the Allies had conquered Sicily and ousted the Germans just the day before. There was a grapevine within the camp and indications that forbidden radio transmissions were being received by the prisoners. Some sympathetic Italians have also been reported as having regularly updated the prisoners with battlefront news. Even if Alvey had been aware of that development, he would not have been able to mention it; the comment would have been censored, and he would have suffered retribution. The final full-length letter from him known to exist was written to Robert Frie on August 18, 1943. He said he presumed that Frie was studying hard, not knowing that Frie was now an Army medic and out of school. Alvey reiterated that his burn scars had almost completely healed and predicted that when he got back "I'll have no evidence of bloody brawling battle on me." The letter closed with, "well, Robin, till I see you again, keep plugging away; I'm looking forward to calling you Doc you know. Alvey."

A little over two weeks after that final letter, on September 3, 1943, the Allies invaded the mainland of Italy, landing at Salerno (Operation Avalanche), Calabria (Operation Baytown) and Taranto (Operation Slapstick). The whole universe was about to change for the captives of Camp 59.

13

Through the Wall

After the invasion of Sicily and the bombing of Rome by the Allies, the Italian Grand Council of Fascism suddenly decided that they had lost all confidence in Mussolini. Hence, on the night of July 24, 1943, King Victor Immanuel III replaced Il Duce with Marshal Pietro Badoglio and had the former dictator arrested. He was held at the Campo Imperatore, a hotel near the Gran Sasso, the highest mountain in the Apennines in the Abruzzo province. Sicily fell on August 17, 1943, and the Allies were then poised to invade the Italian mainland.

King Victor, Badoglio, and others soon engaged in armistice negotiations with the Allies in the hope of winning some favorable concessions for Italy. However, one important impasse that was never resolved was what to do about Germany and its troops then in Italy. Nevertheless, the Armistice of Cassibile was signed on September 3, 1943, between Italy and the "United Nations."

The armistice represented a total capitulation by Italy. However, it also set off a civil war for the control of Italy by the Italian Resistance Movement *(Resistenza italiana)* also known as the Partigiani against Nazi-Fascist elements. It also caused the Germans to flood reinforcements into Italy from the north and to capture about 700,000 Italian soldiers who were then either marooned in prisoner of war camps or forced to fight for Germany on the Russian front. Thousands of other Italian men and boys were conscripted by the Germans for forced labor in German industries.

Under the terms of the armistice, the parties agreed to withhold any public announcement until September 8, 1943. That night, Allied radio in Algiers reported the capitulation, and the Italian government concurrently released the following statement:

> The Italian government, recognizing the impossibility of continuing the unequal struggle against an overwhelming enemy force, in order to avoid further and graver disasters for the Nation requested an armistice from General Eisenhower, supreme commander of allied Anglo-American forces.
>
> The request was granted. Consequently, all acts of hostility against the Anglo-American forces by Italian forces must cease everywhere. However, they may react to eventual attacks from any other source.

That same night, President Roosevelt engaged in Fireside Chat number twenty-six with the American people, and told them the favorable news from the Mediterranean theater but reminded them that Germany and Japan still had to be conquered.

The next day, September 9, 1943, the Allies landed in force on the Italian mainland. The Italian newspaper *La Stampa* carried the banner *"La Guerra E Finita."* But it was far from over for Italy, or for the Allies, or the prisoners of war in camps scattered throughout Italy.

Chaos then reigned supreme on the Italian peninsula. The king and Badoglio gave rise to some resentment among the populace by immediately fleeing to Brindisi and the sheltering arms of the Allies, while the people in the countryside and towns were left to fend for themselves as best they could. Although fascism had supposedly been outlawed, a new Nazi-Fascist alliance was formed in the vacuum and held sway in many areas of Central and Northern Italy.

The situation in Camp 59 and the other POW camps was no less chaotic. Of course, when the announcement of the armistice was made to the prisoners, about September 10, 1943, they were all jubilant, thinking that the war was over and that the Italians were now our Allies. But the ecstatic mood was tempered by what would happen next. Scuttlebutt said that the Allies would reach them in just two to three days and that they should just stay in place. The official position was set forth under the infamous "stay put order" issued from MI9 in Whitehall, London. In essence, the Allied prisoners were ordered to remain in the camps under penalty of courts martial. This caused no small amount of consternation, given that in both the British and American armed forces, it was the duty of every soldier, sailor, and airman to escape, in order to tie up and redirect as many enemy resources as possible in a search effort.

The electrifying announcement and misguided stay put order were followed by several days of anxious waiting. There are many accounts of the next few days that have been written about or verbally reported by the survivors. Many of these accounts have the Italian guards abandoning their posts and simply going home. Others state that the cooks walked out as well but that the remaining Red Cross parcels were passed out to the prisoners. Meanwhile, the men continued their tunneling efforts and discussed among themselves what they should do.

Some say that the guards inexplicably returned on September 13 but did not occupy the guard towers. The angst of the prisoners was fanned by rumors and misinformation. One report that caused them substantial uneasiness maintained that a column of German armor was headed south to take control of the camp. By September 14, 1943, the mood was tense and the ambient circumstances extremely uncertain and hectic.

There is a report that the prisoners agreed to break out of the camp at midnight with the ringing in the bell tower of the church of San Marco in nearby Servigliano. There was a rumor that Yugoslav rebels would help them all escape. Others determined on their own to smash down the front gate or go over the wall. Nearly everyone who has given an account agrees that many of the estimated 2,000 escapees went through a hole smashed through the stone wall surrounding the camp.

One of the escapees was an American soldier from the First Armored Division named Earl Huddleston, who claimed in a 1944 feature article in Cosmopolitan magazine that he and some others had made poles from the wood of their bunks, hidden them in the brush away from the main gate and then pole-vaulted over the wall. They made it over, but the guards reportedly fired machine guns at the escapers. Huddleston and his band eventually made their way to Allied lines. The story of their adventure behind the lines was authored by Harry T. Brundidge and Ernest Sheehan.

Zulah Ray knew Huddleston and intimated to me that he was more than a little skeptical about the accuracy of the pole-vaulting story. Other features of the article must also give rise to some skepticism. For one thing, Huddleston reported that they crossed the Chienti River just a few minutes later. However, the river adjacent to Servigliano is the Tenna, not the Chienti. Additionally, Huddleston reports at length that he and the others witnessed the rescue of Mussolini by storm troopers sent by Adolf Hitler at Gran Cacco [sic]. But the Campo Imperatore Hotel near the Gran Sasso where Mussolini had been held was about forty-three miles south of Servigliano. Such a distance would have been difficult to traverse over mountainous terrain with enemy traffic constantly on the roads and troops guarding the bridges. It also does not help the veracity of the account that history records that Mussolini was rescued on September 12, 1943, *before* Huddleston and his companions had even vaulted over the wall!

Zulah Ray believed that Huddleston was with the first group of escapees who broke out of the camp on the night of September 13, 1943. He did not believe that Huddleston went over the wall, but rather that he walked through the door. The rest of the prisoners were warned over a loudspeaker that the guards had orders to shoot if any others tried to escape. However, even if Huddleston escaped a day earlier than the majority of the internees, he would still not have seen Mussolini's rescue, which had played out far to the south the day before.

The Huddleston article also asserts that they saw Mussolini rescued by German paratroops jumping from Junkers 52s, and that there were "nearly one hundred twisting bodies in the air in a matter of seconds." The truth is that while *fallschirmjager* (paratroops) were involved in the rescue, they all landed in DFS 230 gliders with a special forces unit commanded by Otto Skorzeny. A parachute drop was not feasible due to the thin air at the 6,000-foot elevation and the small landing zone. Finally, Huddleston reported that Mussolini left by car. But the fact is that that Mussolini and Skorzeny were flown out in a Fieseler Storch, the same type of plane favored by Rommel for his battlefield reconnaissance.

Apart from that, Huddleston claims to have spoken with Pope Pius XII when he visited Camp 59. But there is no record of *Il Papa* visiting Camp 59, although he was known to send his envoys to various camps holding prisoners of all nationalities. Additionally, after making it back to Allied lines, the article states that Huddleston was flown to Palermo and personally interviewed by General Patton. He also supposedly had a personal audience with Italian Marshal Badoglio. While these occurrences are somewhat plausible, I have not been able to verify either of them.

One can only speculate as to the reason for so many glaring factual liberties. They could be attributable to intentional misdirection or propaganda by the Allies to hide from the enemy the fact that American and British intelligence knew the true facts. The article does explain that the "complete factual story" could not be told until after the war. Also, it is common knowledge that prisoners returning to Allied control were told not to talk about their experiences because too many escape details might jeopardize the men still behind the lines.

However, the controversial reputation of one of the authors of the article may explain the tall tale aspects of the Huddleston story. Harry T. Brundidge was an old-school journalist who was always trying to dig up a major scoop ahead of the competition. He was not so much concerned about veracity, as the sensational value of any given piece. For example, he published an alleged interview with Al Capone even though Capone denied that the interview had even taken place. After the war, he went to Japan in the hope of scoring an interview with the emperor or Hideki Tojo. Frustrated at his lack of success, Brundidge focused on "finding" the woman known to GIs in the Pacific theater as Tokyo Rose. Although there were various women in Japan thought to be traitors to the United States who broadcast radio propaganda to American troops, the name Tokyo Rose was never used in the broadcasts. That was just a composite title fabricated by the troops.

Brundidge and a reporter named Clark Lee went to Japan and located a woman named Eva Toguri D'Aquino, an American citizen who had been trapped in Japan when the war began. She was one among many English-language speakers compelled to work for the Japanese on radio broadcasts emanating from Tokyo. But her radio name was actually Orphan Annie, not Tokyo Rose. In fact, the name Tokyo Rose was actually used by the troops long before D'Aquino was ever involved in the *Zero Hour* broadcasts from Radio Tokyo.

Lee and Brundidge promised to pay D'Aquino $2,000 for her story. She and her husband were in desperate need of money. Not realizing the potential consequences, she signed a statement identifying herself as Tokyo Rose and told them the entire account of her tenure at Radio Tokyo during the war. Brundidge promptly claimed to have the exclusive story on Tokyo Rose. He connived with the occupation authorities to call a press conference, where she answered reporters' questions in a forthright manner. Brundidge also gave her "confession" to the US government and suborned the perjured testimony of a witness. She was arrested in Yokohama and held incommunicado for a time.

After public pressure mounted and fervor was drummed up by columnist Walter Winchell, Eva Toguri D'Aquino was brought back to the United States and tried on eight counts of treason. She was convicted of one trumped-up count, sentenced to ten years in prison and a $10,000 fine. She served more than six years and was released in 1956. She never saw her husband again. But after it was discovered that two witnesses at her trial had given perjured testimony and been coached to lie by government operatives, D'Aquino was pardoned by President Gerald Ford on January 19, 1977. Brundidge never paid her the $2,000 and welshed with the excuse that she was a criminal. He helped to frame her and ruined her life for the glory of a scoop made up out of whole cloth.

So much for the journalistic integrity of one of the authors of the Huddleston escape account. In any case, my point is not to discredit Huddleston, who performed his solemn duty to escape, but to show how muddled the various escape accounts have since become, particularly when coupled with the passage of time, the sensationalism of the press, and the conflation of several memories.

The notorious stay put order is also the object of disagreement in the Camp 59 survivors' escape accounts. After the Italian armistice, there were an estimated 80,000 Allied prisoners in Italian camps. There was a concern among some in the British command of the potentially negative consequences of a mass breakout. The situation in the countryside was uncertain. There were still Fascists everywhere, and the Italian farmers did not have enough resources to feed themselves. Also, it was thought that the Allies would probably roll into the camps within a matter of days. Thus, according to popular history, the head of MI9, Brigadier Norman Crockatt, and his cohorts, including Bernard Montgomery, issued the infamous order P/W 87190 on June 7, 1943.

> In the event of an Allied invasion of Italy, officers commanding prison camps will ensure that prisoners-of-war remain within camp. Authority is granted to all officers commanding to take necessary disciplinary action to prevent individual prisoners-of-war attempting to rejoin their own units.

MI9 had the stay put order broadcast to the camps in Italy. Instructions were surreptitiously communicated to the POWs through the weekly BBC radio program of the Reverend Ronald Selby Wright. The senior Allied officer in each camp was therefore required to enforce the infamous order, which was directly contrary to standard armed forces policy. In Camp 59, this responsibility fell squarely upon the shoulders of British doctor Captain J.H. Derek Millar after the man of confidence, Sergeant-Major Hegarty, became overwhelmed and unable to deal with the issue. Captain Millar had rendered superior medical treatments to the prisoners despite being handicapped with primitive equipment and little or no appropriate medicine, other than laxatives and iodine. Many men have credited him with saving their lives.

An account by historian Dr. Giuseppe Millozzi in his dissertation "Allied Prisoners of War in the Region of the Marche and Prison Camp at Servigliano" reveals that Dr. Millar enabled all of Camp 59's estimated 2,000 POWs to escape because he defied the stay put order. This act of defiance was said to be based on an agreement between Millar and the Italian commandant, Colonel Bacci, that the men could flee the camp if Millar accepted full responsibility. Because of Dr. Millar's defiance of an unequivocal order, he was threatened with punishment by the British but was ultimately decorated for his role in the escape. Dr. Millar's published *Memoirs* relates this same version of the facts.

However, there are several supplemental accounts by escapees that cannot simply be disregarded. They are referenced here for the sake of a complete historical record and not to cast a negative light on Captain Millar, who is worthy of the utmost respect.

First, Keith Argraves, Kenneth Lightbody, Robert J. Noah, and Raymond Cox have all claimed that men rushed the front gate of Camp 59 on the night of September 14, 1943, and were shot at by Italian guards. Others such as James Kavana and Clarence Dust have affirmed that the escapees were shot at. Many were said to have been wounded or killed. Some claimed the prisoners streaming from the camp fought back with sticks, stones, and knives made from tin cans. Argraves tells the story of the gate rush in his book *Keith Argraves Paratrooper*, by George W. Chambers, and unequivocally claims that eight brave Scotsmen were killed. Lightbody, Noah, and Cox all told me that men were actually shot, except they did not assert that the victims were Scotsmen. Question: If the prisoners were free to go because Captain Millar claimed full responsibility, why was the front gate stormed with the consequence of prisoners being fired upon, and injured or killed?

Second, Zulah Ray has written an extended account of the escape in his self-published book, titled *Zulah Dawson Ray: His Stories*, by Evalynn Quisenberry. He unequivocally states that the "English doctor" in charge of the camp tried to calm the prisoners by advising them that they were now under the authority of the commander of Camp 59 and would take orders from him, otherwise they would be up for courts martial. He then avers that the

English doctor mandated, "You are ordered to remain in camp until the Allies reach you."

Zulah Ray maintained that the English doctor came on a loud-speaker as the prisoners were starting to leave the camp and spoke to them "as a father speaks to a child when he realizes he is no longer in control," advising them that the commandant said they could leave the camp, but asking them not to leave the area or go into the countryside. If they left, they could still sleep in the camp. The doctor said that the Italian people did not have enough food to feed themselves, so they would leave the gates open so the prisoners could go in and out anytime they wanted to. According to Ray, this message was reiterated several times. Ray went on to say that about a quarter of the POWs did as the doctor asked and remained in the camp. Ray told me that frankly, it was reprehensible to him that so many elected to stay in the camp when it was their solemn duty to escape.

A British SAS soldier, Sid Dowland, who escaped from Camp 59, has confirmed Zulah Ray's version of the facts. Richard Dorney wrote about Dowland's exploits and escape experience in his book, *An Active Service.*

> The prisoners knew only that the Italians were being driven back, so it was a great surprise when the Commandant of Campo 59 announced the news of Italy's capitulation. There was a great deal of confusion. The Commandant told them that the Germans would probably take over the camp. The men speculated what the Nazis would do with them. Some thought there would be no change, others thought that they might be transported to Germany. Some even suggested that the Germans wouldn't bother to come, as they would be fighting the allied advance.

The senior officer in the camp, a British Captain, issued an order forbidding the men to try and escape. No doubt he feared that there would be a massacre if they tried to break out in a disorganized fashion. To the amazement of the prisoners their guards were reinstated, they couldn't understand it. The commandant had told them that they should leave before the Germans arrived. Why were the guards suddenly back in place? Everyone seemed confused, even the Italians. The SAS men got together to discuss the situation and they agreed unanimously that they would break out as soon as they could. Some of the group tried unsuccessfully to escape straight away and were soon returned to the compound.

Charlie Smith confirmed that the men were ordered to remain in Camp 59 by the British officers. In his own postwar memoir written by his wife, Ruby Simon Smith, he recalls the circumstances as follows:

> We got word the British troops would be in the area in ten days. Meanwhile the POW British officers more or less took over and advised us to remain in the compound. They placed non-commissioned officers outside the compound to watch for Germans who might try to come and recapture us.

Third, most of the prisoners of war I contacted have recounted that a hole was smashed through the wall of Camp 59 enabling the men to escape en masse. The outline of this hole in the wall and its repair can be seen to this day and has been the subject of countless photographs. Others have described how a door was broken down in the showers. If the prisoners were free to leave the camp at will, why was it necessary to knock a hole in the wall or break down a door in the showers?

In general, the Americans have related to me that they just decided to get the hell out of there. It is clear to me that they made their decisions to escape without any deference to Captain Millar or the desires of Colonel Bacci. But it is also true that none of them were privy to Captain Millar's negotiations with Colonel Bacci. Yet, I must query if Millar and Bacci just bowed to the inevitable and decided to let the men go if Millar accepted full responsibility, thereby preventing the Fascist Bacci from giving orders to shoot the escapees.

Without any doubt, as a caring physician, Millar always had the men's best interests at heart. Still, it is an incomplete account to the effect that Captain Millar simply defied the stay put order and allowed around two thousand prisoners to escape and seek safety, or ensured that they were able to escape. That conclusion does not tell the whole story. There should be no doubt that Millar at first obeyed his superiors and actually issued an order forbidding the men from escaping. It is far more likely that the prisoners were going to escape regardless and that Captain Millar realizing this, then did what he could to prevent further bloodshed at the hands of Bacci and the Italian guards. There is no doubt whatsoever that Millar did sign an agreement with Colonel Bacci to accept full responsibility.

It is difficult to account for so many contrary reports about men being shot and killed if the men were simply allowed to leave. Argraves in particular was an extremely religious and seemingly credible individual. It is doubtful that he would include in his account the demise of the Scotsmen if that was completely untrue. Many others reported shots being fired during the escape, which is also inconsistent with the "free to leave" contention. There should not have been any reason whatsoever for the guards to fire if Colonel Bacci had ordered his men not to fire, even if just over the heads of the escapees.

Many of the Yanks and Brits just wanted to get as far away from the camp as possible. Some have said that they were too weak and suffering from malnutrition to get very far. This was particularly true of the tankers, who were not used to walking as great a distance as the infantrymen were. Others claimed to have traveled twenty-five miles during the first night and following day. Meanwhile, at other camps throughout Italy, including Chieti, once the Germans swept in, the prisoners who had obeyed the stay put order were all loaded into cattle cars, which were attached to northbound trains. It is estimated that as many as 50,000 Allied prisoners who obeyed the stay put order in Italy were swept up by the Germans and transported to Poland and Germany. It is curious, that the notorious stay put order could not be found after the war. Thus, it appears that the order was purged from the files to protect the reputations of those who generated it.

The ex-prisoners of war I spoke with all contended that most of the Camp 59 escapees were rounded up and recaptured by the Germans in the first two weeks after the escape and then shipped by rail to camps in Germany and Poland, although they did not learn the destinations of the trains until much later. They claimed that the men who built fires and stuck to roads as among those who were recaptured first.

While some escaped in large groups of ten to fifteen men, they quickly deemed it advisable to split up. At the time of the escape, according to a notepad still kept by Ila Van Arsdale, the widow of Harry Van Arsdale, Alvey was in the same hut as her husband, Harry, along with Zulah Ray, Woodrow Byrd, Dan McAnally, and Edwin Martin "Matt" Majeski. Zulah Ray said that when the shower door was broken down, he was standing in his hut with Kenneth Robertson and Woodrow Byrd. He did not see his other buddies, Charlie Lum or Johnnie Ford, so he and Robertson and Byrd left without them. Kenneth Lightbody told me that he escaped from the camp with Ray Skinner and J.B. Tackett. Lightbody and Tackett were together the entire time until the Allies liberated the area about nine months later.

Life on the run was an excruciating ordeal that daily threatened their very survival. The escapees were starving, exhausted, and suffering from exposure. They did not know who to trust. The towns were filled with sympathetic Italians as well as those who would turn them in for the monetary reward without thinking twice. Some took refuge in churches. Many found shelter with the local *contadini* (countrymen). Others actually joined the partisans. Zulah Ray told me that some simply gave up and went back to the camp. Many kept moving south into the unknown and some elected to hunker down in what became familiar territory before winter set in. Again, as far as they knew, the Allies would soon be there. But that was long before the interminable delays at Anzio and Monte Cassino.

They had many close calls. The Germans roamed through the woods and brush, spraying machine gun bullets at random. They lobbed grenades into caves thought to be occupied by the escapees, or burned piles of straw they believed to be their beds. Sweeps were made by the Germans in patterns of concentric circles of five miles radii from the camp. The enemy picked up more prisoners as each ring tightened. It was a dangerous, fluid situation. Partisans were regularly killing Germans and *fascisti* and vice versa. But the escapees by and large were just seeking enough food and shelter to survive.

In October 1943, Badoglio issued a proclamation to the Italian people telling them to help the escaped Allied prisoners and promising them a reward. The Allied air wings also dropped leaflets saying essentially the same thing. Efforts were also made to drop supplies to the prisoners on the run, but many recount that the Fascist Blackshirts got them all. Units were also organized to lead the escapees to freedom. Even the OSS was involved. But that group's primary focus was to help the partisan resistance. The escapees were even informed that there were submarines and other boats waiting to pick them up offshore near Ancona.

Shortly after the mass escape from Camp 59, a terrifying, massive earthquake struck the village of Offida, just fifteen miles from Servigliano. Many people were killed, including the men, women, and children of Italian families trying to help the former prisoners of war who were all just trying to get home.

14

Brave Men

In the quest to discover the truth about what actually happened to my namesake during and after his escape from Camp 59, I encountered a number of brave ex-prisoners of war who were of immeasurable help to me in more ways than they could ever imagine. They, or their surviving friends and family members, provided oral histories, while others committed their unique and common experiences to writing. Each provided another piece of the puzzle and entrusted their stories to me, unconditionally. Due to the need for brevity, not all accounts can be related here. But I trust that those soldiers, sailors, and airmen whose accounts are summarized below fairly represent the entire band of brothers who escaped from Camp 59 on September 14, 1943.

I feel the need to apologize to all the British and other Allied prisoners of war who escaped at the same time as the Americans, for not being able to include all of their accounts. However, there was no Internet to speak of in 1991 at the time I undertook my research, and I had no other means or leads to contact any survivors in England and other places around the world. Fortunately, Dennis Hill at Indiana University has done a superlative job in his blog of presenting numerous profiles of many other survivors. Also, within the past twenty years, a number of memoirs have been published by British survivors and others who have posted entries on the Internet that serve to fill in many of the gaps. Thus, all sources taken together create a tapestry of the shared experience of these brave men. It is entirely fitting that I am summarizing these stories on Veterans Day. What follows is an exemplar of a unique chapter in world history and of the men who participated in the real Great Escape.

Zulah Dawson Ray

Zulah Ray was the first ex-prisoner of war from Camp 59 that I met. In 1992, my wife, Shannon and I had dinner with him and his wife, Marie, at a banquet in Clackamas, Oregon, sponsored by the Western Chapter of the American Ex-Prisoners of War organization. After the banquet, we adjourned to Zulah's hotel room, and he did his best to answer all of my questions about the camp and the aftermath of the escape. He was extremely generous with his time, and when we parted, he gave me a copy of his self-published book, *Zulah Dawson Ray: His Stories*. His book is replete with details of his experiences commencing with day one of the Battle of Sidi Bou Zid, thence into captivity, followed by life on the run, and his eventual repatriation.

Zulah originally hailed from a farm in Blooming Rose, Missouri, but at the time I met him, he was a Californian, having retired from the oil business and living in Los Angeles. Other escapees he had been in touch with over the years included Kenneth Robertson, Charlie Lum, and Kenneth Lightbody. Lum and Robertson were in Bakersfield, California, and Lightbody was also living in California, in Orange County. After I had established contact with Raymond Cox, I was able to provide each of them the contact information for the other, and it is my understanding that Zulah and Raymond visited a number of times by telephone.

It was from Zulah that I learned most of my information about the convent hospital at Camp 204, in Altamura near Bari, Italy.

Zulah did not really remember my uncle, but I attribute that to the passage of nearly fifty years and the fact that Alvey did not survive the war. Yet, he and Zulah were both tankers in the First Armored Regiment who were burned in the skirmishes at Sidi Bou Zid on different days, taken to the same field hospital and confined in the same Italian camps. Further, they had common acquaintances who were in Alvey's battalion and also taken captive at the same time. Thus, I am sure that given the circumstances, he knew my uncle at one time and interacted with him a great deal in the hospital at Camp 204 and their final prison, Camp 59.

Zulah's account is also remarkable for the details surrounding the escape and its aftermath, providing vivid descriptions of the Italian people they encountered and the food and sustenance they were able to scrounge, including garlic-drenched snails.

Most significantly, he talked about the overall experience of how it felt to be hunted like animals, and the uncertainty of living day to day. There were many occasions when they narrowly escaped recapture by the Germans. Zulah speaks with considerable admiration about the friendliness and generosity of the Italian people who helped them and were quick to shout warnings when the Germans were coming.

Shortly after the escape, they were joined by an escapee named Charles Gallo, from New Haven, Connecticut, who spoke fluent Italian. One time, while they were with Gallo they approached an Italian villa. A stately woman named Lady Funero appeared at the door and offered them some wine. She also gave them fresh homemade bread and some cheese. They stayed with her for three weeks before moving on. All the while, Germans continued searching for them. But the Americans did not just take from her, they worked on Lady Funero's estate to show their gratitude.

While they were still at Lady Funero's estate, an American plane swooped over the hill where they were standing. It was olive drab with white stars painted on the fuselage. The plane came in so close they could see the pilot. The next thing they knew, they saw a pillar of black smoke arise from the road a mile below, quickly followed by the chatter of machine gun fire. The plane had strafed two German trucks, and four enemy soldiers were killed. The Allied planes made frequent strafing runs against German vehicles. The roads were composed of white limestone, which enhanced visibility for the pilots, particularly at night under a bright moon.

Some of the local men became nervous about the strafing attack and the dead Germans and asked Zulah and his companions to leave. Because the attack had hit trucks on the main road, the Germans began using secondary roads, some of which were closer to Lady Funero's estate. That night, the GIs slept in a nearby cave they had been steadily preparing.

While at Lady Funero's, a farmer ran in from the field shouting "Tedeschi! Tedeschi!" ("Germans! Germans!). Ray, Byrd, Robertson, and Gallo sprinted for their cave. Suddenly, they heard a loud boom, which shook the countryside. They heard women scream and thought that the house had taken a direct hit. They had also felt what they thought was an explosion nearby. A short time later, two other escapees came up the trail. They were Zulah's friend, Howard Reese, and a buddy. They had been mistaken for Germans.

But what about the bombs they had heard? Reese told them that it was an earthquake. Loosened bricks pounding on the tin roof had sounded like explosions. None of them had ever experienced an earthquake, and the Offida quake of October 3, 1943, was a violent tremor that caused a great deal of property damage and killed a lot of people.

Lady Funero became very fearful, and Gallo told them that they had to move on. She and the other women cried when the Americans left and gave them some bread and cheese for the journey. Gallo quickly found another farm family, and the other three set out together. Soon, near Montefalcone, they ran into Raymond Cox, whom they all knew. Cox was a coal miner from West

Virginia, and he was helping a farmer named Primo Nazareno Mecossi in his wheat field when they came upon him. Raymond told them that Primo had a brother named Alfredo who might be able to help them.

Alfredo did help. The three actually stayed with him for four months. They learned a great deal about the Italian culture while there, and Zulah reminisced at length about wine and bread making as well as sporting activities and festivities.

Most significantly, he told of the deep snow the area had starting around Christmas 1943. It was so deep that the Germans could not get into the area and the evaders could not get out. Zulah related that once the snow melted at the end of February 1944, the Germans began patrolling again and raiding houses looking for escaped Allied prisoners. Soon after, the three of them were hiding under a terrace wall when four Germans stopped and sat down right above them, enjoying a cigarette break. The GIs were afraid to even breathe. Then, the Germans dropped their cigarette butts and continued their patrol.

Zulah, Robertson, and Byrd left their hide and could see that the four Germans had linked up with two more on patrol. What follows is Zulah's account of what I believe is his memory of Alvey's recapture and execution:

> They went across a little valley up to a house where we knew two Americans from P.G. 59 were hiding. We knew that one of them was from Kansas. We saw the Germans go into the house and come out with the American soldiers, ex-prisoners of war like we were. They prodded the scared men in front of them at pistol point. They took them down the road out of sight. We heard several shots. Later that day the Italians wept when they told us the six German soldiers shot our American men in cold blood. This was the time Alfredo

said we should go on. It was no longer safe with him. Primo, Alfredo's brother told us with tears in his eyes that the bodies of the American soldiers were taken away by the Italian people and given a decent Christian burial.

Although my uncle was from Indiana and Martin Majeski was from South Carolina, I believe that this incident recalled by Zulah Ray was the same recapture and execution reported by Raymond Cox, who was staying with the Mecossi family about 400 yards away from the Viozzi house where my uncle and Majeski were staying. Due to the distance, and the ensuing years, Zulah may have confused either Alvey or Majeski with Ray Skinner, who was actually from Kansas. Skinner, who was one of Alvey's friends from D Company, First Armored Regiment, did make it home to Kansas.

Zulah emphasized to me the fear and anxiety this created in the ex-prisoners of war who were still on the run. But by the grace of God, he and all of his companions made it home and lived to tell about the horrors they had all witnessed.

Raymond Cox

The American Ex-Prisoners of War provided me with a copy of their membership directory. The directory was a tremendous resource that not only listed the current addresses of the ex-POWs, but also identified their units and the prison camps where they had each been held. In 1992, I found Raymond Cox then living in Russell, Kentucky, near the borders of Ohio and West Virginia, and wrote to him. He called me and excitedly said over the telephone that just before receiving my letter, he had been reading the newspaper when the words "Santa Vittoria" flashed before his eyes. He told me that he was staying in the Mecossi family farmhouse about 400 yards from where my uncle and Majeski were recaptured, which was between Montefalcone and the hilltop town of Santa Vittoria in Matenano, three miles distant.

Raymond said that Newton and Majeski were killed "early in the morning." He was concealed nearby and heard the shots that I believe were simultaneously heard by Zulah Ray and his friends after they saw the SS take the two Americans from the house. But Raymond said that he later heard from Primo Mecossi that the Americans in the nearby farmhouse were captured by the notorious brutal Fascist in that area, Captain Settimio (Septimius) Roscioli and then murdered by him and his men. But since he did not witness the events, Raymond allowed that it could have been the SS, also reported to have been in the area.

He did not remember my uncle by name but probably knew him in Camp 59, even though Raymond was not a tanker, but an infantryman from the Forty-seventh Infantry, Ninth Division. Raymond was captured at the Battle of El Guettar, Tunisia, and transported by plane to Camp 98 in Palermo, Sicily. Later, he was moved to Camp 59. After the armistice they got word that the Germans were on the way, and he and ten others broke out of PG 59 the night of September 14. He said that they were all weak and starving but had walked all night to get six to seven miles from Camp 59 to the area near Montefalcone en Apeninno where he met Primo Mecossi.

One detail he remembered that coincides with other accounts is that the family who had sheltered the Americans suffered the burning of their house and possessions. Also, in Raymond's opinion, he thought the two Americans were taken because the house was too close to the road and was the first place that the Germans searched that day. When I visited the house in the summer of 1999, I discovered what Raymond meant. Now a villa, it was just off the main road leading to Santa Vittoria and clearly visible from all four sides.

Raymond told me that the family the two Americans had

been staying with never would have given them up, but he believed that a spy had reported them to the Germans. He said "someone snitched, because the Germans had never gone there before." Raymond also offered that it may have motivated by revenge against the POWs due to a sexual assault upon an Italian woman by some Canadians who had imbibed too much local wine. According to Raymond, Charlie Smith had given the Canadians a thrashing for their mistreatment of the woman, but after that, the Italians cut off the wine supply for all of the escapees. For whatever reason, Charlie Smith does not mention this incident in his own memoir, *Wine, Cheese and Bread*, written by his wife, Ruby Simon Smith. Still, it was a vivid memory for Raymond. Charlie Smith advised me in a letter in 1992 that he and some others had been drinking wine with Alvey and Matt in early March 1944 and never saw them again. They heard about the execution of the two men by grapevine news.

Raymond told me that Santa Vittoria in Matenano was a Fascist stronghold, while the nearby town of Penna San Giovanni was in the grip of the rebels, led by a Yugoslavian lieutenant who was constantly raiding German convoys. Cox knew the paratrooper, Manuel Serrano, whom the POWs called Romeo and also heard that Serrano had joined the partisan brigades.

He mentioned that he also knew that fellow escapee John Procko had stayed in nearby Montefalcone for a time and was sheltered by a priest. He said that a man and a woman came to the church one day, claiming to be Americans. Raymond suspects that the visitors were with the OSS. They were either trying to arrange a food drop for the escapees, or a rescue. Raymond said that the priest was afraid to tell them he knew where the escapees were hiding. Nevertheless, Raymond said that there were supply drops in the area by the Allied planes. In fact, they were told to light a fire one night and a plane would circle Montefalcone and drop supplies.

Although they lit night fires and watched for three straight weeks, there was never any supply plane over Montefalcone.

But one night, there was a full moon shining across the valley to the village of Force. Raymond said the Allies dropped seven chutes of supplies intended for the stranded escapees, but the Blackshirts got every one of the bundles. There was also a plan to rescue escaped POWs near Ancona by submarine and other boats. The Allies were going to take eighty to ninety men out at a time. He said that paratroopers came into the area and escorted some evaders to Ancona. The first group got out OK, but when the second group started for the boats, the Germans spotted running lights and opened up on them with machine guns. He knew that Serrano's group of partisans also worked behind the lines to rescue POWs on the run.

Raymond also told me of other atrocities perpetrated by the Germans and Fascists in the vicinity. Specifically, he said that seven escapees had been found dead under a bridge over the River Tenna. They had been stripped and shot. He also related that the SS had killed nuns and priests and burned a monastery about seventeen miles away because they had dared to shelter the Americans. He said many more escaped English and American prisoners were summarily executed in Comunanza.

One day in June 1944, after the last of the retreating Germans had sped from the area, Primo Mecossi loaned Raymond a bicycle, which he then rode to Ascoli-Piceno into the Polish lines. He was debriefed by the Poles, who were at the spearhead of the British Eighth Army along the Adriatic coast. When he learned that the Poles had arrested Roscioli's brother, Raymond and some other escapees pleaded for his life, because according to Raymond, although Roscioli was an ardent Fascist and war criminal, his brother had actually helped the escapees.

Raymond emphasized repeatedly to me that the POWs never

would have survived without the Italians who helped them and called the *contadini* "the most decent race of people." He died in 1994.

Charles Lum

In 1991, Pete and June Fix had a potluck at their home in Portland, Oregon, for members of the Western Chapter of the First Armored Division Association. Pete had advertised the gathering in the newspaper, and I called him and asked if I could attend. He graciously invited me and my wife to his potluck. At that gathering, I met a number of veterans of the First Armored Division who had fought in campaigns in North Africa and Italy, including Clifford Larkin, of F Company, Second Battalion, First Armored Regiment. Clifford was captured at the Battle of Sidi Bou Zid, with Alvey, but was transported directly to a prisoner of war camp in Germany. I also met Hubert "Herb" Olson, who told me that Charlie Lum was captured at Sidi Bou Zid but escaped and was "running loose in Italy for a while."

I spoke with Charlie Lum by telephone and also corresponded with him by mail. Charlie was in F Company, Second Battalion, First Armored Regiment, and was wounded and captured at Sidi Bou Zid on February 15, 1943. He basically mirrored the experiences of my uncle and was also at Camps 204, 75, and 59. He was friends with Everett Gregg, Alvey's tank commander, who was also from Bakersfield, California. At the time I spoke with Charlie, he said that Gregg had already passed away some years before.

Charlie told me that he remembered my uncle's name from PG 59. He said that he recalled that Alvey and an escapee named Ferree Grossman were staying about a mile from where he was. The Italian people were amazed to see a Chinese American in their midst and would say "Chee nay see — Chee nay see," whenever they saw him. But soon after the escape, the Germans spotted

Charlie lying in a vineyard. He was recaptured and sent to a POW camp in Germany.

When he entered the German camp, Gregg was there to shake his hand. Gregg immediately warned Charlie, "Keep your mouth shut; there are spies in here." Gregg said not to talk about what happened with any strangers. When the war ended, Gregg shook Charlie's hand again and said that he had an important paper to deliver to Allied headquarters and would see him at home in Bakersfield.

The mothers of the men held captive in Italy and Germany developed a communication net to glean whatever news they could about their sons. My grandmother Susie corresponded with Agnes Gee, Charlie Lum's sister, as well as the mothers of Lee Kaser and Ray Skinner. In one letter, Mrs. Gee said that Charlie had been recaptured and sent to Germany. The family found out about it from a ham operator on the East Coast who had picked up a radio transmission from Berlin. She also said that Kenneth Robertson, one of the men with Charles, had made it home to Bakersfield and was then on furlough.

Kenneth C. "Trapper" Robertson

I never met or talked to Kenneth Robertson. He died several years before my search began. But I did learn that he was in F Company, Second Battalion, First Armored Regiment, and wounded and captured at Sidi Bou Zid. There is no doubt that he and my uncle were well acquainted, having been in the same battalion, then in the same convent hospital at Altamura together, followed by months in Camp 59.

He was nicknamed Trapper because of his philandering ways. Trapper had a magnetic appeal to the ladies. He claimed that he would just go out at night and set his "trap line." I have already related the humorous accounts about Trapper in the hospital and the jests made by the others about his wound in the buttocks. He also had a severe shoulder wound and wore the same shirt with the bloodstain for more than a year until he was repatriated.

Zulah Ray recounted that one night while they were all sleeping in a shed, he had just drifted off to sleep when Robertson let out a "painful, deep-throated, wailing, howling scream." He and Byrd bolted out the door and asked, "Where's Trapper?" They looked back in the shed. Robertson was still in bed. He had had a nightmare. His bare feet had become tangled in a bundle of sharp twigs used for fuel, and he dreamed that a wildcat had him by the feet!

One day, living up to his reputation as a ladies' man, Trapper set out alone to visit seven sisters he knew were staying in a house across the river. The escapees had previously been warned not to cross the river. A short while later, Zulah and Byrd looked on helplessly as a convoy of Germans approached the house. The Germans entered the house and emerged with Trapper and took him away.

It was not until after the war that they learned Trapper had survived. Surprisingly, these Germans had treated him well. In fact, they had put him to work driving their truck for a matter of weeks. His captors stopped for dinner one night, and Trapper asked them if he could relieve himself in the bushes. They told him that he could. He went out of their sight and never came back. Somehow, Trapper reached the Allied lines and got home before Byrd and Ray!

Kenneth Lightbody

Kenneth Lightbody was in E Company, Second Battalion, First Armored Regiment. He was wounded and captured after Sidi Bou Zid and sent to Camp 59. On the night of September 14, 1943, he escaped with J. B. Tackett, Ray Skinner, Robert Linker, and two others. I spoke with Ken and met him at his home in Yorba Linda, California.

Ken told me that he eluded capture by the Germans near Sidi Bou Zid for three days. From his hiding place in the rocks, all he could see were German tracer rounds arcing through the sky. But the Germans found him and transported him to a hospital tent in Sfax. After that, he went to the convent hospital in Altamura and then on to PG 59.

After the escape from Camp 59, he said that he and Tackett were on the run together for nine months, spending most of their time near Comunanza, about fourteen miles from Servigliano. They had reached Comunanza on the very first day after the escape. Ken mentioned that Tackett had been the driver of Zulah Ray's tank and that he had been killed in a car accident in the late 1950s.

Although much farther from Camp 59, Comunanza was not a safe place for POWs. Ken remembered that about thirty British and American soldiers were recaptured by the Germans, lined up against a stone wall in the town and gunned down by machine gun fire. After the war, Ken visited Comunanza and noted that you could still see the shell holes in that wall.

Ken also related that there was a raid conducted by partisans and Americans on a jail near Comunanza in order to free some captured POWs. He said that three Fascists were shot in the head and left in the road. After that, it was hard to find a Fascist. As we parted, Ken gave me a baseball cap emblazoned with the patch of the First Armored Division. He died in 2011.

Ferree Grossman

Herb Olson also told me of another tanker who had been held captive in Italy and escaped named Ferree Grossman. I located him and wrote a letter asking several questions. I was particularly interested in what Grossman had to say because he had been in D Company with Alvey, and was wounded and captured at Sidi Bou Zid, then sent to Altamura and PG 59.

Grossman sent me a detailed reply. He escaped from PG 59 with Herman Noble, another member of D Company, and Albert Butacavoli from Brooklyn, New York. Ferree told me that the

Germans were only searching for POWs for a short time after the escape and after they had recaptured many of the escapees, there was very little military activity for a long while. Ferree attributed the relative calm to the fact that there were few main roads in the area and the towns were all very small.

He said that things were fairly quiet until about Christmas 1943, when the escapees began hearing rumors of Fascists searching for them. But around December 31, about four feet of snow fell rapidly, which paralyzed all means of transportation and removed the fear of the Fascists for some time.

About March 1, 1944, the snow began to melt and road traffic resumed. The family that Ferree and some others were staying with became scared and asked them to leave. As they were walking around the area, they stopped at the place where Alvey was staying and they visited for a while. Ferree said that my uncle was in good physical condition and that there were some burn scars on his face, but they were discolorations, rather than deep scars.

Grossman's group found another place where the people agreed to look after them and gave them food and a place to sleep. Shortly after arriving at the new place, they heard that Alvey and the other escapee he was with had been recaptured and executed by the Fascists. He said they all were scared, but believed that Alvey and the other POW were the only ones who were shot.

One puzzling aspect of Grossman's recollection was his account that there was a Welshman with Alvey at the farmhouse the day Grossman stopped to see him. I attribute this to the fact that he may not have known Martin Majeski, who may have been wearing British clothes, as many Americans were, and assumed that he was British. Or, the family who sheltered Alvey also sheltered an actual Welshman for a while. But there is also a far more sinister possibility. Regardless, Grossman was very specific about calling the other man he saw a Welshman.

When the Allied forces reached the area, Grossman and the

others were staying near Falerone, outside Fermo. They were repatriated, and he returned to the USA.

Robert J. Noah

Robert J. Noah was with the Eighteenth Infantry of the First Infantry Division, ("The Big Red One"), captured in North Africa on December 23, 1942. He escaped from Camp 59 the night of September 14 and tried to get as far away from the camp as he could. Robert told me he and some others broke down a door at the back of the compound and were fired on by a guard. They were forced to hide in slit trenches nearby until the firing stopped.

Significantly, Robert remembered that they were warned to stay away from Santa Vittoria. He said that he and his buddy Milton Hanks were privates and although they met some NCOs in the area, the senior enlisted did not want them around. They wound up in Monte San Martino.

In 1983, Robert and some of his family members returned to Italy and visited Monte San Martino. One of the Italians that had sheltered him asked, *"Roberto, ti ricorda Roscioli?"* ("Robert, do you remember Roscioli?") Noah replied that he did, and the Italian just shook his head and uttered, *"Egli era un uomo cattivo."* ("He was a bad man.") I then asked Robert about Roscioli's fate, presuming that he had been captured by the Allies and executed because he had murdered, or been implicated in the murders of so many British and American soldiers. To the contrary, Robert told me, Roscioli had survived the war and died of natural causes about 1956 or 1957. Noah was as disgusted as I was about this turn of events. He said that money was at the bottom of the failure to fully prosecute. History also tells us that the after the war, the Allies became fully focused on defeating Communism and less and less about justice for the ex-POWs who had been mistreated or killed.

When the Polish forces reached Fermo, Robert and the others

turned themselves in. After the war, he worked for the Veterans Administration until his retirement.

Francis Gallo

Captain Francis Gallo was not in Camp 59 and was never imprisoned with my uncle Robert. Nevertheless, I wanted to include him in this tribute to the brave men I have come to know over the years. His story is so compelling that I had to retell it here. Captain Gallo was a doctor in the First Armored Division, captured in North Africa. He was treating our wounded on the front lines as the Germans appeared on the horizon. Although he had numerous opportunities to escape, Captain Gallo allowed himself to be captured so that he could continue treating our men.

He was interned at Camp 21 for officers near Chieti, southeast of Servigliano. I first learned about "Doc" Gallo from Joseph S. Frelinghuysen, a lieutenant in the US Army who had been captured on November 28, 1942, in the first race to Tunis, and was also in the camp at Chieti. Frelinghuysen wrote an account of his time as a prisoner of war on the run in the Italian countryside in his book, *Passages to Freedom*.

Frelinghuysen tells how Gallo helped him learn Italian. Gallo was from the Hartford, Connecticut, area known as Winstead and had grown up speaking Italian. Frelinghuysen details how the Senior British Officer (SBO) attempted to rigidly enforce the stay put order. The expectation was that the Allies would be there any moment, so the officers in the camp generally complied. However, on September 15, 1943, a German Storch observation plane made a pass over the camp.

The SBO had threatened any man who tried to escape with a court martial. When they saw the swastika on the plane, the POWs cursed him with bitter obscenities. Still, the order was enforced, to the point that a British patrol knocked a ladder from a wall and arrested the two would-be escapees. The SBO told the men over a loudspeaker that they would be "collected" by the Allies in a few days.

But five days later, the men began seeing German trucks outside the gate. By dawn on September 21, 1943, there were German paratroopers manning the guard towers. The prisoners were ordered into the courtyard and loaded into trucks. The officers were all taken south to Camp 78 at Fonte d' Amore, where there was a railhead. But before that, Frelinghuysen escaped with Dick Rossbach in broad daylight. Doc Gallo and some others later jumped from a train just outside of Florence. But due to the infamous stay put order most of the POWs in Chieti went on to prison camps in Germany and Poland.

I later heard from Dr. Erly "Frank" Gallo, in Hartford, Doc Gallo's son. He said his father had passed away about four years earlier. For some time, I believed that the "Gallo" with Zulah Ray and remembered by Charlie Smith was the same Doc Gallo that had jumped from the northbound train. However, the Gallo near Montefalcone was Charles Gallo. It is interesting however, that both Gallos were from Connecticut.

Robert Linker

The first details about what happened to my uncle were provided by Robert Linker, a tank gunner in F Company, Second Battalion, First Armored Regiment. Linker was captured with the others at Sidi Bou Zid and was interned at Camp 59. After the war, he met up with family friend Jack Hunter at Camp Atterbury, Indiana, and provided Hunter with the details of Alvey's murder. Hunter returned to Logansport, and it is said that he went to my uncle Red's house to tell him but paced up and down on the sidewalk both saddened and reluctant to report what he had learned from Linker.

It is known that Linker was from Fort Wayne, Indiana, and that my grandmother later made a trip there shortly after Hunter's visit, presumably to speak directly with Linker.

I tried to locate Robert Linker myself and wrote a letter to a Vern Linker in Decatur, Indiana. Vern Linker called me and said that he was Robert's brother. At that point Robert had been dead about twenty-five years, having passed away in November 1966. Vern told me that Robert had died of cirrhosis of the liver, which the family attributed to the inhalation of fumes from the tank engine and batteries.

Manuel Serrano — The Partisan from Brooklyn

One of the most dashing individuals to escape from Camp 59 was Manuel Serrano, a Puerto Rican from Brooklyn, New York. Serrano was a paratrooper with the 509th Parachute Battalion who was captured while on a mission to blow up a bridge in Tunisia. The day after the escape, Serrano met three Yugoslavs who were headed south to join an Italian partisan encampment near Sarnano, about sixty miles away. Serrano asked them what the partisans did. They told him that they killed Germans and Fascists. Serrano said that was good enough for him, joined their band and headed south with his new acquaintances.

Serrano was the subject of a feature article in *Yank* magazine in 1944 titled "The Partisan from Brooklyn." When I wrote to Armie Hill, Dennis Hill's father, he was gracious enough to provide me with a copy of Serrano's story. Serrano had numerous harrowing experiences with the partisans. Fascists were caught and hanged, and German convoys were attacked. One time, Serrano heard that six Allied escapees had been murdered by the Fascists near Comunanza. The evaders had been forced to dig their own graves and were stripped of all identification and clothing. The dead soldiers were then taken to a convent. After seeing them, Serrano vowed to kill a Fascist for each one of the dead soldiers. He also said that he then knew for the first time what it meant to be a partisan.

Ironically, after the Germans had retreated from Le Marche province, Serrano returned to Servigliano, where he celebrated with the local *contadini* and the partisans who were all welcomed home. In 1999, my wife and I arrived at the site of the former Camp 59. The local historian, Angelo Paci, gave us a personal tour of the grounds. After we were finished, he showed me the original blueprints for the camp. Then he mentioned that the American actor Manuel Serrano had visited Servigliano after the war. My research indicates that there were about fifteen movies and television shows in the 1950s and 1960s with a Manuel Serrano in the cast. That actor died in 1982. That the actor was the same Manuel Serrano is a distinct possibility.

Dan McAnally

Dan McAnally was one of the prisoners in Alvey's hut, according to a list that had been compiled by Harry Van Arsdale. McAnally was in the First Armored Division and shipped out to Ireland on the *Queen Mary*. Dan was captured in Tunisia and taken to Palermo, where he was loaded on a bus with a sign that read: "Americani: Chicago Gangsters." The prisoners were marched through the streets, where the citizenry heaved rocks and spat upon them.

McAnally was on a tunnel detail at Camp 59, and in the mass escape of September 14, 1943. He kept going south for two days until some nuns gave him food and shelter and tended to his blistered feet. Although he was recaptured by the Germans, he simply walked away from a work detail unloading their trucks. Then he was taken captive with a group of civilians for yet another work detail carrying water.

The five Germans made him hold a mirror while they shaved. One of them threw the dirty water on Dan. But an air raid blared, and McAnally ran off to the nearby river. Somehow, he made it all the way south to Bari. Dan was awarded the Bronze Star for his escape, in addition to the Purple Heart for a hand wound. But, he said, "I never got the Good Conduct Medal."

He spent his postwar years as a security guard at a community college in Pennsylvania. I heard from Mary McAnally, Dan's wife, in 1992. He had already passed away, but she was kind enough to provide me with a campus newsletter article about Dan's escape that was published for Veterans Day, 1980. Mary also told me that Dan said the reason he survived was because he went off by himself and traveled only at night.

Keith Argraves

Several of the ex-prisoners I contacted mentioned a soldier named Keith "Doc" Argraves, who they said was a real inspiration to them. It took a while to discover any details about him, because most said his last name was "Hargraves." In any case, Argraves was a medic in F Company, Second Battalion, 509th Parachute Infantry Regiment. He was a very religious man who did not smoke or drink, and many of the POWs looked up to him and the other paratroopers in Camp 59.

I found the details concerning Argraves by contacting Charlie Doyle, a member of the 509th Parachute Association ("Geronimo"). He in turn, put me in touch with Warren Decker, another paratrooper who escaped from Camp 59 with Argraves. Charlie also provided me with a copy of a book published in 1947 by the Seventh-day Adventist Church, titled *Keith Argraves Paratrooper*, by George W. Chambers. Charlie Doyle had some remarkable wartime experiences of his own with the 509th. In fact, he wrote a book titled *Stand in the Door: The Wartime History of the Elite 509th Parachute Infantry Battalion*. (Note: The 509th was initially a battalion and was expanded to a regiment during the war.) Charlie's book is now extremely rare and commands prices in the hundreds of dollars, if you can even find it.

In his own book, Argraves describes the breakout from Camp 59 and flatly states that they rushed the camp gate and that Allied soldiers were killed. After they were out, Argraves was on the run with Warren Decker, Alfred Nastassi, Tony Cole, Dan Cole, and Mahlon Black. He dedicated his book to each of them. The men were quickly disconcerted by a Fascist radio broadcast in a village that told the people to be on the lookout for escaped Allied prisoners and promising an 1,800-lira reward, and an equal amount from the Germans, dead or alive!

Decker told me that they were holed up in the mountains above Ascoli-Piceno, not far from Santa Vittoria. He said there was an Italian woman in the vicinity who regularly turned escaped Allies into the Germans for the reward. He had a vivid memory of the 1943 earthquake they all experienced. Decker also told me that Argraves had died in Klamath Falls, Oregon, in 1974.

Argraves's account recalls the murder of several escaped prisoners. While scouting a road, he saw several fellow prisoners cut down by machine guns. Several escapees from PG 59 told me that Argraves had spoken of a plan to commandeer a boat and sail across the Adriatic to Yugoslavia. Argraves later recalls that they had heard that a boat was waiting for them at the coast. So they headed for the Adriatic.

His band arrived at the appointed place and waited three days after the first boat left. They saw some boats just offshore. But when one of the vessels stabbed the shoreline with a searchlight, they knew it was not a rescuer. Then the enemy opened fire. Prisoners fell in the sand, dead or wounded. Argraves and his team escaped the hail of bullets and tried one more time to escape by sea. However, the German flag on the approaching boat convinced them that they needed a Plan B.

Argraves may or may not be describing the rescue attempt near Ancona planned by the British and American intelligence services, which was recounted by Raymond Cox. It mirrors some of what really happened there in that the first boat made a clean getaway, while the next group of men was less fortunate and were fired upon. Keith's group went back into the mountains. This time, they joined a group of partisans. They fought with the guerillas and in one skirmish, Keith acquired some badly needed medical supplies. The band was then living in a cave.

Keith related in his book that five feet of snow fell between January 1 and 2, 1944, and that was followed by another foot. They had to dig out and fashioned snow-shoes from saplings, then went into the village and were welcomed into the home of an Italian captain. Later that night, a German ski patrol crept into the village and rounded up eighty escaped POWs, including Argraves and his companions. Argraves says that the Germans demanded that everyone produce identification. About forty of the escapees had none. So, Argraves said that the Germans lined those men up and shot them down in cold blood.

Those who had identification were taken to a Fascist prison, then to Camp 53, where Argraves saw Jewish women and children tortured and killed. They were moved from camp to camp, then to Germany. But while en route, they were bombed by our own planes near Florence, with great loss of life. The survivors were forced to bury the dead. Germans put the living on another train headed to the Brenner Pass. However, Argraves and some others cut a hole in the boxcar and escaped again. Some went to a nearby monastery, but Argraves headed south alone. Yet, he was caught by Fascists and turned over to the Germans.

Another train took him to Austria, but Argraves escaped again. Nevertheless, he was recaptured by a sentry near a bridge and put on another train for Germany, landing at Camp 7-A near Munich, then 3B near Berlin. In early 1945, Argraves and a group of other medics were exchanged for captured German nurses and sent to Switzerland, then to France and homeward bound.

Joseph P. Meredith

Joe Meredith was a squad leader with Company A of the Sixth Armored Infantry Regiment and fought in the initial invasion of

Oran, Algeria. His outfit was bound for Tunis on November 12, 1942, and told to mop up a few scattered German paratroopers. But he wrote that, "It looked like the whole German Army hit us. Nothing was common, but confusion."

One of the men captured with him was Dan McAnally. They were sent to Camp 66 near Naples, then to PG 59. Meredith told me that he was in the mass escape on the night of September 14 and said, "I heard that there were thirty-nine killed that night."

The next morning he was with Holland, Lipps, McGee, Collins, and Lindsey. They split into two groups of three. He left with Collins and Lindsey. Later, he heard that the other three were recaptured. Joe also recalled that five feet of snow fell around January 1, 1944. An old Italian man told him he had never seen so much snow at one time.

He said some of our boys lived in caves and as a result froze to death. Then, when the snow melted some were crushed by cave-ins. Joe related how they were shot at four times but all three made it back when they found a Polish pack mule outfit on July 3, 1944.

Elmer Reece

Elmer Reece escaped from Camp 59 the night of September 14, 1943. His group lived in the woods until they were taken in by an Italian family. They stayed at their farmhouse for four months. Reece poignantly recalled the Offida earthquake of October 3, 1943.

> While there, an earthquake occurred. Among other damage thereby caused, the floor of a grain storage building collapsed and suffocated a baby girl in the farmer's family. She was buried in a makeshift grave on a nearby hillside following an emotional, mourning family procession up the hill. A young girl between sixteen and eighteen (perhaps the infant's godmother) carried the tiny lifeless body on her head to the grave

site. This earthquake and the baby's death was another terrifying experience. It has also been a lingering sad memory over all these years since that time.

After four months, someone betrayed Reece's group to the local Fascists. They were transported by truck to a railroad station and loaded into cattle cars. They arrived in Frankfurt, Germany, and were bombed by Allied planes. Reece's box car was not hit, but others did not have the same luck.

Reece was sent to a work camp, but the Germans started marching them aimlessly from place to place for fifty-eight days as the Allies drew nearer. One day, the guards deserted, and they were rescued by an American tank column. During the long forced marches, Reece had lived mainly on turnips and scraps that could be bartered from farmers along the route. He told me that he "had enough turnips for a lifetime, and to this day, they are far from a favorite vegetable."

James Kavana

James Kavana was captured on December 23, 1942, at Medjez El Bab, Tunisia, when his tank was destroyed by enemy fire. He awakened in a Tunis field hospital and was transported by air to Camp 98 in Palermo, Sicily. He escaped from there just three days later, but was wounded and recaptured. The Italians then sent him to Camp 59. James met my uncle when Alvey first arrived at the camp, and they talked frequently as they were both tankers.

He said that most of the talk was about the outside world and escape. They spent a lot of time digging tunnels with the British, but according to James, these were discovered because of Cypriot informants. One time, James was disciplined by being thrown into a "stooping chamber." He also said that Alvey was put in one because he talked to him frequently. Kavana also busied himself learning the Italian language. He said it was easier for him than some others because he had studied Latin in school.

Regarding the escape from Camp 59, James said that they knew what was going on outside after the Italian capitulation and decided that on September 14 at midnight, they would all escape when the church bells rang in Servigliano. He told me that when the bells began to ring, the men went over the walls and through the gate throwing sticks and stones and knives fashioned from tin cans. James also stated that "Many of the POWs were shot and killed or wounded at the time."

He related that all of them were suffering from malnutrition. James himself dropped from 165 pounds to 95 pounds, and said Alvey also lost weight. The last time he saw Alvey was just after the breakout, and he had always wondered what happened to him.

After his escape from the camp, James recalled as did Zulah Ray that the Germans were making circles of the camp in five-mile radii and closing in on the escapees each day and rounding up escaped prisoners. He and another prisoner he traveled with tried to keep outside of the circles.

Kavana went to Ancona because he heard from the Italians that the Americans were sending in landing craft to pick them up. Unfortunately, James was wounded again and captured by SS troops and transported in a Red Cross bus to Macerata. But he said that on the way, they executed their guards and escaped in the bus. Kavana then joined a group of partisans comprised of Czechs, Yugoslavs, and Poles.

James was again recaptured together with a group of Italians and loaded on a train for Germany. En route, the train was bombed by British aircraft. James escaped once again and headed south. He met up with an Italian Alpine officer who took him to his home in Penna San Giovanni, not far from Santa Vittoria. Kavana remained there until the Germans had retreated and made his way to Foggia airport. He said that he compared the war to deer hunting, except that this time, the deer shot back.

After the war, James submitted a claim to the War Claims Commission for reparations against the Badoglio government for failing to furnish him with food as required by the Geneva convention before he was repatriated. The War Commission found that the Italian government was in full compliance with the terms of the armistice agreement and denied Kavana's claim.

Charles K. "Red" Simmons

Red Simmons spoke about the numerous rumors the escapees heard about their buddies being executed. He heard one story about two Americans who were invited to eat at a farmhouse with an Italian family. Then, some German soldiers walked in. They gave the POWs the impression that they had nothing to worry about and sat down and ate with them. They told jokes, laughed, and had a great time. After they were done eating, the Germans gave the escapees some cigarettes and they all went outside. A short time later, the Americans were shot.

He never did find out what their names were, but the Italian people buried the POWs on their property and put a wooden cross on each grave. It was said that for the longest time, two crows would perch on the crosses and fly back and forth. Red did not know the meaning of that legend.

After the mass break from Camp 59, he and some others made it all the way to Monte San Martino the first night. They stayed there long enough to get their bearings and then gradually walked all the way to Foggia and the Allied lines.

Homer A. Lewis

Homer Lewis remembered both Manuel Serrano and Keith Argraves. He said that Argraves enjoyed watching him play checkers with Russ Merritt. Homer also recalled that as they were

breaking out, Argraves said that he was going to head for Porto
San Giorgio to steal a boat and make for Yugoslavia. He never
saw Argraves again, but after the war, he wrote to an address that
Argraves had given him in Portland, Oregon. However, the letter
was returned to him undelivered.

He and Argraves shared an Oregon connection because Lewis
had worked in Civilian Conservation Corps camps at Kirby and
Crater Lake in 1939, and Keith's father had a ranch close to there.

Clarence M. Dust

Clarence Dust and a buddy stuck together at the time of the mass
breakout from Camp 59. They were shot at by the guards as they
ran out. They were fed by the Italians until they joined a guerilla
band in the mountains and started attacking the Germans going
through the main highway.

Dust was in Camp 59 for nine months before escaping, and
behind the lines for an additional nine months. He remembered
the host of bed bugs the prisoners had to contend with. He was
in the First Armored Division with a half-track unit when he was
badly wounded and captured in the fall of 1942.

Steve Schweitz

Steve Schweitz was captured at the Battle of El Guettar, Tunisia.
He was wounded and operated on at a German MASH unit. Schweitz was taken to a Red Cross hospital ship and transported to
Bari. He was in the hospital there for about three months, then
arrived at Camp 59.

Schweitz said that the prisoners received BBC news from an old
Italian priest, who was caught and executed by the guards the next
day.

He and eight others escaped the night of September 14 and lived
with the Italian people for about two months. They helped out by
working in the fields. The evaders got in contact with the Italian

underground and planned their escape to the sea. The Americans were supposed to pick them up, but when they arrived at the coast, the Germans opened up with machine guns. They took off, but two were killed and four recaptured.

Steve was recaptured by the Germans and sent to Germany, until liberated by the Russians.

Leo E. Keating

Leo Keating was with Company C of the Twenty-seventh Field Artillery, which was attached to Combat Command C with the First Armored Division. He was captured at Djebel Bou Aqukaz on December 6, 1942, near Tebourba. They were attacked by many German Mark IV tanks.

Keating told me that when the prisoners flooded out of the gates during the mass escape from Camp 59 that "some machine gun fire was heard." Many went into the mountains and worked the fields with the farmers. Keating was about twelve miles from Ascoli-Piceno and contacted elements of the Eighth Army there after the German retreat. He was fed and transported to Foggia airport.

Leo closed his letter to me by saying the following:

> We in the 1st Armored Division were all buddies. I know you want to know more about your uncle. I would say you should think of him as a hero who fought and died for his country, for he truly was.

Gerald W. "Tex" Rowland

In one of his letters home as a prisoner of war, Alvey told them to let George Kienly know that "Tex Rowland is here with me." Rowland and Kienly were both in the Thirteenth Armored Regiment of the First Armored Division. Tex was a tank gunner like Alvey.

I located Tex Rowland in Bay City, Texas, wrote to him, and in response to my letter, he literally called me from his sickbed. I could tell that he was on oxygen and having extreme difficulty breathing, so I did not pester him with questions. Tex did not remember Alvey or George Kienly. Nevertheless, Tex asked his son Joe Rowland to send me whatever documentation he had.

Joe took the time to accumulate and copy Tex's documents for me. They told the complete story of Tex's escape from Camp 59 and return to the Allied lines. Joe said that he had not seen most of them before and that his dad "had talked some about his war years, but there is so much more that I'm sure he has chosen not to talk about." Joe went on to say that Tex was saddened by the treatment of my uncle and his buddy at the hands of the enemy.

Tex was wounded in the leg and captured during the Kasserine campaign on February 21, 1943, and spent three months in the hospital. He was then transferred to Camp 59 and was involved in the mass escape five months later. After nine weeks on the run, he succeeded in reaching the Eighth Army lines on November 21, 1943.

Rowland spent much of the time behind the lines with the family of Pietro Angelini in Rotella, not far from Santa Vittoria. Pietro wrote letters to Tex after the war expressing some very emotional sentiments. Tex had them translated from Italian into English. When I traveled to Italy in July 1999, I stayed at the Hotel Farfense in Santa Vittoria. I met a man there named Alfredo and showed him the letters written by Pietro Angelini to Tex. Alfredo then offered to call Rotella for me to see if we could find Pietro Angelini. He did reach someone by phone in Rotella who said that Pietro was no longer there. Consequently, I did not pursue it any further. Nevertheless, the letters serve to show the mutually warm relationship between the escaped prisoners of war and the Italian people without whose help they almost certainly would have perished or been quickly recaptured.

• • •

These summaries accurately represent the high caliber and distinct qualities of the men who endured the trials and indignities of protracted imprisonment and then did their duty to escape and harass the enemy. They were all too humble to have thought of themselves as the Greatest Generation. But they and their companions, both British and American, are all heroes and an inspiration to the enduring spirit of free people everywhere.

The Newton boys ca. 1920. Left to right: Joseph Norman Gray Newton; James Glenial ("Red") Newton; and Robert Alvey Newton.

Robert Alvey Newton, Indiana schoolboy, ca. 1925.

Lifelong friends out fishing:
Robert Alvey Newton and Robert J. "Doc" Frie.

At the Boy Scouts training ship:
Robert Alvey Newton with Joe Kienly.

Robert Alvey Newton, camping in the Indiana woods.

Robert Alvey Newton with the canoe he and Doc Frie built.

Cousin Nell Loraine Alvey and
Robert J. "Doc" Frie test the homemade canoe.

Robert Alvey Newton.
(U.S. Army official photo.)

Robert J. "Doc" Frie,
WWII medic.
(U.S. Army official photo.)

March 1942: A last photograph with his family as Robert Alvey Newton leaves for Fort Dix, NJ and the war. They never saw him again. Left to right: Father, Claude Lee ("C.L.") Newton; Robert Alvey; mother, Susie Newton; and brother "Red" Newton. Not pictured was younger brother Joe Newton, who was serving in the U.S. Army Air Force.

Second Battalion, First Armored Regiment, First Armored Division, Northern Ireland 1942.

Second Battalion, First Armored Regiment, First Armored Division, Northern Ireland, 1942. (U.S. Army official photo.)

The five man tank crew, training in Northern Ireland at Mount Panther, summer 1942. Left to right: Philip Caldwell, driver/machine gunner; Lee Cole Kaser, radio operator/cannon loader; Robert Alvey, 75mm gunner; Alphonse "Al" Urbanovsky, assistant driver/machine gunner; and Everett Gregg, tank sergeant/commander.

Another photograph of the tank crew at Mount Panther, Northern Ireland, summer 1942, before the invasion of North Africa. Left to right: Robert Alvey, Everett Gregg, Lee Cole Kaser and Philip Caldwell. Al Urbanovsky missed this photo because of a blackjack game.

Prisoner of war Camp 59, Servigliano, Italy,
as it appeared in 1943.
(Courtesy of Associazone Casa della Memoria)

Post-WWII photo of Camp 59 prisoner hut.
(Courtesy of Associazone Casa della Memoria)

Plaque at the entrance to the site of the former Camp 59 commemorating the 50th anniversary of the mass escape the night of September 14, 1943. The plaque was placed by the Associazone Casa della Memoria ("House of Memory Association"). The English translation reads as follows: "After the Armistice of 8 September 1943, 3000 Allied prisoners escaped through a hole they dug in the west side of this field. They will always be grateful for the immediate and courageous generosity of the Italian people."

July 1999: Interior of the former Camp 59 prison camp site. After the war, the site was converted to a recreation field.

The railway station at Servigliano, Italy, as of July 1999. This was the last stop for the arriving Allied prisoners who were marched to the adjacent Camp 59. The railway station now houses a memorial museum for Camp 59, sponsored by the Associazone Casa della Memoria.

July 1999: The author, right and Dino Viozzi, left, examine the patched hole in the wall through which the prisoners escaped from Camp 59 the night of September 14, 1943.

Gates of Camp 59 with prisoners standing in formation during WWII. (Courtesy of Associazone Casa della Memoria)

July 1999: Touring the site of the former Camp 59 at Servigliano, Italy. Left to right: Shannon Newton, the author's wife; the translator; Dino Viozzi; Angelo Paci, the town historian; Giampietro Viozzi; and the author.

Front section of U.S. Army topographic map obtained by Joe Kienly
showing the approximate locale where Robert Alvey was executed
by German troops on March 9, 1944, six months after his escape.
Doc Frie used this map when he traveled to Italy in 1964 seeking
information about his friend who had been killed there 20 years earlier.
Note the "x" marking the spot in the lower left-center of the map.

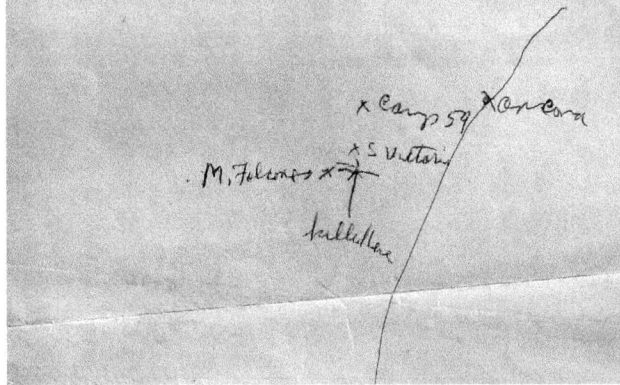

Reverse section of topographic map containing Joe Kienly's handwritten notes and a rough sketch of the place where Robert Alvey was killed by German troops. Joe Kienly drew an "x" marking the place near Montefalcone where his friend was believed to have been executed.

Summer 1964: Members of the Viozzi family gather around their farmhouse dinner table. The family patriarch, Pietro Viozzi sits at the head of the table. The Viozzis told the author in 1999 that Pietro treated Robert Alvey and Martin Majeski like his own sons. The two escaped prisoners worked on the farm and made wooden toys for the children.

Summer 1964: Tony Cruciani (far right) and his wife stand with members of the Viozzi family viewing the former gravesites in the cemetery at Santa Vittoria in Matenano where Robert Alvey and Martin Majeski were buried at night by the contadini.

July 1999: Dino Viozzi points to the site beside the Aso River where Robert Alvey and Martin Majeski were executed by German troops the morning of March 9, 1944.

July 1999: The Viozzi family gathers around the author and his wife Shannon at the head of the table at the home of Gino and Adele Viozzi in Campiglione di Fermo, Italy. The Viozzis were no longer farmers and had relocated to the Fermo area after Doc Frie's 1964 visit.

*The author, far left and his wife Shannon visit with Zulah
Dawson Ray, who was in Robert Alvey's hut at Camp 59 and
part of the mass breakout the night of September 14, 1943.*

*January 2009: The author's cousins Marilyn Newton Williams,
third from left and Sue Ann Newton Jargstorf, fourth
from left, visit the Viozzi family in Fermo.*

Indiana University

holds in reverent memory
Robert Alvey Newton

who died in the service of his country. His name has been inscribed on the permanent honor roll of his Alma Mater with the hope that his sacrifice may help those who come after him to live peaceably in a free world. Bloomington, Indiana. May 1, 1946.

President, Indiana University

The honor roll certificate issued by Indiana University on May 1, 1946, in memory of its alumnus, Robert Alvey Newton.

Kaywoodie pipe belonging to Robert Alvey Newton with myriad of inscriptions.

Part VI

BESIDE THE RIVER ASO

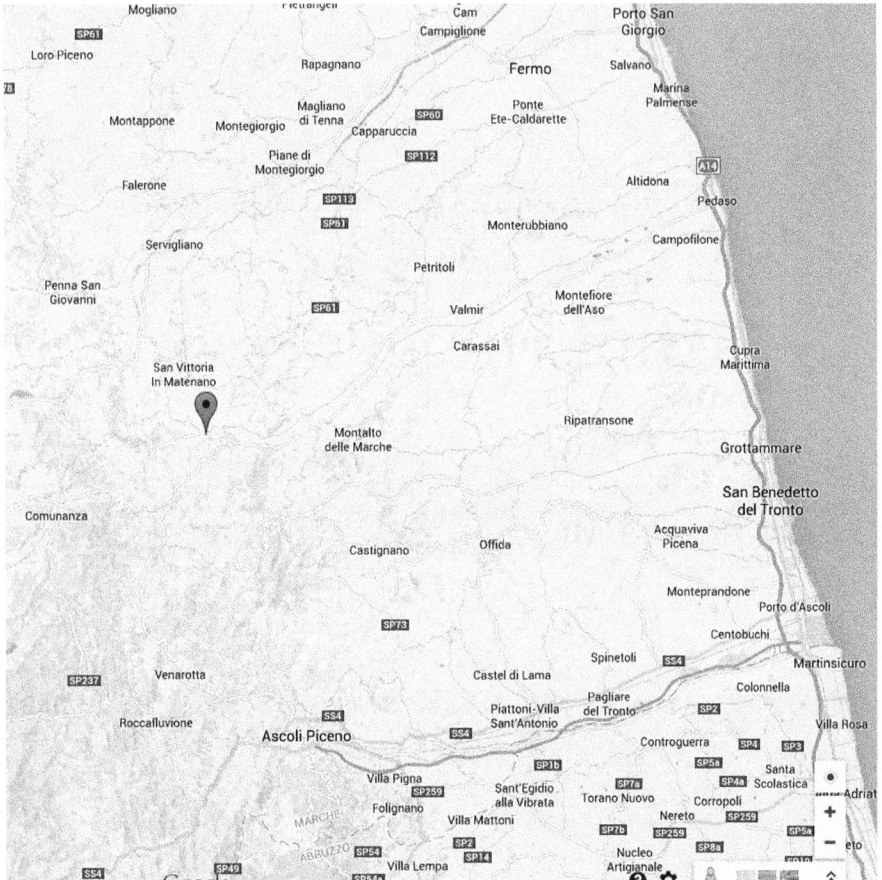

Map of Central Italy, showing vicinity of execution site of Robert Alvey Newton in relation to Camp 59, Servigliano, the Adriatic coast and other villages where escaped prisoners of war were concealed while the final events in the book took place. (Map data: Google Maps)

15

Beware the Ides of March

According to many historians, the Greek tragic dramatist Aeschylus was the source of the adage, "The first casualty of war is the truth." This is certainly the predicament when it comes to the truth regarding my uncle's capture in North Africa, his subsequent escape from Camp 59 and murder at the hands of the Axis. Time and distance worked against concrete resolution. Repatriated vets were warned by the US government not to talk. Family members were too devastated to press for answers. That, coupled with the fact that eyewitness testimony and hearsay are inherently unreliable, produced a mystery that required years of detective work to unravel.

This chronicle could never have been documented in such detail without the help of the friends and family members who preceded me as well as the ex-prisoners of war and iron soldiers of the First Armored Division and their loved ones who cared enough to help me even fifty years after the events in question. Then too, I am particularly indebted for the assistance of ardent researchers Dennis Hill and Brian Sims. I have already set forth the reports of Zulah Ray and Raymond Cox, who were a matter of yards from the scene of this war crime. What follows are summaries of various other accounts concerning the deaths of Alvey and Matt

Majeski that vary only slightly, yet nevertheless made it difficult to definitively close the case until very recently.

I very much regret that I have very little information about Matt Majeski beyond the fact that he was a member of the Seventeenth Field Artillery, was captured at Sidi Bou Zid on February 14, 1943, was wounded in the knee and walked with a limp afterward. The Viozzi family knew him as "Martino." I did write to Majeski's family in Anderson, South Carolina, but they did not to reply. Therefore, I did not press them. Still, Alvey and Matt were bound together in death, as in life at Camp 59 and on the run. Their shared experiences are certainly well related by their fellow escapees who made it back.

For fifteen agonizing months, Alvey's family and friends did not hear anything from or about him from August 1943 until November 1944. My grandmother, desperate for news, wrote to the War Department. In reply, she received a letter from the War Department dated October 5, 1943, which stated:

> The Provost Marshal General directs me to reply to your letter of 18 September 1943, regarding your son, Corporal Robert A. Newton.
>
> The status of American prisoners of war in the hands of the Italian Government is uncertain at this time. It is assumed that all have either been transferred to German Custody or returned to duty with our forces. When further information is received concerning their status you will be notified.

The family was also provided with interoffice correspondence addressed to a Jim Puett at the *Chicago Daily News* dated May 19, 1944, which read in relevant part as follows:

> The American Red Cross says that the address you gave us for Corp. Newton is no longer sufficient because

when the Americans invaded Italy all prisoners of war were removed to occupied Italy or into Germany. Some of them escaped however, and they are now with the Italian underground.

While my grandmother wrote to other mothers and family members of the men known to be with Alvey, six more months dragged on without any word. She heard from Mrs. Gee that Kenneth Robertson was home and that her brother Charles was still in Germany. The most dreadful news for any mother came by a letter dated November 7, 1944, from the chaplain of the First Armored Division, followed by a letter dated November 8, 1944, from the adjutant general of the War Department.

It is with deep regret that I am conveying to you the sad announcement that your son, Corporal Robert A. Newton, was killed in action on 9 March 1944, in Italy.

The great sorrow this message brings to you is most understandable and I realize your desire to know the circumstances attending your son's death. The report received in the War Department states that Corporal Newton, who was previously reported a prisoner of war of the Italian Government, apparently escaped and it distresses me to advise you that he was shot by Italian Fascists. Your son's death was confirmed by the Italian with whom he and a companion, who was also shot, were living.

That was the only official account the family knew for twenty years. They all believed that Italian Fascists had done the deed. It is apparent that Robert Linker's account to Jack Hunter and presumably my grandmother did not vary in any material respect. The family may have learned from Linker that the companion also killed was "a Polish kid." The only thing my own father ever said was that his brother and the other soldier were discovered hiding in a barn when the enemy poked in the hayloft with their bayonets. Supposedly, the two POWs were then given cigarettes and shot. In the interim years, Joe Kienly had done some investigation before he left the army, which resulted in the location the general area where Alvey was killed, near Montefalcone. Joe subsequently provided Doc Frie with a topographic map of the area near Montefalcone marked with an "X," stating, "Alvey killed here."

What the family could not have known about, or seen, due to their SECRET and CONFIDENTIAL designations, were War Crimes files Nos. 16-203, 16-396, and 16-34, generated immediately after the war in Italy had ended by the US Army War Crimes Office of the Judge Advocate General. With the able assistance of Kenneth Schlesinger at the National Archives, I was able to obtain copies of these files in 1992. The entire process took about a year. In any case, there are numerous affidavits from American escapees that shed light on the crime and in some cases, obfuscate a clear picture of what happened.

It does appear that the investigation into the murder of Alvey and Matt was closed on April 24, 1947, based on an earlier entry in the file:

CASE HAS BEEN FULLY INVESTIGATED AND PRESENTLY AWAITING APPREHENSION OF ACCUSED.

The various accounts, including testimonies that follow, were gleaned from these War Crimes files. I have maintained the original typos and misspellings for historical accuracy.

Herman Ira Noble

Corporal Herman I. Noble was a member of D Company, Second Battalion, First Armored Regiment and escaped from Camp 59 on

September 14, 1943. On July 1, 1944, he provided this sworn statement to the adjutant general:

> I, Cpl. Herman Ira Noble, 38023144, formerly a member of the First Armored Division, do hereby certify that I escaped from an Italian POW camp on 14 September 1943. After escaping, I remained in the vicinity of St Victoria-in-Matenano until I returned through the allied lines 27 June 1944. While in the locality mentioned above, I learned of the death of Cpl Robert E Newton, formerly a member of Company D, First Armored Regiment, First Armored Division. I learned of the death of Cpl Newton through an Italian civilian who, on 11 March 1944, told me that Cpl Newton had been staying at her house about three miles from St Victoria. She told me that he, together with another American (name unknown), had been captured and killed by the Fascists on 9 March 1944. She showed me a note written by Cpl Newton, and I recognized the handwriting to be that of Cpl Newton. I was told by this civilian, and later by others, that the two soldiers had been buried in the St Victoria cemetery. I do not believe that the graves are marked.

Arthur S. Elliott

On May 16, 1944, Staff Sergeant Arthur S. Elliott, of Company C, 133rd Infantry gave the following sworn statement about the murders of Alvey and Matt:

> I, S/SGT. Arthur S. Elliott, 20701801, formerly a member of Company C, 133rd Infantry, certify that I recently escaped enemy territory. While in hiding, I met two other escapees who were living in a nearby

house. Cpl. "Mat" (first name unknown) Magersky had been a member of the 5th Artillery; Pfc Robert Newton was a soldier of the 1st Armored Division. On the afternoon of 2 March 1944, the Italian with whom they were living confirmed the rumor of their death. They had been found shot by Fascists. They were buried two days later at San Vittor. Fact of death in each case is, I believe established beyond a reasonable doubt.

Curiously, there is also a recorded and indexed account in the file attributed to Staff Sergeant Elliott that provides additional details.

> Sgt. Arthur S. Elliott, 20701801 (MISC. Report No. 86 -19 Jun 44): Source stated that two Americans were killed near S. Vittoria, Italy, early in March 1944. They were Robert Newton of the 1st Armored Division and Cpl. Majursky of the 5th Artillery, 1st Infantry Division. He believes they were killed by Facsists in German uniforms. He spoke to the Italian who dragged their bodies out of the river and who saw the shooting, and from him got the story s follows: The two Americans are buried at S. Vittoria. They were sleeping in a stable near the river, and upon awakening one morning, they saw German trucks coming up the road to the stable. They rushed to the back door, but more Germans were coming from that direction. Not knowing whether the Germans were going to stop, they called to the family in the house near the stable that they would stay in it. The trucks, however, did stop, and the Germans came to the stable and said to the two Americans, "You are prisoners." One of the Americans had on a combat suit which was dyed and the other had on wool pants

and a field jacket, both dyed. The Germans put them on a truck, took them to the river, took off their shoes and jackets, kicked them in the river and shot them. It was believed that spies had a hand in this affair, as the Germans knew exactly where the two Americans were.

Francis A. Thomas

Francis A. Thomas was formerly a member of A Company, Eighteenth Infantry, First Infantry Division. He was interned at Camp 59 and escaped on September 14, 1943. The following are excerpts from an affidavit he provided to the judge advocate general, which is dated September 26, 1946. He was by then a civilian, living in Muskegon, Michigan.

> Q. State what you know of Settimio Rocsiolli and his activities.
>
> A. He was the Marshall of all the Fascist troops on the Adriatic side of Italy. He worked closely with the Germans and was extremely cruel. Through Caesaroni Ocari, Italian civilian, I learned that Rocsiolli was directly responsible for the killing of Robert Newton of Logansport, Indiana. Caesaroni Ocari got this information from the people in whose house Newton had been hiding. Rocsiolli found Newton in their house and killed him. . . .
>
> Q. Can you describe Fausto and tell of his activities?
>
> A. Fausto was about 5'10" tall, 185 pounds, heavily build, olive complexion, brownish red hair, oval shaped face, and a broad nose. He was the companion of Settemio Rocsiolli at all times and was present at the killing of Robert Newton, and other victims of Rocsiolli.

In his affidavit, Thomas also spoke about the executions of

Allied POWs in Comunanza, and other war crimes, which are covered in considerable detail later.

Walter John Simon

Walter Simon was also a member of A Company, Eighteenth Infantry, First Infantry Division. He was also a prisoner in Camp 59 and escaped the night of September 14, 1943. He gave the following testimony in an affidavit dated June 26, 1946:

> Q. State what you know of Settemmio Rocsiolli and his activities.
>
> A. He was Marshal of San Vittorio and was working closely with the Germans. He was a confirmed blackshirt and was extremely cruel. I would say that he was personally responsible for the capture of a large number of allied prisoners and I know of at least two Americans that he killed. Their names were Sam Mangreschi of Philadelphia, Pennsylvania and Robert Newton of Logansport, Indiana. These two men were caught in an Italian home by Settemio Rocsiolli and another Italian named Fausto, who was a shoemaker in Force Italy. Rocsiolli ordered Mangreschi and Newton out of the house and as they stepped through the door they were shot down by Rocsiolli and Fausto, using machine pistols. Settemio Rocsiolli was about 5'8" tall, 170 pounds, stocky build, brown eyes, brown hair, ruddy complexion, round cherubic face, small nose and very swaggering attitude. He was named "Little Caesar" and "Mad Rocsiolli."

Neil E. Torssell

Neil Torssell was a technical sergeant with the Ninety-ninth Bomb Group, Twelfth Air Force, shot down on July 5, 1943, during a raid on Sicily and taken prisoner. He made the breakout from Camp 59, the night of September 14, 1943. Torssell provided an affidavit to the judge advocate general on August 22, 1945. He confirmed that there were shots fired at them during the escape but did not know if anyone was hurt. Torssell gave this testimony about the murder of Matt Majeski and Alvey:

> Q. State what you know of your own knowledge of the killing of T-4 Martin Majeski.
>
> A. It happened in the morning. The convoy was going up the road — the house he was staying in was just off the road — and the convoy stopped there because they needed supplies. This Martin and another boy were sleeping in the stable and they happened to find them. They made the boys take all the food and clothing — anything they could use — out of the house and they made the owner of the house get hay from his own hay stack and put it under the beds and then light the fire himself. They took the boys with them and went near the Aso River. The Germans asked the boys to get out of the truck because they wanted them to get some wood to do some cooking. The boys were reluctant to do it and finally when they were convinced and had their backs turned, they shot them in the back of the head and just shoved a little snow over them. The next day the Italians came and picked them up and gave them a decent burial.
>
> Q. Who told you about this?
>
> A. The people that lived right next door to the house that was burned. He lives near San Vittoria. These boys were killed the 9th or 10th of March, 1944. This fellow that told me about it lived in the States for about fourteen (14) years and he could speak good English.

Torssell may have spoken with either Primo or Alfredo Mecossi. According to Raymond Cox, one or both of them had lived in Canada or the United States before the war and spoke good English. Arthur Elliott also said that Tony Augustini, who witnessed the murders, also spoke good English and Torssell could have talked to him. Of course, all of this is speculation some seventy years after the fact.

Laurence Danich

PFC Laurence Danich was a member of D Company, Second Battalion, First Armored Regiment, who was wounded and captured at Sidi Bou Zid, and taken to the same hospitals as my uncle before being transferred to Camp 59 and later escaping. There is no question that he knew my uncle well after their years of service and subsequent imprisonment together. On September 10, 1945, he gave the following testimony regarding the circumstances of Alvey's death:

> Q. Are you familiar with the circumstances of the killing of Corporal Newton?
>
> A. Yes.
>
> Q. Where and when did this incident occur?
>
> A. This killing took place in the Village of Penna, Italy, near the Pescara River, in January 1944.
>
> Q. State what you know of your own knowledge of this killing.
>
> A. In January 1944, while I was an escaped prisoner of war from Camp Serigliano, heading for Bari, Italy, I saw Corporal Newton, first name unknown being led out of a house in the outskirts of Penna by German troops. I was standing on a hill overlooking the scene, about four blocks away and I saw German SS Troops shoot and kill Corporal Newton. I later examined Corporal Newton's body and found 17 slugs in the body and

head. He died instantly. The German SS Troops had also cut off a class graduation ring from Corporal Newton's little finger.

Q. Do you know the background concerning why Corporal Newton was in Penna?

A. Corporal Newton, like myself, was an escaped prisoner of war. We were both wearing civilian clothes. Corporal Newton and I served together in the First Armored Division. The only other background information I have concerning him is that he was from the State of Indiana. After making my own escape, I was informed that Corporal Newton was staying in an Italian farm home at Penna. I myself was staying in a farm home nearby. I had visited with Newton on the morning of the day he was killed, in January 1944, exact date unknown. I left Newton and returned to my place of hiding in the Italian farm house. Later I received a warning that German SS Troops were making a search of the area, so I immediately left my place of hiding. Apparently Corporal Newton was not warned in time of the coming of the SS Troops and was caught. I saw Corporal Newton being led off and then saw the German SS Troops shoot and kill him. He was killed with German submachine guns.

Q. Can you identify any of the German personnel responsible for Corporal Newton's death, either by name, physical description, unit, or organization?

A. I cannot identify any of the German personnel personally, but I know that they belonged to the German SS because of their black uniforms.

Danich was incorrect about the town and river near the scene of the murder. Penna (San Giovanni) is about eleven miles from Santa Vittoria in Matenano and about fourteen miles from the River Aso where the killings took place. He was also a bit off with his dates. My uncle and Majeski were killed in March 1944, not January. But Danich should be afforded a pass on these inaccuracies because this testimony was eighteen months after the events in question. Even so, his basic testimony about the recapture and murder lines up extremely well with the memories of other eye witnesses, including Zulah Ray and members of the Viozzi family to the effect that Robert and Martin were killed by the German SS.

Kenneth G. "Bull" Seldon

Bull Seldon was a corporal in the 168th Infantry Regiment, Thirty-fourth Division, and a demolitions expert captured at Bizerte, Tunisia, on December 1, 1942. Seldon was transferred to Camp 59, and in the same barracks with Matt and my uncle. He escaped on September 14, 1943. Seldon provided the following testimony on September 5, 1945:

> Q. What information do you possess regarding the killing of Corporals Edwin Majeski and Robert A. Newton, American Prisoners of War, near San Vittoria, Italy sometime in March 1944, at the hands of an unidentified German soldier?
>
> A. I do not have any direct information and all that I know about this incident is what has been told to me.
>
> Q. Tell the story which you heard.
>
> A. My first knowledge that Corporal Majeski and Corporal Robert A. Newton had been killed was acquired about in May, 1944 while I was being held at Stalag III-B, Furstenberg on the Oder, Germany. Several men from the First Armored Division, and with whom I had been held as a Prisoner of War in PG-59, Servigliano, Sicily, were brought into Stalag III-B. One of these men, whose name I am not certain

of but which I believe is either McGinn or McGinnis, told me that Corporal Majeski and Corporal Newton were buried in San Vittoria, Italy. The story was that they had been shot by the Germans and buried by the Italians. McGinn, or McGinnis, was very positive as to the graves of these men being at San Vittoria because either he or some of his buddies with him, saw their dog tags hanging on the cross mark at the graves. After learning of this incident, I made an effort to contact and talk to all the men who had been at PG-59 whenever they would be transferred to Stalag III-B. I heard rumor stories from other men but none of them were very clear or definite. . . .

Q. Did you have a personal acquaintance with either Majeski or Newton?

A. Yes. Majeski and Newton, as well as myself, were part of a group of approximately 980 American Prisoners of War who were being held at PG-59, Servigliano, Sicily. I had become acquainted with both of them. On 14 September 1944 the Italian guards abandoned PG-59. Immediately thereafter the 980 American prisoners left the camp and I know that Newton and Majeski went with the group. That is the last I saw either one of them. Most of these men were loose shifting for themselves in the mountains of Italy and many of them were captured and returned to the prison camps. The others were attempting to work their way back to the American lines and I imagine that Majeski and Newton were working their way back to the American lines at the time of their recapture. Majeski was somewhat handicapped by reason of an injured knee which would not permit him to move around as rapidly as he would like to. I know that some of these men were in this mountain area for as long as 6 months before recapture and that the Germans were constantly sweeping this area for the escaped men.

Seldon had also been held at PG 98 near Palermo, Sicily, before being transferred to PG 59 and obviously erred by saying Servigliano, "Sicily." To date, I have been unable to locate any record of a "McGinn" or "McGinnis" who may have been held at Camp 59. Also, the mass escape was in 1943, not 1944. Still, Matt Majeski was known to have a leg wound just as Seldon remembered. Bull Seldon died in 1946, less than a year after giving this testimony. He was only twenty-nine years of age.

Worth Columbus Hampton

Staff Sergeant Worth Hampton was married to Matt Majeski's cousin, Virginia Lee Majeski. He and Matt entered the army together and were close friends. Hampton and Majeski were both in Battery F, Seventeenth Field Artillery. Although Hampton was not interned at PG 59, he met Bull Seldon in Stalag III-B, and Bull told him what had happened to Matt in Italy. The following are excerpts of the testimony given by Worth Hampton on August 8, 1944, regarding Matt's death:

> Q. State what "Bull" Seldon told you about that incident. . . .
>
> A. A few days after Italy surrendered to the Allies, most of the Italians left this camp and Seldon stated that he broke out with the other prisoners and that on the night he left, he saw Majeski making a bedding roll and preparing to leave also, but this time according to Seldon, Majeski's leg wound had about healed, although he still limped. In March 1944, some more Allied prisoners of war came through Seldon's village

and told him that three (3) escaped American prisoners were lying dead at a cross roads near San Victoria.
Seldon stated that some of the escaped American prisoners with him, but not himself, went to San Victoria
and found these men. They positively identified Majeski,
whom some of them knew well and they buried all
three of these men near the cross roads. It is understood
that these men were dressed in various odds and ends of
clothes but they were not armed. The Americans who
buried these men took their dog tags and other papers
and gave them to the mayor of San Victoria to hold for
American authorities. Seldon knows the names of these
escaped American prisoners who buried Majeski and
the other two (2) dead prisoners.

Robert J. "Doc" Frie

In the summer of 1964, my uncle's lifelong friend, Robert J. "Doc"
Frie traveled to Italy with the fraternal organization, the Sons of
Italy. He and his wife, Edie, went with their good friends in the
group, Tony Cruciani and his wife. By happenstance, the group's
itinerary included a visit to San Benedetto Del Tronto, on the coast
of the Adriatic Sea, in the province of Le Marche. San Benedetto
is about thirty miles east of the Montefalcone – Santa Vittoria area.

Doc and Tony drove to the general vicinity guided only by the
topographic map obtained by Joe Kienly years before, with his
crude drawing of the place where Alvey was killed. How Doc
found the Viozzi family is recounted at the beginning of this book.
Suffice it to say again, that Doc believed that he had been led to
the exact spot and told me that after crossing a bridge, he "sensed
within his spirit that this was the place." I now believe that he
crossed a bridge over the River Aso, not far from the exact spot
where his friend had been killed.

He took a number of pictures of the Viozzi family, the shed

next to their house where Alvey spent a number of nights and days on the run, and of the place Alvey was killed beside the Aso River. Doc then returned to the United States. But when the pictures came back from the developer, none of them had turned out. Consequently, Doc contacted Tony, who was still in Italy, and asked him to return to the area and retake the photos. Tony happily and graciously did as Doc asked. The original negatives and slides of the photographs taken by Tony Cruciani were given to me by Edie Frie after Doc's death in 1986.

I was fifteen years old when I first saw these slides. We were at Doc's home in Miraleste above San Pedro, California, at a summer party. Doc asked me, my dad, and Joe Kienly to come up to his living room and then showed us the slides with a commentary for each one. After they had all been shown, he asked my dad if he should show them to my grandmother. My dad said, "I think she is content with what she knows."

In 1964, there were a greater number of members of the Viozzi family who were eyewitnesses to the recapture and killing than those still alive today. They told Doc that German storm troopers had committed the crime, not Italian Fascists. This was the first time that anyone connected with the family had heard that the Germans had killed Alvey and Majeski. The following is an excerpt from a letter written by Doc Frie to my grandmother on August 15, 1964:

> Alvey was not caught in the loft of an old barn. The retreating Germans (The front lines were only 5 to 8 miles off) rampaged in convoys thru the countryside pillaging and burning what they could not steal for food etc. Alvey hid in the wooded draw when the convoy came through and was caught by the merest trick of fate when a single jeepload of drunken storm troopers caught him after he came back to dinner. The people

think some despicable informer told the Germans but
they were never able to find out.

Doc did not speak Italian and relied upon Tony Cruciani's translation of what the Viozzis were telling him. There are a number
of features of this report that are at odds with other eyewitness
accounts and the historical record. For one thing, the front lines in
early March 1944 were a great deal farther than five to eight miles
away. In fact, the Allies were hung up at Monte Cassino until
May 18, 1944, and the breakout from Anzio did not happen until
May 23, 1944. Cassino is about 175 miles from Montefalcone and
Anzio is about 203 miles southwest from there. Allied forces did
not enter Rome until June 5, 1944. Then too, the Polish II Corps
did not reach the Aso River until about June 20, 1944. Even allowing for the arrival of forward elements in the vicinity before June
1944, there is still a disparity of months. Be that as it may, the
identification of the killers as German storm troopers is absolutely
consistent with what other eyewitnesses later contended.

In July 1999, my wife and I traveled to Italy and found the
Viozzi family. The surviving brothers who were eyewitnesses were
all the younger brothers. Giuseppe Viozzi was then nineteen;
Dino Viozzi, sixteen; and Gino Viozzi, ten. They were all adamant
that Roscioli was not involved and that the Germans had killed
"Roberto" and "Martino."

By the year 2010, I was fairly well convinced that we had
heard the last of the accounts regarding the circumstances of the
murders of Matt and Alvey. Then I received an email from Dennis
Hill at Indiana University with an attached interview taken from
a feature published by Italian historian Filippo Ierano titled *Antigone nelle Valle del Tenna*. The interview was given by Cesare Viozzi
to Ierano in July 2001, and was itself titled *"Avevano Appiccato Il
Fuoco,"* ("They Set It On Fire").

The interview was translated from the Italian into English by

Anne Bewicke-Copley. Anne is a lawyer living and working in Oxford, England, and is the daughter of the Sixth Lord Cromwell. She and her husband own a house near Montefalcone Appennino. They travel there frequently, and Anne has honed a keen interest in the stories of the *contadini* and their interaction with Allied escapees. In fact, she has authored magazine articles on that subject.

Cesare Viozzi is a cousin to Giuseppe, Dino, and Gino Viozzi. He was also one of twenty-eight family members in the house the fateful day when Alvey and Matt were recaptured and killed. Here are excerpts from the 2001 interview of Cesare by Filippo Ierano:

> Early one morning we saw German troops coming along the road for Santa Vittoria. We were scared and immediately made the two prisoners escape and they hid themselves in a ditch. Word went round that the Germans were withdrawing. As soon as all seemed quiet, we told them that they could return. After a bit, whilst we were at the table having breakfast, we realized that two soldiers on two motorbikes, including sidecars, were coming in the direction of our house. No one expected anything like this, and in fact the two Americans were with us at the table. We didn't even have time to think of any solutions before the two Germans began to shout, ordering us to come out and threatening us with their weapons. We never understood how but they recognized the two Americans immediately and they took them.
>
> It could only be that a spy had informed them. Otherwise it was impossible that they could have recognized the prisoners, dressed like us, in such a short time. Threatening them with their weapons, they made Robert and Martin get into the sidecar and they left. We followed them with our eyes, we were very afraid,

and from afar we saw them stop in a little wood on the River Aso, near to Ponte Maglio. A few seconds later the Germans fired several shots and killed the Americans. Then, the two soldiers got on their motorbikes and returned to our house. I escaped with some of my cousins, all boys and hid behind a hedge. The Germans made everyone come out of the house, and my parents were even forced to carry out into the farmyard a poor old aunt who had been bedridden for years.

One uncle wanted to do something, but as the weapons were pointed at them, his brothers told him to keep still; there could have been a massacre with all the women and children in the farmyard. We boys, who'd managed to flee, watched everything from afar. They immediately began to set fire to everything, entering the rooms with torches setting fire to things. My poor desperate mother, notwithstanding the threats, beat the flames trying to put them out. . . .

They loaded all of our goods onto their bikes. Given that we had butchered four pigs some months before, there was a lot of stuff. They also set fire to the stables, but luckily my uncles managed to save the animals which were inside. . . .

Before leaving they fired at the walls of the house and maybe threw some little bombs against the windows, terrifying everyone and shattering the glass. Another soldier arrived, and seeing that we had a horse, ordered us to give it to them. The retreating Germans wanted to take everything. The fear was so great that even our three dogs didn't bark. . . .

The next day a *contadino* brought the bodies of the two Americans to Santa Vittoria by horse and cart, for burial. The stupid thing was that he claimed payment

from us for the transportation. Crazy stuff. The house
was gravely damaged, the flames made the roof unsta-
ble and the frame was almost non-existent. All summer
we had to undertake difficult reconstruction work. . . .

Our family suffered the most in the vicinity, but no
one ever regretted having given hospitality to those
poor boys.

Cesare Viozzi also reported that the Germans came upon two
boys playing on a broken-down lorry and shot them dead. There
is also today a weathered plaque on the wall of a nearby farmhouse that memorializes the murder by the Germans of a David
Viozzi, who was "assassinated" on June 15, 1944. That was more
than three months after Alvey and Matt were killed. According to the Viozzi family, David was not related to them, but was
killed because the retreating Germans stopped at his house and
demanded food. Someone in the household refused, and David
was killed in retaliation.

The eyewitness accounts are unanimous in reporting that
German troops committed these war crimes. Still, it is intrigu-
ing that Roscioli was fond of riding around on a motorcycle while
wearing a German uniform. In fact, he was not a captain, but a
sergeant-major in the German army and used to accompany the
Germans on raids looking for partisans and escaped prisoners.
Roscioli was repeatedly mentioned by the repatriated prisoners
of war as being the primary suspect in so many atrocities against
escaped Allied soldiers as well as Italian civilians. He bragged
about killing thirty Allied POWs, and it was said that he was
so cruel that the Germans accompanied him just to temper his
barbarity. However, I must conclude that the Viozzis either knew
Roscioli, or knew of him and perhaps had encountered him in the
vicinity before. In any case, they would have been able to discern
if one of the renegades was Roscioli or any other local Italian, as
opposed to a German or other foreigner.

One account that is most difficult to reconcile is that provided by Herman Noble. He was in the same company as Alvey and knew him well enough to distinguish his handwriting. But, according to Noble, the woman from the Viozzi family that gave him the note written by Alvey told Noble that the Fascists had killed him. Could it be that the *contadini* simply referred to both the local Fascists and their German counterparts as *fascisti*? The Italian language does have the terms *Nazifascisti* and *Nazifascismo*. But it is far more likely that the woman would have used the word *Tedeschi* for Germans. Although this is speculation, she may have been simply repeating the scenario that Primo Mecossi related to Raymond Cox, that Roscioli had shot Robert and Martin.

In Shakespeare's *Julius Caesar*, the soothsayer warns him to "beware the ides of March." Technically, the warning is referring only to March 15. Yet, ever since then, that reference has been perpetually imbued with a sense of foreboding. For the men still behind the lines, the wanton killing of these two American soldiers and other rumored murders of their fellow POWs filled them with deep anxiety and chilling apprehension.

16

Crimini Di Guerra

The unprovoked killing of these two poor sons (*poveri figli*) was not the only atrocity committed by the Nazis and Fascists in the area. Although rare, in terms of the headcount of those prisoners of war who did come home from Italy, the known incidents of war crimes were characterized by extreme cruelty and wanton barbarity.

On October 18, 1942, Hitler issued his infamous, secret Commando Order stating that all Allied commandos operating behind the lines were to be executed immediately without trial. This was in direct abrogation of the laws of war, yet German commanders who did not carry it out were themselves subject to extreme punishment. The German general staff knew this order was illegal and only printed it in twelve copies. In the spirit of this barbarous directive, after the mass escape from PG 59, the German commander in the area of Servigliano issued the following warning to the Italian people on September 22, 1943:

COMMANDER OF GERMAN TROOPS

WARNING

Citizens:

Anyone who hides or assists enemy prisoners of war (English, American, Cypriot, Canadian, etc.) and who doesn't denounce them immediately to the German Commander of Servigliano or to the local police will be arrested and treated according to the martial law of the German army, that is, with the sentence of death.

Anyone who assists by capturing and presenting prisoners of war or by furnishing information which assists in their capture will be rewarded in cash a sum from Lire 1000 to Lire 10000 depending upon the information provided.

Servigliano, September 22, 1943
THE COMMANDER OF
THE AREA OF SERVIGLIANO
Lieutenant Stein

This was not an isolated incident. The following year, the governor general in Ascoli-Piceno issued the following order on May 2, 1944:

To the Mayor of the Community of Comunanza

Today the 2nd of May 1944 have been shot by order of the German Command four English and two Americans, the reasons for the execution of the prisoners of war are following:

The mentioned English and Americans have plundered the homes of farmers and terrorized them, the inhabitants of the same northwest of Amandola.

Prisoners of war of this kind are still being in the great number in the vicinity of Comunanza, and four your benefit I am rendering this announcement in public. In that way it shall be for the population of

Comunanza and understood among the farmers as a lesson. For the benefit of the population, therefore, else for all Italy I will give this order change.

1. Who concedes asylum and nourishment, or a favor in any kind to prisoners of war or bandits, will be shot.

2. Any citizen of Comunanza who knows the whereabouts of a band of prisoners of war must give immediate communication or else be shot.

That the Americans and English are enemies is still proven by the recent fact, when they came back and machine gunned a cart with oxen, on the highway Comunanza Amandola, though it was not a military objective.

This announcement to the population of Comunanza is of my part the first and last. We came here to assure the population a life more tranquil and undisturbed. For this I am firmly resolved to render all necessary measures to obtain this promise.

Signature of the Commandante
Unrau

This outrageous atrocity described in the foregoing communiqué regarding the cold-blooded murder of ex-prisoners of war in Comunanza has been recalled by a number of survivors of Camp 59 who were camped nearby.

Moses "Moe" Melmed

The foregoing "manifesto" was obtained by Camp 59 escapee Moses "Moe" Melmed, Company A, Eighteenth Infantry, First Division. Melmed translated it from the original Italian. He gave the army a copy of the original as well as his translation in his affidavit dated August 16, 1946.

Comunanza was about ten miles from the Montelparo – Santa Vittoria area. A number of men, including Ken Lightbody and Manuel Serrano, reported the murders of the escaped Allied POWs in Comunanza. Moe Melmed gave the following testimony about this incident:

Q. Are you familiar with the circumstances surrounding the deaths of six allied prisoners of war at Comunanza, Italy, on or about the 15th of March 1944?

A. Yes, I am familiar with circumstances surrounding the deaths of six allied prisoners of war at Comunanza, Italy, but to the best of my knowledge the date was on or about 2 May 1944.

Q. Please state what you know.

A. A few Italian friends and prisoners of war who have witnessed this execution told me about this. They were shot outside the cemetery of Comunanza in the early morning by a firing squad. I was also told that they had to dig their own graves. The names of the executed prisoners were impossible to obtain, although we, my Italian friends and my comrades, tried very hard. . . .

Q. Have you any further information regarding atrocities against allied prisoners of war?

A. There was two men who particularly known to be anti-allied and pro-fascist, Sittermio Rosciolli and Fausto. Sittermio Rosciolli was a fascist official in San Vittoria, and he used to spy on all anti-fascist activities in that region. He used to ride in a motorcycle from place to place, looking and spying on the Italians and terrorizing them. Fausto was his assistant, and lived in Force, Italy, terrorizing this vicinity.

Q. Are either of these men still alive?

A. I don't know.

Leroy Thurman

Leroy Thurman escaped from Camp 59 on September 14, 1943. He was hiding on a rooftop in Comunanza and witnessed the murder of recaptured prisoners of war. He provided the following testimony in his affidavit of May 1, 1945:

Q. Did you witness the shooting and killing of 4 American soldiers and 3 British soldiers near Comunanza, northern part of Italy, during March 1944?

A. Yes.

Q. State what you know of your own knowledge about that incident.

A. On 14 September 1943, I successfully escaped, along with approximately all of the soldiers at Camp 0-59, northern part of Italy. It is my opinion there were some 1100 soldiers, mostly British, confined at this camp at the time we escaped. I roamed the hills in the northern part of Italy evading being captured and during March 1944 I was at Comunanza in the northern part of Italy and was informed that the Italians had a searching party in that community looking for escaped prisoners of war. A friendly Italian family where I was staying and who were feeding me suggested that I go on top of their roof at this Italian home so in the event searching parties should come in their house I would not be located. I did go to the top of the roof and was lying there when about 9:00 P.M. at night I heard a commotion approximately 100 yards from the house where I was on the rooftop and I looked in that direction and noticed there was a large cemetery. The moon was shining bright and I could distinguish some American and British soldiers and many Italian soldiers in this graveyard. The Italian soldiers set up a

guard detail and continued to walk around the cemetery all night. At daybreak during the same morning
of March 1944 I noticed four American soldiers, three
British soldiers and three Italian children in the center
of the Italian soldiers and each were given a shovel or
some instrument and each were digging a hole in the
ground which gave the appearance of a grave. About
9:30 or 10:00 A.M. the graves were dug by each of the
four American soldiers, three British soldiers and three
Italian children, said children being about 15 years of
age. Each of the American soldiers and British soldiers
and Italian children were apparently ordered to stand
at the foot of each grave whereupon one Italian officer,
description of rank I cannot give, walked by each one
and shot each soldier, both American and British, and
each Italian child and they were shoved in the grave
and buried by the Italian soldiers.

Manuel Serrano

Manuel Serrano was nearby with the partisans at their forest
hideout and later saw the bodies of six executed Allied prisoners
at Comunanza. On September 18, 1945, he gave the judge advocate
general an affidavit containing the following testimony:

> Q. Did you witness or have you been told of any atroci-
> ties or mistreatment of American citizens?
> A. Yes. I have information concerning the killing of
> six allied soldiers at Communanza, Italy on or about
> the middle of March, 1944.
> Q. State what you know of this incident.
> A. On or about the middle of March, 1944 at Com-
> munanza, Italy, in the Province of La Marche, six
> allied prisoners were executed. The shooting occurred

toward evening. I heard that these six allied soldiers (five Americans and one British) had already escaped the Italians and were living in the vicinity of Comunanza when they were apprehended by Italian Fascists and were ordered executed by a firing squad. I did not see the actual shooting, but I did see the six bodies approximately six or seven hours after the shooting, about midnight. The bodies had apparently been bayoneted and their identification and possessions removed. I knew that some of the men had been in my hut, but due to the condition of the bodies, I wasn't able to actually identify them because they were badly mangled. Therefore, I can't furnish any of their names.

Q. Do you know the names or nick-names of any of the perpetrators of this crime, or can you give a physical description of any of them?

A. The only party I would hold responsible for the death of these allied soldiers was a Fascist by the name of Rosholli (FNU), who was a sort of Provost Marshall for the areas around Comunanza. I only saw him a couple of times and was never near enough to be able to give a description of him. I heard that Rosholli was responsible for at least 22 allied prisoners being killed, although I do not remember who told me. I am sure he was responsible for the death of these six allied prisoners.

Guss Oliver Teel

Guss Teel was a private with A Company, Eighteenth Infantry, First Division. He was from Roswell, New Mexico. On September 14, 1943, he escaped from Camp 59 at Servigliano and made his way to Comunanza with some other guys from his outfit. He provided the following testimony on August 26, 1946:

Q. Are you familiar with the circumstances surrounding the deaths of six allied prisoners of war at Comunanza, Italy, on or about 15 March 1944?

A. I was not an eye-witness to this crime, but became familiar with the circumstances through the local people of Communanza, Italy.

Q. Please state what you know. . . .

A. On or about 15 March 1944, I heard some of the men discussing a letter they had picked up in town from the Governor General at Ascoli Piceno, to the Mayor and people of Communanza. This letter stated that the six allied prisoners had been participating in terroristic activities and other crimes; that they had been captured and tried by a military court and had been sentenced to death and were to be executed on that same afternoon. About 2:00 o'clock PM we could see from our hiding place about a mile away, a group of guards marching down the road with six men, who appeared to be their prisoners. We could not see them very plain because of the distance. These men were marched to the cemetery, lined up against a wall and shot to death. . . .

Q. Who was directly responsible for this execution?

A. I think the Governor General of Ascoli Piceno, an Italian civilian, whose name I do not remember, was responsible for the execution. Our informants told us that the firing squad was commanded by a German officer, a lieutenant.

Q. Do you know if any of the local people were involved in the execution?

A. I am certain that Settimio Rocsiolli, Marshal of Santa Vittoria, and his two brothers, Julio Rocsiolli and Fiori Rocsiolli, were involved in the execution.

Q. State what you know of Settimio Rocsiolli and his activities.

A. He was a strong Fascist long before the war and the leader of the "blackshirts" in the Province of Ascoli Piceno. He was the Marshal of San Vittorie and was working very close with the Germans. He was a very cruel individual, and we were told that he was responsible for the capture of a large number of allied prisoners. One of our men, Private Walter Simon, Company "A", 185th Infantry, 1st Division, told me that he had personal knowledge of at least two American prisoners that Settimio Rocsiolli had shot to death. I am not familiar with the details of this crime as I was nowhere around the area where it happened.

Q. Can you describe Settemio Rocsiolli?

A. He was about 5'4" tall, weighed about 150 lbs. stocky build, ruddy complexion, small nose and an arrogant attitude. I do not remember what the local people called him for a nickname, but the majority of the people of Communanza disliked Rocsiolli very much.

Walter John Simon

In the previous chapter, I included excerpts from the affidavit of Walter John Simon relative to the murders of Alvey and Matt. Simon was at Comunanza and also provided the following testimony pertaining to the execution of six escaped Allied prisoners of war:

Q. Are you familiar with the circumstances surrounding the deaths of six allied prisoners of war at Communanza, Italy on or about 15 March 1944?

A. Yes.

Q. Please state what you know.

A. After my escape from Servigliano I managed to join up with about thirteen other escaped prisoners and we hid out in a small hunting lodge near Communanza,

Italy. We were in close contact with the people of this
town for they were assisting us in hiding, giving us food,
etc. and also whatever information they could obtain
from any sources concerning the Nazi and Fascist
troops in the area. We saved all the leaflets dropped
by allied and enemy planes and any additional leaflets
or publications we could get a hold of. I went to the
hideout one morning (the morning of 15 March 1944)
to get some pistols and when I arrived one of the other
men showed me a letter from the Governor General
at Ascoli Piceno to the Mayor and people of Commu-
naza which said that six men had been executed that
afternoon about 2:00 p.m. From our hideout, which
was far up the side of a mountain overlooking the town,
we watched these six men taken under 30-men guard,
to the cemetery where they were first shown six open
graves, then lined up against the wall and shot. . . .

Q. Who was directly responsible for this execution?

A. I would say that it was either the Military Governor, a man whose name I do not know, or the Governor
General at Ascoli Piceno, an Italian civilian whose
name I do not know. The firing squad was commanded
by a Lieutenant, but I do not know whether he was
German or Italian, although I believe he was German.

Q. Can you give any names of persons actually
involved?

A. I am pretty sure that Settemio Rocsiolli, Marshal
of San Vittoria, and his two brothers, Julio Rocsiolli
and Fiori Rocsiolli, were involved in this killing.

Francis A. Thomas

Excerpts from the affidavit of Francis A. Thomas relative to the
murders of Alvey and Matt were also set forth in the prior chapter.

Thomas was also at Comunanza with other soldiers from his company and provided the following testimony pertaining to the execution of escaped Allied prisoners of war:

Q. Are you familiar with the circumstances surrounding the deaths of six allied prisoners of war at Communanza, Italy on or about 15 March 1944?

A. Yes.

Q. Please state what you know. . . .

A. One day, Caesaroni Ocari, an Italian civilian who had befriended us during our hiding out period brought to us a letter signed by a German General and addressed to the people of Communanza. I do not remember the name of the German General but this letter stated that six men and one Italian had been caught and court-martialed, and convicted of rape and robbery against the people and that these seven men were to be executed in a few days. On the day set for the execution we watched from a hidden position near the scene of the execution. We saw the seven men taken, heavily guarded to the cemetery, where they were forced to dig their own graves. After doing this they were lined up against a wall and shot. . . .

Q. Do you possess a copy of the "Manifesto" which you mentioned above?

A. No. I turned the copy which I had in to the United States Military authorities in Algiers, Africa when I returned to duty. Pfc. Moe Melmed another member of our group of escaped prisoners of war had a copy of this document but I do not know what he did with it. Caesaroni Ocari, the Italian civilian, possessed a copy of this "Manifesto." . . .

Q. Who was directly responsible for this execution?

A. I would say that a German Officer, a General, was directly responsible. I do not know his name but know that he was in command of troops in Communanza and at Ascoli Piceno. The firing squad was composed of Fascist troops and commanded by a German Lieutenant.

Q. Can you give the names of persons actually involved?

A. Settemio Rosciolli was the Marshal of all Fascist on the Adriatic side of Italy and an Italian named Fausto were involved.

I am convinced despite the significant variations in the reports of the execution of the Allied prisoners of war at Comunanza, that the witnesses were all recalling the same event. The most obvious disparity concerns the date of the execution. Only Moe Melmed produced a copy of the manifesto pertaining to the execution of the six prisoners. While that document is dated May 2, 1944, most of the others testified that the murders occurred on March 15, 1944. (Serrano says mid-March.) This may be attributable to the fact that the interrogators kept asking the men to state what they knew about the circumstances surrounding the deaths of six prisoners of war "on or about 15 March 1944." Perhaps the men were anxious to state what they knew and being unsure of the precise date up to a year afterward, did not deem it imperative to correct the interviewer whom they presumed had superior knowledge as to that aspect of the investigation.

These accounts also vary regarding the time of day, as well as the number and identification of the people who were killed. Then too, there are slight variations regarding the execution itself and whether the hapless soldiers were required to dig their own graves, or lined up against the wall and brought down by a firing squad.

Time and again in the accounts set forth in this book, we have seen how eyewitness accounts are inherently unreliable, and that people can all view the same thing, yet recall the events through different lenses. As an attorney, I have over the years seen this happen time and again. You can only shake your head in amazement at how peoples' perceptions can be so different. In our own era, we only have to remember the diversity among the testimonies of eyewitnesses to John F Kennedy's assassination to understand just how much human perceptions can vary. One woman even swore that Jacqueline Kennedy had a dog on her lap!

The truth is that memories often fail to present accurate versions of critical events and that is why effective cross-examination is usually called for in a court of law. Forensic psychology has demonstrated through scientific tests that memory is highly adaptable. Memory can be manipulated. It is a reconstruction, not a true record. Other sources flood the brain and fill in the gaps. In this case, men from the same unit reinforced certain aspects of the case while failing to incorporate others. Finally, each eyewitness filters what he sees through his own biases and experiences.

Still, there should be no doubt regarding the main gist of these accounts. A vicious and heinously cruel war crime was committed at Comunanza, whether a month or three months before the Germans abandoned the Province of Le Marche and streamed north just ahead of the encroaching Allies.

There were numerous other war crimes perpetrated in Le Marche and throughout Italy during this same time frame, which are too numerous to recount here. But among the most notorious are the slaughter on Monte Sole, the Boves Atrocity, the Marzabotto massacre, and the Sant' Anna massacre. The Italian civilians were regularly slaughtered by the German occupiers who suspected that they were helping escaped prisoners or assisting the partisans. For example, on November 21, 1943, the Germans murdered 128 Italian people, including 34 children under the age of ten and a month-old baby, near Pietransieri just because the village was suspected of helping the rebels. Only one six-year-old girl survived because she was shielded by her mother's body. The Germans left the bodies in the snowbound woods of Limmari, and the victims were not buried until the following spring.

One historian has estimated that on average, the Germans killed 165 civilians and escaped POWs per day between September 8, 1943, and May 8, 1945! That estimate does not even include the partisans who were killed in running battles with the Nazis and Fascists. In addition to the summary execution of POWs and partisans witnessed by Keith Argraves, there were three others in March 1944 that are highly documented.

Montedinove

UK researcher Brian Sims provided me with documentation from the British archives detailing the murders of three escaped British soldiers and the Belgian agent sent to rescue them behind the lines. These men were all arrested by the Germans, shot and dumped under a bridge at Montedinove on March 10, 1944, the day after Alvey and Martin were executed just a few miles away. The British soldiers were L. H. J. Brown, Daniel Hollingsworth, and Thomas White. The Belgian rescuer shot with them was named Mario Mootis. As in so many other instances, Roscioli was said to have assisted in the recapture and murder of these brave men.

Ardeatine Caves Massacre

Another war crime of particular moment is the massacre of 335 Italian men and young boys at the Ardeatine Caves *(Fosse Ardeatine)* just outside of Rome on March 24, 1944. This mass killing was in retaliation for a partisan bombing in Rome that resulted in the deaths of German SS policemen. Innocent Italians were rounded up by the Nazis and transported by truck to the caves, where their hands were tied behind their backs. Then they were machine-gunned in groups of five. As more and more groups were killed, the victims were forced to kneel on the dead bodies of the groups who preceded them in death.

The killing took nearly all day, with the dead being stacked as the sun rose higher in the sky. After the systematic killing spree ended, the Germans set explosives and sealed the caves to hide their crime.

There were two German commanders primarily responsible for the slaughter, Erich Priebke and Herbert Kappler. Priebke escaped justice by immigrating to Argentina. But he was brought back to Italy in 1994 and subsequently sentenced in 1998 to life imprisonment, which actually amounted to house arrest in his lawyer's home! Priebke passed away of natural causes at the age of 100 in October 2013. Kappler was caught by the British and sentenced to life imprisonment. He died in Germany in 1977.

Operation Ginny II

Yet another war crime involving Allied prisoners of war occurred on March 26, 1944. The murdered men were behind the lines on a mission known as Operation Ginny II. It was preceded by Operation Ginny I, which took place February 27–28, 1944. In the first raid, fifteen operatives with the clandestine American OSS (Office of Strategic Services) boarded PT boats bound for Stazione de Framura, Italy, on the Ligurian Sea, to commit sabotage behind the lines. But they were offloaded too far south of the target and aborted the mission.

Operation Ginny II was launched on March 22, 1944, with the same objective. The commando unit was also landed at the wrong spot but pressed on with the mission. They were all captured on March 23, when an Italian fisherman saw their rafts pulled up on the shoreline and told the authorities. The Germans then swept the area and captured all fifteen US soldiers holed up in a barn.

History records that Field Marshal Albert Kesselring, commanding general of all German forces in Italy, ordered the summary execution of the Americans, and German General Anton Dostler issued the actual execution order. This was of course a blatant violation of the Geneva convention but was in full compliance with Hitler's Commando Order. Some German officers did try to intervene to prevent the execution, but they were overruled. On March 26, 1944, the captured Americans, all of whom were in uniform, were gunned down by a German firing squad and dumped in a mass grave.

Dostler was found guilty of war crimes by an Allied court, sentenced to death and executed by a firing squad on December 1, 1945. Kesselring almost suffered the same fate. He was found guilty of war crimes and sentenced to death on May 6, 1947. But Winston Churchill, Clement Atlee, and others intervened on his behalf, and the sentence was commuted to life imprisonment. Yet, he was released in 1952 and died a natural death in Germany in 1960.

This is just one blatant example of the selective justice meted out in the face of overwhelming complicity in the barbaric assassination of prisoners of war and Italian civilians in 1944.

17

Mad Roscioli

In his war crimes affidavit, Walter Simon revealed that Settimio Roscioli was pejoratively dubbed Little Caesar and Mad Roscioli. Given the notoriety of the brutish Roscioli, and his repeated implication in so many war crimes, it should be expected that he would have faced the application of swift and sure justice once the Allies took control of the Le Marche region. Sadly, that proved not to be the case.

Roscioli was from the village of Monte Rinaldo in the region of Le Marche. Monte Rinaldo was about eighteen miles from Ascoli-Piceno and nearly five miles from Santa Vittoria in Matenano. He was known to travel from town to town on a motorcycle, terrorizing the *contadini*, who were generally an apolitical people and just wanted to work their family farms in peace. A number of Allied escapees have vivid recollections about Roscioli and his motorcycle. But he was also known to drive a Fiat Topolino automobile. Topolino means "little mouse" in Italian. But in Roscioli's case, "little rat" would have been a far more appropriate appellation.

Mad Roscioli was ably assisted by three other disturbed villains, Fausto Poloni, a shoemaker from the village of Force; and Arturo Vannozzi and Gino Bascioni, originally from Belmonte. My research indicates that Poloni was tried and convicted of war crimes in Ancona. What his punishment was and whether he served any part of it is not readily available. As far as I have been able to determine, Vannozzi was arrested and indicted for robbery and aiding the enemy but was released under a postwar amnesty program. Bascioni, on the other hand, is still listed on the Central Register of War Criminals of the United Nations War Crimes Commission and wanted by the United Kingdom for murder. I am purposefully omitting the use of the adjective "alleged" in connection with the crimes committed by these four despicable cowards.

For a time, I believed that justice had been meted out by one of the Camp 59 survivors. In March 1992, I heard from William T. Miller of Avoca, Indiana, formerly a half-track driver with the Sixth Armored Infantry, First Armored Division. He escaped from Camp 59 and linked up with a group of partisans. William told me that shortly after escaping, he acquired an 8 gauge shotgun. He and the others heard that Roscioli was coming, so they lined up along the road and as he approached, they opened up. William said, "I gave him both barrels." He also said that the more POWs Roscioli killed the more money he received from the Germans. Consequently, there was no hint of any regret on William's part for having dispatched the Fascist on the motorcycle, whoever that might have been. Regarding his time as a prisoner of war behind enemy lines, William then confided, "I still suffer every day. I saw things in Italy I'm still mad about."

I have no doubt that Miller dispatched some Fascist on a motorcycle. However, it was not Settimio Roscioli. There is a possibility that the rider was one of Roscioli's brothers, Julio or Fiori. Still, Robert Noah told me with a tone of extreme disgust that he had returned to Italy in the 1960s and learned that Settimio Roscioli had survived the war and died of natural causes in his own bed.

Roscioli was regarded with the utmost disdain by everyone but his Fascist cohorts and Nazi overlords. After the war Camp 59 escapee Walter Simon kept in touch with the *contadini* who had sheltered him. They sent him a newspaper article about Roscioli that he provided to the war crimes investigators on September 26, 1946. No translation of the Italian was provided. However, the following is a translation prepared in 2013 by Natasha Ferrotta-Baretta, an Italian student at New York University:

Roscioli, Criminale di Guerra
The Photographer Tells

We heard a motorcycle in front of the entrance to our building. I was working in my darkroom on developing photos of children. They rang my bell; my wife went to open the door; they came towards the darkroom and a pale face and two waxy white hands came towards me. "Roscioli is looking for you," they said. I looked around the room for my family members. The film started to burn and the children's' smiles began to disappear. I moved toward the exit.

"Good morning," I said. There was Roscioli. He was wearing a tunic, smelled of gasoline, and had two large dirty hands. He wanted to be photographed. I was hesitant. My baby girl was crying in the kitchen. My wife answered for me, "Yes," and quickly went to get my camera. I took his photo in a courtyard. He smiled happily. He left saying he would be back.

A few days went by. One morning, under the Bridge of Devils, they found massacred corpses that had been shot and thrown off the bridge. I decided to go down there with others from my area. Once there, I wanted to go down there with the warrant officer of the Carabinieri. It was not possible. The name Roscioli was on their tongues like poison. Once arrived at the site, a woman was screaming frantically. The bodies were strewn under the bridge. They told me it had to do with ex prisoners. When I was back on the road, a group of German soldiers drove by. They didn't take care of us. They didn't take care of anybody.

After a few days, Roscioli came back to me. He wanted his photographs. He left happy, satisfied. He smelled of something unidentifiable that gave nausea. He left on a motorcycle. He didn't know that I had hidden in my garden the photos of his victims. The Italian press these past few days has been interested in the capture of Settimio Roscioli, who operated in our area as one of the most violent criminals of this war. Rosciolli had also been wanted by the Allies in a case involving murdered British and American soldiers. We publish today these photographic documents of the blood bath taken under extraordinary circumstances by the photographer Carlo Baffoni of S. Benedetto del Tronto.

The photographs taken by Carlo Baffoni show an upper body cameo of Roscioli brandishing a submachine gun held diagonally across his chest. He was smiling and physically resembled a demented Telly Savalas. Just below Roscioli's photo, Baffoni has captured three of Roscioli's victims in death. They have bullet holes in the face and upper body. It could not be determined at that time from the undated newspaper article whether they were British or American. The one certainty is that they were just trying to get home. But as the photographer remembered regarding the townspeople and witnesses to that crime, "The name Roscioli was on their tongues like poison." Roscioli regularly killed civilians and escaped prisoners of war in cold blood and deserved nothing less than summary execution once he was caught.

On January 3, 2014, I received a late Christmas gift from the United Kingdom. Dennis Hill conveyed an e-mail to me with attachments from a British researcher named Brian Sims. From his country's national archives Brian had uncovered a wealth of files and documents pertaining to the murders of Alvey and Martin, in addition to the killings of the three British soldiers and a Belgian agent at Montedinove that was described and depicted by Mr. Baffoni. There is no doubt that these are the same incidents, since one of Baffoni's pictures is identical to the photograph in the British archives identifying those two men as Daniel Hollingsworth and David White.

As I understand it, over the course of several years, Brian has been researching the death of his own father and 813 other British prisoners of war who were crammed into the holds of the Italian cargo ship SS *Scillin*, which was torpedoed and sunk by the British submarine HMS *Sahib* off the Tunisian coast on November 14, 1942. No information was made public about the sinking until 1996, and Brian was instrumental in ferreting out information and finally providing the truth about what happened to the victims' families.

Brian was researching war crimes matters for Dennis Hill, and Dennis had asked him to check if there was any information in the British archives regarding the deaths of Alvey and Martin. Brian uncovered approximately 83 pages of investigative records specifically pertaining to the recapture and summary execution of Martin and Alvey. These reports fill in the gaps and provide amazing details about what really transpired on March 9, 1944. They are virtually moment by moment and explain how the two ex-prisoners of war were taken and killed by a German special forces unit, with Roscioli arriving at the scene of the crime and speaking to the German commander about a half-hour later. The records Brian provided were the product of an extensive investigation by the British 60 Section, Special Investigation Branch, which included numerous affidavits and translated statements of eyewitnesses.

At Montedinove, the photographer Baffoni tied Roscioli to the killings of the three British prisoners of war and the Belgian agent who was trying to lead them to safety, based on the statements made by his countrymen at the scene. He also references the fact that Germans were in the same area and with an indifferent air, passed by Baffoni and the others. But regardless of the culpability issue, Noah's recollection of justice denied turned out to be entirely correct. Further research revealed that after the Allies had established control of the Le Marche region, Roscioli fled to Rome, hoping to take advantage of the anonymity afforded by a distant, large city. However, on May 21, 1945, he was recognized by the parents of an Italian partisan whose execution he had ordered and was quickly arrested by the carabinieri. Roscioli's capture was reported in the *Toronto Daily Star* and *Ottawa Citizen* newspapers. Both articles represented that Roscioli was "charged with responsibility for the execution of more than 200 Italian patriots and their supporters and of numerous Allied prisoners."

As far as I have been able to determine to date, Roscioli was tried for war crimes before the Extraordinary Section of the Assize Court in Pesaro, and sentenced to thirty years. But he only served a fraction of that time and was released under an amnesty program. Also, it appears that the Italian government actually tried him for multiple war crimes against the Italian people and not due to his culpability for atrocities committed against escaped Allied prisoners of war. Unfortunately, neither the US nor British governments appear to have mandated that he be tried by Allied tribunals. With few exceptions, Italians were not tried by Allied courts for war crimes, as the Germans and Japanese were. Nevertheless, English and American agents did investigate Roscioli and knew that escapees had repeatedly named him as the prime mover in the murders of countless escaped prisoners of war.

Given the enormity of the documented atrocities, the reaction of the Allied and Italian governments was utterly anemic. It appears that pragmatism prevailed over justice. Their wanton failure to provide warranted follow through was particularly egregious given the fact that no postwar German tribunal ever issued a single, binding verdict pertaining to war crimes committed on

Italian soil. Only five German soldiers were ever sent to prison for war crimes perpetrated in Italy during World War II. Further, notorious Nazi Gerhard Sommer, although sentenced in absentia to life imprisonment by the Italians for war crimes in Italy, including the massacre of 560 civilians in Tuscany, lived as a free man in Germany to the age of 92.

This is not to say that the individual war crimes investigators failed in their duty to bring Roscioli and his ilk before the bar of justice. Special agents working for the British Special Investigation Branch and the US Army's Judge Advocate General's War Crimes Office, tracked down leads provided by Italian civilians and repatriated prisoners of war who were debriefed upon crossing back over the lines. In most cases, the former prisoners had been discharged and returned to civilian life. However, many were not even located and asked to provide affidavits until up to two years after the atrocities they had witnessed or heard about.

I believe that this inordinate delay coupled with reliance upon rumor and hearsay was a prime contributing factor to the lackluster response. Then too, there appears to have been little coordination between the Allied and Italian governments regarding the apprehension of the accused and the prosecution of notorious war criminals such as Roscioli. The most telling example of the latter failure were the following entries in the US War Crimes file dedicated to Roscioli and the Comunanza murders:

> Settimio RUSHOLI has not been reported to this office as a prisoner of war in United States custody.
>
> 2 Jun 1945

> Last Name, First Name RUSHOLI, Settimio
> NO RECORD
> Enemy P.W.I.B. Wash. D.C.
>
> Aug 21 1945

In fact, Roscioli had been captured in Rome on May 21, 1945 and was actually in the custody of the Italian government. Then there is a document in the US war crimes file on the murders at Comunanza with the following heartbreaking entry:

> 2. Above referred case has been administratively closed
> by this section and complete file transmitted to British
> authorities for further action.

The file materials provided by Brian Sims contain a four-page report dated April 8, 1946, regarding Settimio and his brother, Fiori Roscioli. It was authored by a first lieutenant in the Italian army named Alberto Orlandi and is addressed to Field Head-quarters War Crimes Branch, JA Sec, HQ MT OUSA. Orlandi's report is an investigation into the criminal activities of both Rosciolis. That report affirms that Settimio Roscioli was a Fascist sergeant-major collaborating with the Germans in the Ascoli-Piceno area and alludes to the fact that he had been apprehended and was then in the custody of the British in Naples.

Orlandi's report speaks of the various categories of evil deeds perpetrated by Settimio Roscioli and also mentions that he was the chief inspector for the Fascists of all of Ascoli-Piceno and commanded all of the Fascists in all of the towns in the province. The report further claimed that Roscioli was helping the Germans stationed at Montalto Marche and Petritoli with mopping up oper-ations. A few weeks after his capture, Roscioli was interrogated by CSM B. Cohen of the Special Investigation Branch regarding the killing of Alvey and Matt. Here is his report:

> On the 10th July, 1945, accompanied by Sergeant Major
> MOTTRAM of this Branch and Official Interpreter,
> PANICCIA Claudio, I went to the Civil Prison,

ROME, where I saw Roscioli Settimio, who was held
there in custody.

I said to ROSCIOLI, through the medium of
PANICCIA, "I am C.S.M. Cohen of the Special
Investigations Branch, Corps of Military Police and
I am making enquiries regarding the shooting of two
escaped prisoners of war, about 09.30 hours on the
9th March 1944, near the River ASO, S. VITTO-
RIA-IN-MATENANO, ASCOLI Province, and
I have reason to believe that you know something
about it." ROSCIOLLI was then formally cautioned
in Italian and after the caution had been administered,
I instructed the interpreter to ask ROSCIOLI if he
desired to make any statement. ROSCIOLI replied, "I
do not know anything about it."

Roscioli's lack of candor is no surprise. Nevertheless, in recog-
nition of his "exemplary" services, the Germans provided Settimio
Roscioli with a complete German uniform. Orlandi's report not
only places Roscioli at the site of the murders of six Allied prisoners in Comunanza, but asserts that Roscioli himself was among
those who fired the fatal shots.

One of the most striking revelations made by Orlandi about
Roscioli was the following:

Roscioli, however, did not always carry out his criminal
actions personally. In fact, a known tactic of Roscioli
was that of almost never being present at arrests and
executions of Allied prisoners and partisans, but to
arrive a few minutes after the events had taken place.

Orlandi goes on to relate that Roscioli had a civilian automobile at his disposal, which is most likely the Fiat Topolino that others have described, and was frequently seen at the head of or in the midst of German columns engaged in antipartisan activities and the search for Allied escapees.

The most curious aspect of the US war crimes files pertaining to the murders of Alvey and Martin and the Allied soldiers at Comunanza is that although the affidavits and investigative entries focus primarily on Roscioli, he and Fausto Poloni are included on the list of *witnesses*. They were wanted for questioning. But the named accused were all Germans.

The Americans did investigate the crimes and actually took into custody former German soldiers associated with the Brandenburg Division. In fact, the army had in custody individuals named Josef Siene, Hermann Miller, and Frank Werner, who were also purported witnesses to the war crimes. A docket sheet in the file states that the names of the accused are "LT. FRANZ ROMMEL; LT. (UNKNOWN) HOSSFELD; LT. (UNKNOWN) FISCHER; and other unknown." There are also twenty-four other individuals with German names on an attached witness list. Yet, it did not appear from the US files that any disposition or trial of anyone on the part of the Americans ever occurred for the murders of Alvey, Martin, or the six Allied prisoners executed in Comunanza. The docket sheet is dated June 17, 1946, and has the following notation at the bottom:

CASE HAS BEEN FULLY INVESTIGATED AND PRESENTLY AWAITING APPREHENSION OF ACCUSED.

There is also a document dated April 24, 1947, in Alvey's war crimes file number 16-34, which states:

Subject War Crimes Case was administratively closed

by this section and complete files forwarded to War Crimes Group USFET for the reason indicated in attached letter of transmittal.

A document prepared the very next day, April 25, 1947, partially explains what transpired with the US investigation of his death:

> There is forwarded herewith the complete files of this office relative to a case which appears to have been a war crime committed by German personnel against US Prisoners of War. Investigation of the case over a long period of time indicates that most of the accused are either in Germany or other areas under your jurisdiction and therefore the investigation cannot be completed in this theater.
>
> In view of the imminent close-out of this theater and the necessity of terminating War Crimes investigations on 1 May to permit the completion of cases now ready for trial, this case is forwarded to you for necessary action in accordance with the War Department policy that you will assume the residual war crimes functions of this theater. It is believed that this will permit you to review these files and to request information deemed necessary from this area which might not otherwise be obtainable if transmission was not made until after the close-out of this theater.
>
> There are in custody in this theater the following named individuals:
> SIENE, Josef
> MILLER, Hermann 81 G 684 H
> Request you advise us at once of the disposition you desire made of the individuals in question, and also that you advise of any further information you may desire

from here. We will continue to assist to the extent of our ability so long as this office remains in existence even though our staff has been reduced to become almost ineffective.

TOM H. BARRATT
Colonel, JAGD
Theater Judge Advocate

There is no reply in the file and no further requests for information or any semblance of any resolution. Thus, it appears that because the war had been over for two years, offices were being closed and personnel reassigned or discharged, the ball was completely dropped by the United States. No apprehensions of the accused were ever reported and no disposition whatsoever was ever made.

It must also be noted here that the US government's abandonment of pursuit may also have been attributable to certain rather galling political considerations. In particular, with the end of World War II, the threat of Communism assumed far greater importance than justice for the murders of prisoners of war and Italian civilians. Communist groups were very powerful in Italy after the war. Northern Italy was completely in the Communists' grip, and Soviet-sanctioned Socialism threatened to take control of the entire country. The American government was very active in countering this threat with money and major intervention by the CIA. Although the Soviets spent ten times the amount of the monetary support proffered by the United States, the Christian Democrat party, backed by the Americans, prevailed and was largely responsible for Italy's recovery and postwar economic success.

Nevertheless, the way this pragmatic policy played out is worthy of the utmost contempt. Not only did the authorities fail to pursue Nazi and Fascist war criminals, they actually employed their services to counter the Reds in Italy! The CIA went to considerable lengths to protect war criminals. There was now an active rivalry with the Soviet Union, and the defeat of Communism was elevated above all other considerations. Former Nazis and Fascists were not only given safe haven in the United States and Italy, they were employed by their own clandestine services. Most likely, some of them were even provided with security clearances!

One extreme example is the claim made by Karl Hass, a former SS major captured several times and held by Italy for an investigation into his role in the Ardeatine Caves massacre in March 1944, involving the execution of 335 Italian men and boys. In 1997, when he was 83 years of age, Hass gave an interview to the German publication *Der Spiegel.*

> Hass, a former SS major, told the magazine that in 1947, an officer with US military counterintelligence found him in the small town of Ascoli Piceno and said: 'We have more important things to do than to keep capturing you. Now, we have a common fight — against international communism.'

Hass then began working at a US military radio station in Austria. The US government provided him with an alias and sent him to Rome to spy on Italian Communists. I have already reported in this book how SS Captain Erich Priebke was eventually convicted decades later for his role in the Ardeatine massacre, but his long delayed "punishment" turned out to be "house arrest" at his lawyer's residence in Rome.

Apart from outrages such as this, the US Ggovernment unduly delayed the declassification of war crimes files and other relevant records. Many of the war crimes documents set forth above are stamped SECRET, TOP SECRET, and CONFIDENTIAL. Although most files of this nature have now been released, some are still classified. Others have simply not yet been digitized, which requires personal research in Washington, DC, or reliance on government researchers. Germany also engaged in notorious foot-dragging when it came to searching for war criminals harbored within its borders.

There is an Italian counterpart to the Allied diminution or reversal of interest in pursuing war criminals. The situation in Italy had actually been a war within a war. That is, there was an enduring civil war between the partisan and Fascist factions for the political and economic control of Italy. After the war, an absurd result emerged. The partisans who had actually helped win the war by defeating the Axis fell out of favor and former Fascists were restored to power and influential positions in many areas of the country! Many Fascists were given slaps on the wrist or never punished at all. Thus, justice went begging on many fronts.

Turning a blind eye became routine in the postwar environment. Witness the case of one Pio Filippani Ronconi, who was a volunteer for the Waffen SS in Italy. He was a Senior Stormleader, (*Obersturmfuhrer*). Ronconi reportedly served with distinction at Anzio-Nettuno, and was awarded the Iron Cross. After the war, he worked for Italian intelligence and engaged in anti-Communist activities. The fact that he also promoted neo-Nazi causes at the same time was overlooked.

Another example of justice circumvented concerns Colonel Enrico Bacci, Commandant of Camp 59, who was arrested after the war and tried for refusing to allow an emergency operation for appendicitis suffered by a prisoner of war under his charge. The soldier was Sergeant Reley Rudd, who died in the hospital at Ascoli-Piceno on July 20, 1942. Bacci was acquitted because his defense counsel argued that there was poor lighting, meager surgical instruments, and a lack of necessary drugs to successfully perform the operation.

There are even now feelings of nostalgia among some Italians for Mussolini. To them, his atrocities are of no moment. In their minds, he has been rehabilitated. Cabinet Minister Mirko Tremaglia is publicly proud of the fact that he fought with Mussolini's Fascists. Alessandra Mussolini, Il Duce's granddaughter, was elected to national office and has praised him on the Italian talk-show circuit. Thousands turn out at his grave every year to pay respects on his birthday April 28. It is readily apparent that such blindness and revisionism is directly attributable to the failure to resolutely prosecute Italian war criminals. Instead of justice, what the victims received was a charade.

As far as the US prosecution effort is concerned, it was puzzling why some of the documents in the US war crimes files appear to be focusing on the Brandenburg Division. Just that name appears by itself. There were no supporting facts or documents pertaining to the conclusion that German soldiers in that particular unit were involved in the murder of the prisoners of war near Montelparo, or anywhere else in Le Marche province.

Now, due to the efforts of British researcher Brian Sims and Dennis Hill at Indiana University, that mystery has been solved after the passage of seventy years!

18

The Brandenburgers

The US war crimes files contained several unsupported references to the German Brandenburg Division and named three German lieutenants from that unit as the accused. This was the case, even though the affidavits supplied by repatriated prisoners of war cited Settimio Roscioli as the culprit in so many murders. The documents provided by Brian Sims, via Dennis Hill, revealed what must now stand as the core truth.

Prior to receiving the documents Brian had gleaned from the British archives, my own research had disclosed that the "Brandenburgers" were an elite German special forces unit that conducted commando-type operations, including antipartisan missions in many war theaters. They fought in North Africa, the Balkans, and the eastern front, and are known to have committed a war crime in France where in an antipartisan operation, they massacred seventy-two civilians at Vassieux-en-Vercors on July 21, 1944. One of their most notorious missions occurred on May 25, 1944, when 500 of the unit's "specialists" were sent to capture the Yugoslavian partisan leader Josip Broz Tito. But the future president of Yugoslavia escaped just before the Brandenburgers reached his headquarters cave.

The Brandenburgers were highly trained commandos, skilled

in irregular warfare operations behind the lines. They were part of the regular German army but under the control of German intelligence, known as the Abwehr. Each Brandenburger spoke a language or languages other than German and generally had enhanced knowledge about his particular area of operations. They were infiltrators as well as saboteurs and from time to time even wore civilian clothes, camouflage, or the uniforms of their enemies.

However, based on the sparse information available, this unit's Italian operations even now seem to be mere footnotes in its sordid history. They were known to have traveled from the Balkans to Italy just after the armistice for the purpose of disarming Italian soldiers and seizing certain objectives. A Brandenburg Regiment fought at Anzio-Nettuno and the Third Brandenburg Regiment later morphed into Kesselring's Machine Gun Battalion, which was involved in Operation Winter Storm in northern Italy on December 26, 1944. There is an online reference to an Alert Regiment Brandenburg, operating in Italy as of March 5, 1944. Still, I was not able to find any authoritative evidence that any Brandenburgers were involved in the hunt for escaped prisoners of war and partisans in Le Marche region in March 1944. Even a book titled *The Brandenburgers — Global Mission* by Franz Kurowski and yet another called *Brandenburg Division Commandos of the Reich* by Eric Lefevre failed to include any reference to that unit's operations in Italy's Le Marche region.

Yet, elements of the Third Brandenburg Regiment have also been implicated in the massacre of hundreds of Italian civilians at Civitella, Italy, in June 1944. The US records supporting the conclusions reached by special agents after World War II regarding the complicity of the Brandenburgers could not simply be discounted. They were renowned as warrior spies, and it has been said that spies were involved in the murders of Alvey and Matt due to the speed exhibited by the killers in finding them. Entries in the US files simply tersely concluded:

CASE HAS BEEN FULLY INVESTIGATED
AND AWAITING APPREHENSION OF THE
ACCUSED.

Now, based on the records obtained by Brian Sims from the
British archives, the truth has finally come to light. The previously
referenced report prepared by Alberto Orlandi after the war contains the following statement:

> 6. Another particularly important aspect of this case
> was the investigation into German commands in the
> area with which Settimio Roscioli collaborated. There
> were two German companies in the area of Ascoli
> Piceno, one detached at Montalto Marche and the
> other at Petritoli. These units belonged to the Branden-
> burg Division and were specialized in capturing Allied
> prisoners and partisans. Very similar to the SS, they
> were very well organized and equipped for counter-
> espionage activity and especially for the capture of
> Allied prisoners and partisans.

The British war crimes file number WO310/198 specifically per-
tains to an investigation into the killings of Corporal Robert Alvey
Newton and Private Edwin Martin Majeski, United States Army.
The investigation commenced on February 11, 1945, nearly a year
after their murders. It resulted in a series of affidavits and documents that provide a moment-by-moment account of what really
transpired.

A composite picture of the documents in this file produces
the following summary: On November 13, 1943, Alvey and Matt
appeared at the Viozzi family farmhouse. The two escaped prisoners of war had previously been staying at the nearby house of a
farmer named Marini. Pietro Viozzi and his brother Sesto were

the family patriarchs at that time, and they gave the two men food and kept them hidden from the Germans and Fascists. From the record, it appears Alvey and Matt slept in an adjacent stable and also hid in the countryside whenever the enemy was in the area.

During the early morning hours of March 9, 1944, local residents heard many trucks proceeding toward Santa Vittoria and Comunanza. However, because the roads were still impassable due to the deep snow, the convoy turned around and returned to the crossroads near the Viozzi farm. Some have speculated that when the Germans realized they couldn't get to either Comunanza or Santa Vittoria, they turned around and just started the search where they were. Doc Frie later said that "Alvey was captured by the merest trick of fate." He said that when they first went by, Alvey and his companion had hidden nearby, and that although they were given an all-clear signal, they were surprised by storm troopers.

Nevertheless Pietro Viozzi testified that at about 0700 hours, he saw a German convoy proceeding along the road in the direction of Val D'Aso. He warned Alvey and Matt to hide in the stables. This they did. Shortly after that, two men on motorcycles with sidecars detached from the German convoy, which had stopped on the road and drove up to the farm. One of the men on a motorcycle had on a German uniform, and the other was dressed in an Italian military uniform. According to Pietro, the strangers said nothing but immediately began to search the buildings. They entered the stable and found Alvey and Matt and asked them if they were English or American. When Alvey and Matt said, "American," the two soldiers drew their revolvers.

Pietro's recollection about Alvey and Matt being found in the stable varies from the account provided by Cesare Viozzi, in the 2001 interview Cesare gave to Filippo Ierano, which is quoted in Chapter 15. Cesare relates that when the family saw the German convoy on the road to Santa Vittoria they became scared and told Alvey and Matt to hide in a ditch. The two escapees were given the all-clear signal and returned to the farmhouse, but two Germans on motorcycles suddenly appeared and surprised the family at breakfast with Alvey and Matt sitting at their breakfast table. Cesare's account comports with what the family told Doc Frie when he visited Italy in 1964. He said Alvey hid in "a wooded draw" and was seized when he came back to "dinner." Doc Frie showed me a slide of the place he was referring to. The discrepancy in the two accounts may possibly be due to an interpretation error on the part of the person who interviewed Pietro during the war crimes investigation. Alvey and Matt routinely slept in the stable but ate meals with the family, so it is possible that those particular facts became conflated.

According to Pietro, one of the soldiers pushed his pistol into Pietro's chest, grabbed and shook him and demanded to know why the prisoners were there. Pietro did not answer. Alvey and Matt had their hands up in surrender, and Pietro said that the soldiers put them in the sidecar and drove off in the direction of Val D'Aso. Alvey and Matt were driven to the house of a man named Luigi Vergari, who was the local police chief. Vergari had been out of town on business since March 5, 1944, but his wife, Maria Vergari, testified that at about 0900 hours on March 9, 1944, she heard a motorcycle draw up outside her house and saw two prisoners sitting in the sidecar. There was only one German with them, and he had chevrons on his sleeves, which indicated to her that he was a sergeant.

As Maria Vergari continued to observe the men, some German soldiers gave cigarettes to Alvey and Matt, who were by then standing in the yard. About that time, four or five of the German soldiers entered her house and requested food. They spoke Italian fluently and told her that they were Austrians. While they were eating, they saw through a window that their commanding officer was coming toward the house. They told Mrs. Vergari that he was bad man who treated them badly. The commanding officer then entered the house and asked for coffee. The other soldiers quickly left.

Maria Vergari did not know the name of the commanding officer. However, she described him as being very tall and thin, with dark grey eyes and a thin face. He wore glasses and his right eye was nearly closed and crossed. The officer had a dark complexion, with dark brown hair brushed straight back. This description matches a German officer with the Brandenburg Division named Hans Joackim Hossfeld. There is a sheet in the British files bearing his curriculum vitae, including his home address, the names of his mother and father, his educational background, and his military assignments from 1939 to 1944.

Hossfeld, who was with the Sixth Coy, Brandenburg Regiment, held a doctorate in philosophy and worked as a freelance journalist in civilian life. One of his hobbies was playing classical piano. This is an extremely important detail, given the testimony of Count Pier Filippo Marcatilli. The Count stated that German troops were billeted at his villa in St. Paulo during March 1944. Among these troops was a lieutenant named Hossfeld, who was about six feet tall, clean shaven, with a thin face. Hossfeld went out every day searching with his troops for Italian "patriots." The officer's hair was brushed straight back, with a parting. The count remembered that Hossfeld played the piano well. Count Marcatilli also said that the German soldiers occupying his villa wore gray-green uniforms similar to those of the Italian army.

Between approximately 0900 and 0930, according to the testimony of other eyewitnesses, two or possibly three German soldiers walked with Alvey and Matt down by the River Aso just out of sight. Shortly thereafter, the witnesses heard gunshots.

That same morning, the two soldiers said to have taken Alvey and Matt from the Viozzi stable returned to the farmhouse and ordered everybody out. That included Pietro's wife, who was seriously ill and in bed. She died just seventeen days later, and the doctor attributed her quick death to the trauma of that day.

Specifically, the Germans told Pietro that they were destroying the house because he had sheltered the escaped prisoners. They set fire to the house and threw four hand grenades against it. Four rooms were gutted, and a considerable amount of the Viozzis' personal property was destroyed. The Germans took Matt and Alvey's overcoats and also confiscated the Viozzis' food, including several pork shoulders and cured hams. Later the same day, the Viozzis learned that Alvey and Matt had been killed near the River Aso.

About 0930, according to Maria Vergari, her friends Irene and Anselmo Squarcia came to her house. She had been in another room tending to her children, but about that time two German soldiers entered her house and spoke with the officer in charge. The two soldiers then went into another room and proceeded to wash their hands. At approximately 1000 hours, Roscioli arrived in his Fiat wearing a German uniform. Maria did not know Roscioli, but Anselmo Squarcia told her that he was the Fascist Settimio Roscioli. Roscioli also spoke to the German officer and departed.

After the Germans left, Anselmo Squarcia told Mrs. Vergari that he had seen the Germans take the two American prisoners of war across the fields towards the River Aso. He heard two shots and feared that they had been killed. Anselmo had first met Alvey and Matt in October 1943 after the breakout from PG 59 and was very friendly with them. Anselmo said that the Germans who had washed their hands were the same two he had seen escort Alvey and Matt across the fields. The Squarcias then left about 1230, and at about 1500 hours Maria's husband returned from his trip. Mr. Vergari then went into Santa Vittoria, returning home again about 1900 hours.

Luigi Vergari later testified that on his return trip, he had met a German convoy on the road and been stopped by a German sergeant with a revolver. At that point, Settimio Roscioli walked up to Vergari's car and told the German sergeant that he knew Vergari well, whereupon the sergeant told Vergari that he could go.

Meanwhile, Anselmo Squarcia had gone looking for his friends

Alvey and Matt and had found their bodies sprawled in a wooded area by the River Aso. They both had bullet wounds to the head. Their bodies were covered with saplings and the two soldiers were missing their shoes. Anselmo went to the nearby house of a local farmer named Alfredo Rastelli, who agreed that Anselmo should report the killings to Vergari, the chief of police. When Vergari returned from Santa Vittoria about 1900, Anselmo Squarcia was waiting for him and told him what he had discovered. At that point, Vergari telephoned the local brigadier of carabinieri at Santa Vittoria, gave him the information and requested that a guard be placed over the bodies. The brigadier promised to do that.

The bodies of Alvey and Matt lay near the River Aso overnight. About 0930 the next morning, March 10, 1944, Enrico Mangiaterra, the brigadier of carabinieri came to the Viozzi farmhouse and told Sesto Viozzi that two prisoners of war had been killed near the River Aso. He asked Sesto to go with him to see if the bodies were the two who had been staying at the Viozzi farmhouse. About 1500, Sesto went with him and a local doctor named Enrico Corinaldesi to a small wood on the banks of the River Aso. There he saw Alvey and Matt, dead on the ground, covered by the branches of a poplar tree.

Doctor Corinaldesi conducted a postmortem examination of the bodies and prepared a written report of his findings. After the examination had been completed, Sesto helped convey the bodies of Alvey and Matt to the Santa Vittoria cemetery. Coffins were obtained, and they were buried by the town gravedigger, Giuseppe Squarcia.

It also appears from the testimony that Matt had a gold ring on his finger and that the Germans had cut off his finger to get the ring. A gold bracelet Matt had was also missing. The personal effects of the murder victims included two wooden smoking pipes, a pencil, a pocketknife, and some papers containing Italian verbs. Some of the eyewitnesses said that Alvey and Matt were wearing patched civilian jackets, with military shirts and pants. They were also shoeless.

There is a note in the British files to the effect that Alvey and Matt were told that they would be taken to Germany, and were given food and drink as well as cigarettes, while they chatted with the Germans in the yard outside the Vergari house. However, there is no affidavit attesting to those additional facts. But all eye-witnesses agree that the Germans gave the Americans cigarettes before they took their last walk across the fields to the River Aso.

If they were told that they were going to Germany, that would partially account for their lack of any resistance. Alvey and Matt could have also been motivated by the desire to avoid potential repercussions against the Viozzi family, although they could not have known at that time what would befall the Viozzis. The truth about this aspect of the case will never be known. But there is no indication that either of them made any effort to flee what they may have realized was coming as they walked to a very remote spot. They dropped where they were shot.

The files also make note of a persistent rumor among the *contadini* that Settimio Roscioli had himself shot the two Americans after forcing them to drink from the river. Primo Mecossi repeated this rumor to Raymond Cox. Also, the woman from the Viozzi household told Herman Noble that Fascists had killed Alvey. However, there were no known eyewitnesses to the actual shooting as the riverbank dropped below the line of sight from the local houses. Some Italians did encounter the Germans escorting the two Americans toward the river but were threatened by the Germans to get away. The witnesses gave affidavits supporting that story but claimed that they did not see the actual murders. It now seems more plausible that Roscioli had a hand in Alvey and Matt's apprehension and was closely collaborating with the Germans on the morning they were killed, at the same site.

The documents in the British archives are extremely detailed.

There are even photographs of the Vergari house where Matt and Alvey were taken. Additional photos were included of the fields they crossed on the way to the murder site and the wooded area where their bodies were found. There is even a re-creation by British investigators of the positions of the Americans' bodies.

While Hans Hossfeld of the Sixth Coy, Brandenburg Regiment, is the likely local commander of the actual perpetrators, how did the US war crimes investigators also focus upon German lieutenants Fischer and Rommel? That answer was provided by the British archives as well. Included in the materials provided by Brian Sims was an affidavit given by a Padre Stephen Leight at the Collegio Sisto V, Montalto Marche. Padre Leight was of German nationality but spoke English fluently. He testified that about March 4, 1944, a German unit came to Montalto and occupied the Collegio building until about April 13, 1944. There were about eighty German soldiers in the village, commanded by two lieutenants named Fischer and Rommel. Lieutenant Rommel was a nephew of Field Marshal Erwin Rommel. Both men were later determined to be with the Second Battalion, Third Brandenburg Regiment, which was also known as the Bansen Group, named after its overall commander at that time in Italy. Records in the British archives do not clear Rommel and Fischer of any culpability in the deaths of escaped Allied prisoners near Montalto around March 9–10, 1944, but indicate that both men were known to be at their headquarters on March 10, 1944.

An interesting aside is the statement made by Keith Argraves regarding a German priest in the village who betrayed escaped prisoners to the Fascists.

> In the village lived a German priest who claimed that he had been driven from his home in Germany because of his religion. Later events proved that he was a spy. This man quietly passed word on to the Fascists that

escaped Allied prisoners were hiding in and near the village of Falgiano.

There is no proof to date that Father Leight, who was German, and the German priest who informed against the escaped Allied prisoners were the same person. Still, it is noteworthy that Father Leight was at Montalto Nelle Marche, which was four and a half miles from Montelparo, nine miles from Ascoli-Piceno and ten miles from Santa Vittoria, and in the same place that housed the Brandenburgers. I do know that Argraves was not far from the Ascoli-Piceno – Santa Vittoria area when he was first recaptured. Warren Decker, who was with him at the time, told me so.

I believe that Argraves and Decker erred when they called the village where they had been recaptured Falgiano. There is no town by that name anywhere near Ascoli-Piceno. Both may have meant Folignano, which is about six miles from Ascoli-Piceno. In fact, the only Falgiano village is near Reggio Emilia, which is about 250 miles northwest of Ascoli.

One clue that Argraves and Decker are mistaken in this respect is Argraves's recollection in the next chapter that they were taken to a Fascist jail at "Aquazonda." He most likely meant Acquasanta Terme which is only nine miles from Ascoli-Piceno. That interpretation is further substantiated by his revelation that they were next taken to the Fascist civilian prison in Ascoli-Piceno after being marched through that town.

According to Argraves, they were held in Ascoli for twenty days, then road marched to three separate camps before being loaded on a train bound for Florence. Keith made multiple escapes after that, but it does not appear that he was anywhere near the real Falgiano hundreds of miles to the north when he was recaptured the first time. Such location errors are not uncommon, particularly when memoirs are written years later, and without adequate reference points while circumstances are unfolding. It is also not likely that the escapees headed 250 miles north when they were trying to reach the Allied lines, which were then about 180 miles south near Anzio.

Argraves does not name the German spy priest or disclose the source of his information. Perhaps he was still constrained by the army's admonition not to talk about his experiences in detail, particularly since he had probably been debriefed once repatriated. Even so, the tip provided by Argraves may prove to be highly relevant and warrants further investigation. However, if the town with the traitorous priest was actually Folignano, then the turncoat cleric referred to by Argraves could not have been Father Leight, simply because he was in Montalto Marche.

It does bear mentioning here that the Nazis did infiltrate the Vatican with apostate German Catholic priests who spied for Hitler. In fact, they had a network that filtered down to the parish level. Some of the more notorious covert priest operatives included Albert Hartl, an unethical monk named Herbert Keller and Georg Elling. But the worst villain of them all was the devilish Austrian bishop, Alois Hudal, of the college for German priests in Rome. To be sure, there were many innocent German Catholic priests who had been persecuted by the Nazis who fled to Italy, but there were far too many German apostate spies in the country to simply disregard the ominous threat they posed for escaped Allied prisoners of war.

In his report, Alberto Orlandi of the Italian Army, who was an MI9 (A-Force) operative, stated that it could not be doubted that the capture and killing of the four Allied prisoners at Ponte del Dragone, Montedinove, previously alluded to, was carried out by German troops stationed at Montalto Marche. Those troops were under the command of Lieutenant Fischer and Lieutenant Rommel. Orlandi described Fischer as of "medium, but robust build, elementary school teacher in Sudetendland, spoke French and was very severe." Lieutenant Rommel was also described by

Orlandi thus: "Said he was nephew of German General Rommel. Attended University of Tubingen in Wurttenburg; commanded armored car unit."

I recently discovered an online photograph that gave me a great deal of pause. The caption showed a German soldier decorating a Christmas tree in the hospital of Loughborough Prison Camp, northwest of London. The caption said that the soldier was Dr. Karl Heinz Rommel, the nephew of Field Marshal Erwin Rommel! It could be that Rommel had more than one nephew and that the individual in the photograph was not the person affiliated with the Brandenburg Regiment. Then again, the Rommel photographed could have been the same man. There is also an unrelated online newspaper article in the UK Guardian dated May 9, 2001, and titled, "Rommel's Nephew Linked to War Crime." The account relates that "SS Lieutenant Rommel of the Second Battalion, Third Brandenburg Regiment," was a prime suspect in the killings of the British soldiers and Belgian agent in the Province of Ascoli-Piceno (Montedinove). The article closes with the following curious statement: "The files released yesterday say attempts were made to find Rommel at least until 1948, but do not report if he was ever caught." Hence, there is still a great deal of follow-up to do.

Padre Leight testified that he did not know the regiment at Montalto Marche, but had heard them spoken about as Brandenburgers. Their uniform was a grey tunic. Significantly, Padre Leight recalled that at times some of the German soldiers in armored cars accompanying the grey tunic soldiers wore black uniforms with a badge representing a skull. All of those soldiers wore soft-peaked caps of the same black color, with long trousers and high boots. That group was composed of men of different nationalities, including Poles, Romanians, and others. He said that this unit was based in Ascoli-Piceno and moved to Perugia after leaving there.

Some surviving prisoners of war claimed to have seen the SS

take Alvey and Matt away. Some witnesses have also referred to the German troops as storm troopers. In any case, it does appear from the evidence that the Brandenburgers were in the immediate vicinity during the March 1944 campaign of terror and definitely involved in the murders of Matt and Alvey and probably at Montedinove as well.

Padre Leight's reference to the skull badge on black uniforms also implicates the German SS. It could have been the Waffen SS, which was made up of various nationalities, particularly late in the war. This is speculation on my part, but it is based on evidence. First, there were German SS and Fascist strike teams reportedly stationed at Montalto and Petritoli in March 1944. Montalto delle Marche is nine miles north of Ascoli-Piceno and seven miles from Montelparo, while Petritoli is about twelve miles distant from the execution site. Second, some of the escaped prisoners of war and Italian *contadini* have affirmed that the killers were German SS, Blackshirts, or storm troopers.

Third, there were two Waffen SS units in Italy that were specifically involved in the hunt for partisans and escaped Allied prisoners of war. They were the Twenty-ninth Waffen Grenadier Division of the SS (First Italian) and the Sixteenth SS Panzergrenadier Division Reichsfuhrer-SS.

The Twenty-ninth Waffen Grenadier Division is also called Legione SS Italia, or simply Italia. This unit was created after the Italian armistice and consisted of Italian volunteers loyal to Mussolini and the new Italian Social Republic he organized after his rescue from the Grand Sasso. The men of this unit initially wore red instead of black SS runes on their left sleeves. However, because they fought well at Anzio-Nettuno in April 1944, SS head Heinrich Himmler allowed them to switch to the usual black runes. He then fully integrated the Italian stepchild into the SS. This unit was also involved in antipartisan activities in Italy and could have been so engaged before and after Anzio.

The Sixteenth SS Panzergrenadier Division Reichsfuhrer-SS was formed in November 1943, and also saw combat at Anzio in May 1944. Before being transferred to Hungary in February 1945, this unit was involved in antipartisan actions against the Red Star Brigade (Brigata Partigiana Stella Rosa) near Monte Sole, Italy. This unit was implicated in two notorious war crimes, the massacre of 560 villagers at Sant' Anna di Stazzema in August 1944, and the mass murder of more than 700 civilians at Marzabotto, between September 29 and October 5, 1944.

Other German units singled out as having committed a large number of atrocities in Italy were the Fallschirm-Panzer Division 1 Hermann Goring, the First Parachute Division, and the 114th Jager Division.

The murders of Allied prisoners of war did not occur in a vacuum. While most of the escapees were hiding out or trying to make their way south to the Allied lines, or the promise of refuge in the Vatican, the partisan units all over Italy were ambushing German convoys and individual soldiers. During the summer and fall of 1944, approximately 5,000 Germans were killed by partisan units behind the lines, with nearly double that number wounded or captured. Hence, the Germans were quite concerned about the danger just behind their lines, particularly in central Italy.

For the most part, the escapees from PG 59 who were recaptured in 1943 were simply loaded on trains bound for Germany and Poland. But in 1944, as the tide of war turned against Germany, its troops and hybrid Italian units gradually became even more vicious and focused on reprisals. Elite hunter units known as Jagdkommandos (Pursuit Commandos), were tasked with locating and killing partisans as well as any Allied soldiers behind the lines. Italian partisans were regarded by the Germans as bandits. The precise status of those captured and the Geneva convention were far from any concern. What mattered was the pragmatic elimination of any rearguard threat and the desire to instill panic and fear in the local populace and prevent them from giving any assistance to partisans or escaped prisoners.

Escaped prisoners of war were caught in targeted sweeps, whether they were involved in partisan activities or not. Some senior commanders regarded them as evaders, and not soldiers protected by the Geneva convention. Also, by this time, the escapees were either wearing ragged military uniforms or had simply adopted civilian clothing because their original garb had become threadbare since being captured, which for some British soldiers had occurred three years before. Some of the eyewitnesses said that Alvey and Matt were wearing patched civilian jackets, with military shirts and pants.

By 1944, the circumstances escalated to the point that Italian civilians were warned by German commandants that anyone who assisted Allied prisoners of war, or Anglo-American agents, or gave them hospitality or food, would be killed by shooting and their houses blown up. They were further warned that their straw and foodstuffs would be burnt and their cattle requisitioned. The Italian people were even required to report to the Germans the hiding places of escaped prisoners of war, or risk execution. Witness the following undated proclamation that was found at the Town Hall in Ascoli-Piceno on April 23, 1945, by British war crimes investigator B. Cohen, the translated version of which reads as follows:

ITALIANS!

With disgraceful treason the English and Americans have been able to penetrate, together with their coloured troops, into the south of Italy. In the territories occupied by them, there is hunger and typhus. Thousands of Italian men are taken away to forced work in the English mines, or they must work as masons fortifying the enemy first line positions. Hundreds of women and Italian young girls are seduced by negroes and Moroccans. Italian children are sent into Soviet Russia, never again to see their parents. Famine, misery, and violations have entered into your country together with the foreign troops.

ITALIANS!

The German Army is fighting hard in the south of Italy to liberate your country from the invader. This fight only can save you, your villages, your houses from the horrors of war. Your country and your life is at stake. English and American agents, escaped prisoners of war and foreign plebians have organized in your territory some bands. This favors the enemies of the country. In your interest we shall act to —

ELIMINATE THESE BANDS WITHOUT PITY.

ITALIANS!

Who helps the bands, who assists the prisoners of war or the Anglo-American agents by hospitality, food and clothing, or helps their flight —

HE IS AN ENEMY OF ITALY, AND THE
ENEMIES OF ITALY DESERVE DEATH.

FOR THIS IT IS DISPOSED THAT

He who knows where there is a band and does not give immediate information to the German army —

SHALL BE KILLED BY SHOOTING.

Who gives hospitality or food to a band or to single bandits —

SHALL BE KILLED BY SHOOTING.

Every house in which shall be found a bandit or in which has lived a bandit —

SHALL BE BLOWN UP.

The same shall befall every house from which shots are fired against the belongings of the German army.

In all these cases supplies of hay, straw and food-stuffs will be burnt, the cattle will be requisitioned, and the inhabitants shall be —

SHALL BE KILLED BY SHOOTING.

ITALIANS!

You have in your hands your destiny and that of your country.

DECIDE NOW.

Who decides against the German armies, and with that, against the vital interests of Italy, he shall not be forgiven. The German army shall proceed with justice, but also with inexorable hardness.

THE SUPREME COMMANDER
OF GERMAN TROOPS

PAJ-V-38

Again, every German commander who issued proclamations such as this should have faced the bar of justice after the war and been permanently removed from civilized society. The fact that this type of savagery was not severely punished as an example to the world has given license to an entire generation of copycat war criminals that have plagued the earth since the end of World War II. The signal the Allies sent to these monsters is that there will be no consequences for remorseless inhumanity provided that political exigencies are satisfied.

Finally, the British records unearthed by Brian Sims have revealed a horrible truth about the murders of Allied prisoners of war in Le Marche in 1944. There was a turncoat British soldier and ex-prisoner of war who gave himself to the Nazi cause and who collaborated with the German units at Montalto Marche to hunt down his fellow escapees. The report prepared by Alberto Orlandi disclosed the following information about this despicable traitor:

> He rendered splendid services to this unit so that he gained the confidence of all the officers. He worked almost always alone and at night, being carried in an armored car to an established point and then left to himself. Dressed in a civilian suit, perhaps dirty and torn, he could circulate and pose as an Allied prisoner looking for companions and still be perfectly at ease. This worked very well because the population of the area is so credulous and uncultured that anyone who spoke any foreign language at all would have been thought a prisoner. He would therefore be given, not only care and attention, but he would be brought together with other hidden prisoners. In this manner he discovered all of the Allied prisoners hidden in the homes of the countryside, succeeding in speaking with

them and winning their trust. Then, with any excuse, he would abandon the group and inform the German command of its whereabouts. Whereupon the German command would send a patrol for the capture. Many, many prisoners were captured in this way. Helping this British prisoner were a few Italians in civilian clothes. It was not possible to establish the identity of the British prisoner used by the Germans as a spy, but his existence is proved by all the friars of the convent of Montalto Marche where the German command had its billets.

In a letter written to my grandmother in 1964 but never delivered, Doc Frie told her about his trip to Italy and said that the family Alvey stayed with suspected that spies were involved, but they were never able to find out. Raymond Cox also claimed that spies had to be involved because the Germans went right to the spot where Alvey and Matt were hiding. The US war crimes files state that "it is believed that spies had a hand in this affair."

When I read the foregoing account confirming the existence of the British traitor, I was haunted by the fact that Ferree Grossman had stopped and talked to my uncle just a few days before Alvey and Matt were killed and said that "there was a Welshman with him." The Welshman may or may not have been the turncoat. The only way for the identity of the traitor to have been revealed would have been to interrogate and properly charge the German commanders, Hossfeld, Fischer, and Rommel. Why that was never done despite specific information about them, their hometowns, and education must remain a mystery, at least for the near future.

There is a curious correlation between the killings of Alvey and Matt at Val D'Aso, the British soldiers and the Belgian agent at Montedinove, and the execution of a Scottish soldier, Sidney Seymour Smith, Signalman, Royal Corps of Signals, near Montelparo on March 21, 1944. A very detailed account has been set forth by Dennis Hill on his Camp 59 blog, and is based on research conducted by Brian Sims. It is readily apparent from that account that either British turncoats or spies pretending to be escaped British prisoners of war were involved in Sidney Smith's recapture and murder.

To summarize, two men arrived at the farm of Giuseppe Mazzoni, where Smith had been staying since escaping from prison camp. One of the men told Smith that he was a British officer. The man spoke English, so Smith was comfortable enough with their story to leave the farm with them. However, something happened to change that perception. As they came to the neighboring farm of Augusta Viozzi, one of the men split off from the group, and Smith asked Mrs. Viozzi for a jug of water. He drank a little and then hit the remaining man on the head. But he was overcome and led away, toward Montelparo.

While walking, they encountered the man who had left them at the Viozzi farm who had during his absence arrested an Italian named Argeo Lupi. The four kept walking toward Montelparo, where they met a group of six to eight men. All but two of them were wearing German uniforms. Smith was beaten by the Germans and then shot in the head and body. The Germans left his body lying in the road. The Italians buried Smith in the Montelparo cemetery.

The investigators reached the conclusion that the killers were members of the "SS Brandenburg Division." One of the witnesses interviewed by the British investigators was fellow escaped prisoner of war John Meyers, who told them that the two men in civilian clothes who came to the Mazzoni farmhouse convinced Smith that they were paratroopers sent to rescue prisoners of war behind the lines. That would explain why Smith willingly left with them. It is also possible that Smith was suspicious of their intentions but left anyway to avoid repercussions for the Mazzoni family.

After killing Smith, the Germans also came after Meyers, but he escaped through a window while being fired upon. Significantly, as in all the other crimes, Meyers said that whilst all this was taking place, Roscioli was waiting on the road by the cemetery in Montelparo.

Argeo Lupi later testified that he heard a rumor that one of the civilians who had accosted him was the Republican Fascist Bascioni from Belmonte Piceno. Bascioni was one of Settimio Roscioli's primary operators in Le Marche.

The Brandenburgers were not an SS unit, but they worked hand in glove with the SS and committed atrocities with the same fervor. Therefore, that is a distinction without a difference. In fact, the Brandenburgers were disbanded later in 1944 and merged into other German units. Many simply transferred to the SS. As the story goes, there were a number of Brandenburgers implicated in the attempted assassination of Hitler in July 1944. After that, the unit fell from grace and was removed from the Abwehr's control.

Padre Leight had remarked that SS troops wearing black uniforms were seen in armored vehicles accompanying the troops he heard others refer to as Brandenburgers. But the SS did not always wear their stereotypical black uniforms, particularly in foreign war zones. Several witnesses reported that the Germans wore grey-green uniforms, known as *feldgrau*. It was not unusual for the SS troops to wear the *feldgrau* of the regular German army. This was because there was such a demand for SS uniforms late in the war that the suppliers could not cope with the demand. Therefore, mixed uniforms and insignia were actually quite common.

Padre Leight testified that some of troops in armored cars wore black uniforms and black caps with a badge representing a skull. The skull and crossbones emblem of the SS on a black hat is a well-known motif of the SS units. However, the SS also wore the skull and crossbones emblem on the left breast of the *feldgrau* uniforms as well as other distinguishing regalia.

Father Leight described the soldiers he had heard were Brandenburgers as wearing grey tunics. For a time, I was perplexed by the fact that he could not definitely identify Hossfeld's unit as being with the Brandenburg division, since I knew that those German soldiers had the word BRANDENBURG prominently tacked to the cuffs of their right sleeves. That unit identifier was embroidered in silver-grey thread on a black wool ribbon band of the dress uniform. However, I discovered that the Brandenburger cuff band was not authorized until August 17, 1944, several months after the murders in Le Marche.

Count Marcatilli also said that the Germans living in his villa, including Hossfeld, wore grey-green uniforms, similar to those of the Italian army. They had belt buckles emblazoned with the words GOTT MITT UNS ("God with Us"). However, such buckles were standard issue for the German army, so that in itself is not dispositive. Pietro Viozzi said that one of the men who rode up to his house on March 9, 1944, had on a German uniform, and the other was wearing an Italian uniform. Again, wearing the uniforms of other nationalities was a common Brandenburger modus operandi. In Italy, they were known to wear captured Italian uniforms in order to blend in.

Regardless of the style of uniforms worn by the perpetrators, which were never completely standardized, it is apparent from all of the above-referenced murders near Montelparo in March 1944, that spies had a hand in each of these affairs. "A" Force special agent Alberto Orlandi stated in his report that the existence of the turncoat British prisoner of war was confirmed by all the friars at Montalto Marche. He also discloses that the traitor managed to speak with all of the escaped prisoners in the surrounding countryside and win their trust. That would tend to rule out a Brandenburger posing as an Englishman. Even assuming an impostor could effectively imitate a British accent, he would still have to fake a life in England as well as correctly describe the details of camp where he was supposedly held. More than likely, it was an escaped British prisoner of war who had crossed over to help the enemy cause.

Orlandi's précis indicates that the traitor was a freelance operator, but there is a remote possibility that he belonged to a group known as the Britisches Frei Korps (British Free Corps), which was organized in January 1944 from a cadre of British Commonwealth soldiers held in German prison camps, designated as the Legion of St. George. This group became part of the Waffen SS. Members of that unit saw limited combat due to questions about the legality of using prisoners of war for that purpose, but they could have been engaged as spies and collaborators in clandestine antipartisan strikes.

The founder of the Legion of St. George, which became the British Free Corps, was a British civilian named John Amery who was living in France at the outbreak of the war and then moved to Germany. He was apprehended by partisans in Milan, Italy, after the war and turned over to the British. He was more of a rabid anti-Communist than an ardent Fascist. Amery was the founder of the unit and the man who proposed to the Germans the idea of a British volunteer force. He personally attempted to recruit British soldiers held in European prisoner of war camps. The Germans also used blackmail and coercion to recruit others. It does not appear from the record that the British Free Corps ever had more than fifty-nine active operatives, who were dispersed to various German units.

Amery's trial commenced at the Old Bailey in London, but before it was over, he entered guilty pleas to eight counts of treason and was hanged by the British on December 19, 1945. Several other turncoat members of the British Free Corps received life sentences involving hard labor, and others received reduced prison time or heavy fines. In sentencing Amery to death, the trial judge made the following pronouncement:

John Amery . . . I am satisfied that you knew what
you did and that you did it intentionally and delib-
erately after you had received warning from . . . your
fellow countrymen that the course you were pursuing
amounted to high treason. They called you a traitor
and you heard them; but in spite of that you continued
in that course. You now stand a self-confessed traitor
to your King and country, and you have forfeited your
right to live.

The founder of the British Free Corps was quickly executed.
Although Amery betrayed his king and country, the salient fact
remains he was neither a British soldier nor a prisoner of war when
he committed high treason. On the despicable scale, it is difficult to imagine a more heinous crime than that of the soldier and
ex-prisoner of war who ingratiated himself with his fellow soldiers
behind the lines and then collaborated with the enemy to recapture and murder them one by one.

Who the Brutus was remains a mystery. Another enigma of
lesser import is the question of how Luigi Vergari was able to
journey to Arezzo in Tuscany, as well as Santa Vittoria in Matenano, during the time the roads were supposedly impassable to
the German convoy because of deep snow.

Part VII

RESCUE EFFORTS

19

Operations Begonia-Jonquil and Darlington II

The clandestine American intelligence operation embodied as the OSS (Office of Strategic Services) played multiple key roles in the liberation of Italy and the rescue of prisoners of war. In addition to gathering and acting on covert information, the OSS kept the partisans well armed and supplied from the air. It also parachuted agents behind the lines in Italy to help coordinate partisan attacks against Axis forces. Further, the organization endeavored to repatriate escaped Allied prisoners of war who were still in enemy-occupied territory.

America's spy agency and the forerunner of the CIA was the brainchild of the legendary "Wild" Bill Donovan. His agency was independent of any other American intelligence operations but interacted with them all. The OSS operated in every theater of war and shared information and resources with its British counterpart, the SOE (Special Operations Executive). The SOE was particularly successful in intercepting and decoding radio traffic of the SS Security Service between Rome and German headquarters in Bonn. Britain's SOE also secretly taped conversations among German prisoners of war pertaining to war crimes and atrocities committed in Italy and elsewhere.

The truth is that without the Allied interception of Axis radio transmissions under the code names "Ultra" and "Magic," we would have either lost the war, or at the very least, it would have been severely prolonged. An elite counterintelligence subdivision of the OSS, known as X-2, was tasked with acting on the secret intercepts. An important function of this unit was to correlate radio intercepts with the information gleaned from the candid conversations of German POWs.

There were numerous attempts by OSS field agents and British special forces units to locate and extract Allied prisoners of war from the regions in Italy then under German control and far from the front lines. The most notable of these efforts was the combined airborne and amphibious raid known as Operation Begonia-Jonquil in October 1943. While the OSS and Free French units participated to some extent in Begonia-Jonquil, it was primarily a British operation.

A few days after the announcement of the Italian armistice, the German command proclaimed on September 16, 1943, that all escaped Allied prisoners of war would be reclassified as "evaders." The German motivation for doing so was to deprive the escapers of their status and protection as prisoners of war under the Geneva convention. There had been approximately 60,000 Allied prisoners held in Italian camps at the time of the armistice. Most had been immediately recaptured. But there were still many thousands behind the lines in desperate need of rescue. Winston Churchill had himself been a prisoner of war during the Boer War in South Africa, and was particularly concerned for the safety of the POWs then on the run. On September 25, 1943, he approved the mission that came to be known as Operation Begonia-Jonquil.

The basic plan for the operation was to introduce airborne and seaborne commando units into four areas along the Adriatic coast from Ancona south to Pescara. Begonia was the airborne component and Jonquil, the seaborne element. The intercepted radio transmissions and other data procured by the SOE and X-2 of the SAS (Special Air Service) guided the planners in establishing the landing zones.

There were two primary British elements involved in the mission, paratroopers with the Eighth Army Airborne and commandos from the SAS. Some of these commandos were highly experienced and had been with the fabled Long Range Desert Group in North Africa.

Begonia-Jonquil had four operational areas along the Adriatic Coast from Ancona to Pescara, designated as A, B, C, and D. Area A was commanded by Squadron Sergeant-Major Marshall; B was led by Captain Power; C was under the command of Captain Baillee and Lieutenant Hibbert; and D was a combined support force marshaled by Lieutenant McGregor, OSS Lieutenant Borrow; and Captain Lee.

Based on the events related to me by former prisoners of Camp 59, I believe that the rescue efforts they described were recollections of what had transpired in area A, stretching from Ancona to Civitanova, or possibly area B, running from Civitanova to San Benedetto del Tronto. This belief is based on the places they were known to be hiding, as well as the striking similarity of their stories to what occurred according to official reports.

The operation did not start well. Evidently, the planners were unaware that in those days the Adriatic beaches basically looked the same from Ancona to Pescara. This resulted in the units being dropped from the air or landed from the sea in the wrong places. But this actually turned out to be somewhat of a blessing in disguise when Allied intelligence units discovered much later that a mole had informed the Germans of the planned drop and landing zones. Could this possibly have been the same turncoat who regularly betrayed his fellow prisoners of war to the Brandenburgers and their SS counterparts?

Originally, the plan called for the Allied prisoners of war to be evacuated by Italian fishing boats and schooners, which were envisioned as good camouflage for the mission. However, this method was scrapped in favor of using LCIs (Landing Craft Infantry).

By mistake, airborne and seaborne commandos destined for areas A and B were jettisoned at the same place. The seaborne forces were landed on the same beach near Grottammare, north of San Benedetto del Tronto. Group C airborne units were dropped too early in broad daylight. There were several other missteps as the mission unfolded, including the arrival of pickup boats at a place where no escapees were even waiting. In that instance, no prisoners of war had been sent to the beach by the inland commando unit. However, by October 24, 1943, approximately 600 escaped prisoners of war were located and led to the rendezvous beaches. But only thirty-seven were actually saved as a result of Begonia-Jonquil.

One particular incident that sounds like what many of the PG 59 survivors experienced was that related by Captain Power in his after-action report. During the night of October 24, 1943, small groups of escaped prisoners cautiously made their way from inland hides to the beach where Power and his men had taken charge of security. The situation was tense as German patrols roamed the area on foot and bicycle and could be expected at any time.

Visibility out to sea was not good. It was a moonless night and clouds obscured the horizon. No boats could be seen. Power asked the escapees to keep still as they kept a low profile, waiting just behind the beaches for evacuation. Power stated that many of the escapes were nervous and making a great deal of noise in the brush. Just after midnight, the prearranged time, Power flashed his signal light offshore. There was no reply. He did it again. Still no answering signal from the sea. On Power's third try, a light pierced the offshore darkness.

According to Power, the escapees in his charge started to crawl from the scrub toward the beach. He whispered for them to stay still, but just then they heard the blast of a shotgun. After a pause, German submachine gun fire filled the air. Most of the prisoners of war ran for cover and scrambled back inland.

There is no doubt that the rescue activity was uncovered by German patrols. The sound of machine guns opening up undoubtedly caused the stampede for safety. Captain Power speculated that many of the prisoners simply panicked, although they still had time to be rescued by the offshore craft without being noticed by the Germans. Yet, the escapees themselves have related that men were killed by the machine gun fire and most of them opted in favor of self-preservation, rather than speculation. In short, they wanted to return to the known where they had a certain amount of control over their destiny, rather than rely on a mission that was in the process of deteriorating.

Some Allied planners later opined that the POWs had lost their soldierly qualities while in captivity. This is a condition pejoratively called "Gefangenitis." The word derives from the German, *gefangen*, which means to imprison, and describes a condition of apathy, neglect, or depression affecting a captive. The condition completely neutralizes or erodes personal initiative, self-confidence, discipline, and military effectiveness.

But I am not so persuaded that the flight inland was in any way attributable to Gefanginitis. First, the men were underweight and severely malnourished having left the prison camp and its 1,000-calorie diet only weeks before. Second, these men did show extreme initiative in breaking out of the camp and foraging for weeks in the mountains, although they had no idea what potential terrors awaited them.

Third, they left whatever safe shelters they had found and headed to the beaches where there were active German patrols. Fourth, while the commandos were armed and could defend themselves, the POWs were not. Fifth, once the German submachine guns roared out in the darkness, there was no way to tell what direction the firing was coming from, or how many enemy soldiers there were. Sixth, and finally, can an escapee be blamed for not crossing an open beach and wading into the ocean when the Germans were alerted and actively looking for promising targets?

Although a total of thirty-seven POWs were rescued by the various commando groups, out of an estimated total of 600 who made it to the beach rendezvous, Begonia-Jonquil is regarded as a dismal failure. It failed for many reasons, including the lack of time to properly plan. The planners and mission executors had to move quickly because more German forces were pouring into the area on a daily basis and were rounding up POWs. Next, the commandos were not provided with radios and had to rely on the unreliable use of signal lights. They did not have proper clothing, such as rain gear, or adequate quantities of food.

Additionally, the *contadini* initially regarded the sudden appearance of foreign soldiers in their midst with suspicion. How could they trust or lend aid to men in slightly different uniforms who might just be different German units? Then too, some of the prisoners of war felt somewhat comfortable with the farmers who were helping to feed and shelter them and were reluctant to leave their "safe" environs in the mountains for the far more visible coastal plains.

Captain Power's group rescued only five POWs. However, to his credit, he and some other commandos remained behind in an effort to locate and evacuate even more men. There is no way to know for sure whether Alvey and Matt were among the escapees who walked from their hides in the hill country to the Adriatic Coast to rendezvous with the rescue boats. But the Viozzis claimed that Roberto and "Martino" were with them the whole time.

A few men have also mentioned that there was a rumor of a submarine near Ancona sent to rescue escaped Allied prisoners of war. I have not been able to determine whether this report has any basis in fact. However, it could have been a version of the rescue attempt in area A under the leadership of Squadron Sergeant-Major Marshall, who did manage to bring back the largest group of twenty-three escaped prisoners of war.

• • •

On the night of May 25, 1944, the Allies tried again to rescue British and American prisoners of war, with Operation Darlington II. A British commando unit left Termoli, Italy, in an LCI bound for Porto San Giorgio, near the mouth of the Tenna River, some seventy miles behind the lines. The British assault team was either preceded or accompanied by a patrol boat carrying US Navy Beach Jumpers who guided the commandos into shore.

The Beach Jumpers were elite units that primarily engaged in tactical cover and deception designed to divert and trick the enemy. In many cases, they simulated amphibious landings to deceive the Germans into thinking they were the primary landing parties while the real attack forces struck the main objective.

Their name is said to derive from an officer who summarized the unit's charge: "To scare the be-jesus out of the enemy." Hence, the unit adopted the initials BJ, which somehow morphed into Beach Jumper. The force was actually the brainchild of actor Douglas Fairbanks Jr., who was on active duty with the US Navy in the Mediterranean theater and had trained with the British SAS. He helped sell the idea in Washington and served to organize the group. Although he did not take part in the Darlington II raid, he was decorated for other combat exploits and is still highly regarded by the veterans of the US Navy Beach Jumpers Association.

Darlington II was the most successful prisoner of war rescue during the Italian campaign. The raiders brought home 127 escaped Allied prisoners of war. By this time, Alvey and Matt were long dead. But it is a tribute to the surviving prisoners of war and their daring rescuers that so many more did make it home.

<u>20</u>

MIS-X — MI9 — IS9

Two years ago, I became aware of a shadowy US intelligence unit designated as MIS-X. The initials stand for Military Intelligence Service-X, and pertain to an agency patterned after the British ultrasecret operation known as MI9. Both of these units masterminded the escape of Allied prisoners held by the Axis around the world. They also provided the escapees with concealed radios, compasses, and maps, and organized a code system for sending and receiving messages behind the wire. MIS-X was so hush-hush that neither the US Congress nor the military itself even knew of its existence.

Because the emphasis of MIS-X was on the escape and evasion of Allied prisoners of war, I postulated that it was a virtual certainty that some or all of the information leading to the German lieutenants being accused of the war crimes derived in whole or in part from the activities of MIS-X. This was confirmed when I recently noticed the designation MIS-X at the top of certain war crimes documents pertaining to the murders of Alvey and Matt.

Unfortunately, MIS-X was disbanded at the end of the war and the bulk of its records were ordered destroyed. There are bits and pieces of MIS-X files in the National Archives and scattered around the country, but it is my understanding that they are not indexed or organized in a readily accessible format. The organization was genuinely invisible at the time and remains nearly so today.

There was also a clandestine group known as MIS-Y tasked with the intense interrogation of Axis prisoners of war, who were brought primarily from Europe to Fort Hunt near Mount Vernon, Virginia, where "enhanced" techniques could be employed.

In 1999, President Clinton established the Nazi War Criminals Interagency Working Group (IWG) designed to expedite the declassification of records related to Axis war crimes. These records would not have been declassified without the establishment of the Nazi War Crimes Disclosure Act of 1998. More than eight million pages of documents have now been released and are available for researchers. The vast majority of these materials are from previously classified files of the OSS and maintained by the CIA since the beginning of the Cold War. Most records of the OSS pertaining to war crimes have been released since 2004. However, some continue to be withheld due to political considerations and other sensitivity issues.

As we now know due to the efforts of Brian Sims, there are large quantities of war crimes documents in the possession of the British National Archives, particularly generated by MI9, and its executive branch known as IS9, which have shed considerable light on the origin of the conclusions reached by the investigators. Additional information may be in war crimes files maintained by the United Nations. However, although those materials are made available to researchers, they can only be reviewed once he or she first obtains the permission of the US State Department, which has an unduly burdensome procedure to obtain that permission. In my view, this type of bureaucratic nonsense serves to impede the revelation of the truth and actually compounds the crimes committed by the Nazis so many decades ago. Still, I am confident that additional facts and hard evidence may emerge from all of these resources, particularly if they gradually become digitized and are then more readily accessible online.

One of the most interesting aspects of MI9 and MIS-X is that some Allied soldiers and airmen were selected in advance of capture for training in the use of secret codes. Once captured, these men were able to communicate with the Allied governments in coded letters to and from the prisoner of war camps. Secret codes were concealed in otherwise innocuous-looking letters home. The coded messages were based on a simple grid system and were never uncovered by the enemy.

MI9 and MIS-X also sent radios, cameras, and escape materials ingeniously concealed in parcels mailed to the prisoners of war. They even set up phony charities so that the Red Cross would not be implicated. MIS-X concealed radio parts in cribbage boards and parts of escape maps were layered into playing cards. Escape materials were also hidden in the heels of shoes in James Bond fashion. It is now known that prior to his capture, Lieutenant Colonel Alger, Alvey's commanding officer, had been briefed by MIS-X in escape and evasion techniques. Alger, and about 300 other captured Allied officers, were detained at Oflag 64 in Poland. While interned there, Alger and his escape committee received approximately twenty "loaded" parcels of escape and evasion materials.

One of the seemingly innocuous methods of smuggling escape aids into the camps was the use of Monopoly and other board games such as Snakes and Ladders. The loaded Monopoly kits were said to have been marked with a red dot on the "parking space" segment of the boards. But once the outer layers of cardboard were peeled away, the prisoners found metal files, compasses, and regional maps. The Allied command also secreted currency of various nations in compartments between the layers of cardboard comprising the game boards.

John Waddington, Ltd., the UK manufacturer of Monopoly games, actually worked hand in glove with MI9 to produce the loaded games. Evidently, the size of the Monopoly box made it easier to conceal a great deal of contraband destined for the prisoners behind the wire in addition to the game itself. But since none of the loaded Monopoly boards are known to have survived the war, some doubt that they were ever actually used.

The secreted escape maps were made of silk, tissue, and cloth. Silk maps were highly favored because they did not make any noise while being unfolded, or while a man was being frisked. Plus, they were extremely lightweight. Apart from board games, compasses were hidden in buttons and pens. There were also loaded decks of cards, known as map decks. When soaked in water, the cards could be peeled to reveal concealed escape maps.

One thing the Allied intelligence services avoided doing was to attempt to tamper with Red Cross parcels, due to the fear that the Germans would use that as an excuse to cut off those lifesaving packages to the prisoners.

MIS-X and IS9 were also actively involved in setting up "ratlines" in Italy behind the German lines. There were subagencies within those groups established for this specific purpose. In Italy, the ratline group was designated as A-Force. One of the A-Force operatives in Italy was Curtis Bill Pepper, who was later an American journalist who worked for Edward R. Murrow and became Newsweek's Mediterranean bureau chief.

At the end of World War II, Pepper stayed behind in Italy in command of a unit that investigated 143 war crimes against Allied personnel. Therefore, I am compelled to conclude that Pepper's A-Force is the ultimate source of the intelligence that led the investigators to Lieutenants Rommel, Hossfeld, and Fischer. This was recently confirmed for me by the previously referenced report of Alberto Orlandi, who was a member of A-Force. Orlandi had this to say about Mario Mootis, the Belgian killed at Montedinove, who was his fellow agent:

> His name was Mario Mootis and he was an agent of I.S.9, then called "A" Force. At the time, Mootis was behind the German lines on a mission. He was known

by me personally as he belonged to the same section of "A" Force as I did, and he had been a soldier in my platoon for a few years.

Curtis Bill Pepper has written seven books since the war, but none of them pertain to his service with MIS-X or A-Force. Most recently, in 2012, he published a biographical novel about Leonardo Da Vinci, titled *Leonardo*. At that time, Pepper was 95 years old.

It is evident that A-Force was a joint operation between the British and Americans based in Cairo. In fact, there is one communiqué in the war crimes files consisting of a transmission to Cairo concerning the Germans being held for questioning. The British even had an "N" Section of A-Force, which during the war was primarily focused on the escape and evasion of Allied soldiers, sailors, and airmen. It is apparent that as the war was winding down in the European and Mediterranean theaters that A-Force immediately transitioned to the investigation of war crimes.

MIS-X and MI9 exchanged intelligence, particularly regarding the investigation of war crimes committed in Italy and elsewhere. They even adopted joint questionnaire forms utilized in the process of debriefing repatriated prisoners of war. Samples of these questionnaires are now available online. At the top of the questionnaires, TOP SECRET M.I.9/Gen/MIS-X is stamped. One document is labeled GENERAL QUESTIONNAIRE PART I. and PART II. TOP SECRET, and the other, Form Q WAR CRIMES, and begins with a set of instructions to the interviewee.

Among the questions asked on the General Questionnaire are:

Were you lectured on escape and evasion? Were you specially interrogated by the enemy? Did you make any attempted or partly successful escapes? Give the names of your companions. What happened to your companions? Did you do any sabotage of enemy factory plant,

war material, communications, etc. when employed on
working parties or during escapes?

Some of the more pointed interview questions were:

> Do you know of any British or American personnel
> who collaborated with the enemy or in any way helped
> the enemy against other Allied Prisoners of War? If
> you have any information or evidence of bad treatment
> by the enemy to yourself or others, or knowledge of
> any enemy violation of Geneva convention you should
> ask for a copy of "Form Q" on which to make your
> statement. (Note: Form Q is a separate form inviting
> information on "War Crimes" and describes the kinds
> of offences coming under this title.)

Form Q begins by defining what a war crime or violation of
the Geneva convention entails, and the following pages are broken
into four divided columns designed to elicit handwritten information from the escapee. These four columns are designated by
the following headings: Date, Camp or Place; Particulars of the
Criminal Act or Violation; Names where known, description,
rank, appointment, unit, etc. of enemy personnel concerned and
any other detail to fix their identity; and Names of other witnesses.

Neither the joint Questionnaire, nor Form Q appear in the
war crimes files for Matt or Alvey, or those pertaining to Roscioli.
Instead, what were provided were affidavits titled "Perpetuation of
Testimony Of . . . ," under the heading of THE WAR CRIMES
OFFICE Judge Advocate General's Department – War Department United States of America. These affidavits in many cases
mirror the types of information sought by the MI9 and MIS-X
forms, which were used as templates for the affidavits typed up by
the War Crimes Office.

In any case, extensive investigative efforts were made by MIS-X, MI9, IS9 and A-Force to identify and locate the Germans and Fascists responsible for war atrocities committed throughout Italy. In a few instances, justice was satisfied, while in so many others, the follow-up efforts of the Allied command were lackluster or nonexistent.

Part VIII

LEGACY

21

The Last Full Measure

Just as his great-grandfather James Irvin Newton had been murdered in cold blood by craven cowards who were never caught, so was the fate that befell Alvey. "Devastating" is the one word in the English language that incarnates the impact Robert Alvey Newton's death had upon his family and friends. They had anxiously waited for more than a year for any news concerning his status. The torment of waiting must have been excruciating, particularly for my grandmother and grandfather. My own father would never say much about it and suffered bouts of melancholy for the rest of his life.

My grandmother, Susie, kept busy reaching out to all of the other Camp 59 mothers in a desperate quest for information about her son. Somehow she established communication with Mrs. Gee, Charlie Lum's sister in Bakersfield, California; Mrs. Mary Kaser, Lee Kaser's mother in Detroit, Michigan; and Mrs. Glacile Skinner of Alma, Kansas, Ray Skinner's mother. Her long agony was over when the letter from the War Department confirming his death arrived in November 1944. But that agony was immediately followed by a heart-rending anguish that only a mother can truly know.

My grandmother also wrote to the War Department for information. There was one terse, generic reply from the War Department about the status of prisoners of war in Italy. It was dated October 5, 1943, from the Office of the Provost Marshal General, Prisoner of War Division, and informed her of the following:

> The Provost Marshal General directs me to reply to your letter of 18 September 1943, regarding your son, Corporal Robert A. Newton.
>
> The status of American prisoners of war in the hands of the Italian Government is uncertain at this time. It is assumed that all have either been transferred to German Custody or returned to duty with our forces. When further information is received concerning their status you will be notified.

Actually, the Allied command in the Mediterranean theater was well aware that thousands of prisoners of war in Italy had escaped from their camps and were trying to work their way back to the front lines. Due to the need for secrecy, even if the military agencies had particular information they would not have shared it with the family members of the escaped prisoners of war. This was an unfortunate exigency of war. They could not have information leak out that may have jeopardized the escapees still behind the lines. The rat line sources also could not be allowed to be compromised. The information they gleaned was TOP SECRET, SECRET, or at least CONFIDENTIAL. What is inexcusable is that it still remained so for decades.

Somehow, my grandmother also came into possession of an Interoffice Correspondence from Elliott Crooks in the Circulation Department of the *Chicago Daily News* to Jim Puett, presumably a reporter or editor for that newspaper in Remington, Indiana. It is dated May 19, 1944, which was months after Alvey had been killed:

> The American Red Cross says that the address you gave us for Corp. Newton is no longer sufficient because when the Americans invaded Italy all prisoners of war were removed to occupied Italy or into Germany. Some of them escaped however, and they are now with the Italian underground.
>
> They suggest that the only way to reach him is to get a new address and if the government has track of him, you can get this information from the Prisoner of War Information Bureau, Office of Provost Marshall, Washington, D.C. When you ask for this information be sure to send a photo static copy of the previous notification giving the address which you quoted us.
>
> I am sorry that we couldn't be of more help, but at least we are all hoping that she finds him.

Grandma Susie even tried to get the press involved. By May 1944, she must have been really desperate for news and must have tried every means at her disposal to locate her son and reestablish communication. Added to that, she was very stubborn, which appears to still be a universal family trait.

Yet, the horrible day arrived six months later. On Saturday, November 11, 1944, a letter dated 8 November 1944 arrived at the family home in Logansport, Indiana, from the War Department, Adjutant General's Office, which began as follows:

> It is with deep regret that I am conveying to you the sad announcement that your son, Corporal Robert A. Newton, was killed in action on 9 March 1944, in Italy.
>
> The great sorrow this message brings to you is most

understandable and I realize your desire to know the circumstances attending your son's death. The report received in the War Department states that Corporal Newton, who was previously reported a prisoner of war of the Italian Government, apparently escaped and it distresses me to advise you that he was shot by Italian Fascists. Your son's death was confirmed by the Italians with whom he and a companion, who was also shot, were living.

The letter goes on to advise her that the Quartermaster General had jurisdiction over the burial of military personnel overseas and to address any inquiry she might have regarding the location of his grave to that official. The letter is signed by J. A. Julio, major general.

Around this time, she also received a letter from the Chaplain of the First Armored Division, who expressed condolences on behalf of the command. Susie had already lost her two-year-old daughter, Mary Anderson, in 1912 when she succumbed to complications from measles, which may have given rise to meningitis. Now, she faced the unendurable once again.

On November 13, 1944, she took her fountain pen in hand and wrote a poignant letter to my father, Joseph Newton, to let him know the awful news. He was then in India, serving with the US Army Air Force, in a sea search attack group hunting Japanese submarines.

> My Dearest Joe,
>
> My dear this is a hard letter for me to write to you but we have at last had word of Alvey. Yes, it is as we have feared all along. He has had to make the supreme sacrifice. Saturday, Nov. 11th a letter came from the War Dept. stating he had been killed in Italy

March 9th 1944. Needless to say my dear boy, you know this has been a terrible blow to us but we are reconciled to God's Holy Will.

My father wrote back to my grandmother and grandfather on November 27.

Dear Mother & Dad:

I received your letter yesterday. Nothing I can say will be of help. If I could only be home with you all now, perhaps it would be easier for you. The poor kid. He had all the bad breaks. I still can't believe he's gone, Mom. Well, he's not. He is still one of those Newton boys. The best of them. He'll always be with us, Mom. And as for prayers, he doesn't need them now, Mom. He was always a good boy. There is no doubt in my mind where he is, and I am sure that he's praying for you and Dad, as I am.

On the line of the letter at the point where my father says, "The best of them," the word "them" is stained with a teardrop.

My grandfather C. L. was also crushed by the news of his son's untimely death. I have been told by my cousins Sue Ann and Marilyn that he always blamed Franklin Delano Roosevelt for getting America into a war and killing his son. He refused to accept any part of Alvey's government insurance, calling it blood money. He tried to express his deep feelings in a poem he wrote in December 1944 and carried in his wallet for the rest of his life.

Anxiously we waited for Alvey, praying that the war would cease, but now beyond that great divide he waits, but waits in peace.

Thank God for the faith that teaches when the

struggle of life is o'er; we shall see him again and be with him forever more.

Robert Frie wrote to my father overseas on January 18, 1945, expressing his feelings about the news of Alvey's death in Italy.

Remember the toast you proposed to the swellest guy we both ever knew? I'm all for it Joe, for that guy occupies my thoughts for a considerable portion of each day. Something is constantly reminding me of him — whenever I consider gentleness, sincerity, friendship and just plain down to earth goodness. I feel his presence. I can't begin to enumerate the millions of fine things that were a part of Alvey. I despise marching and such things, but twenty mile hikes at Camp Grant became almost a pleasure for me when I imagined him walking along beside me with his easy stride and I noticed the things he would notice.

I remember once a couple of months ago seeing a big white crane poised patiently on one leg in some swampy water near Chicago as I passed on the train. Before I passed out of sight, he suddenly plunked his head in the water and withdrew a small fish. Oddly enough, I got all choked up and tears came to my eyes. He was indeed a character in his individualism, but then interesting people are always a little different from the herd, and so was Alvey. Scarcely an hour passes that I don't see the boy in some form or other. I sit here smoking my pipe and I think of him with his old battered pipe in his mouth. I see a good book or just any book; somebody plays a song like "Honeysuckle Rose" or one of his old favorites — or "My Buddy."

I saw a Luna cocoon hanging from a elm out on

the post near the PX; Alvey & I found one down by Georgetown about 15 years ago. So there's always some reminder of his simple, genuine but happy philosophy of living.

I'm glad he never knew I dropped out of med school, but I'd give anything if he were here to eat me out for it.

Doc Frie was an emotional guy, and the tears came easily to his eyes.

The primary reason I know anything about Alvey's time in the army is because Bob Frie kept every single one of his pal's wartime letters, which Doc's wife, Edie, gave to me after he died in 1986. His letters provide a vastly more candid view into Alvey's true psyche than the letters to his mother and father. With Doc, and presumably Joe Kienly, Alvey could express more intimate matters, including experiences with, and observations about, the opposite sex. It was to Doc that Alvey confided that he had actually been burned on the face and hands when the tank was hit, but he asked his friend not to tell Susie and C. L. the truth.

After his death, my grandmother continued her pursuit for the details surrounding his death and burial. As previously mentioned, it is believed that she went to Fort Wayne to visit Robert Linker, a fellow PG 59 escapee and member of the Second Battalion of the First Armored Regiment. Presumably, she found out about Linker from family friend Jack Hunter, who encountered Linker at Camp Atterbury, Indiana, as they were mustering out after the war. Susie also continued writing to the Army. As she was instructed to do in a prior letter from the provost marshal, she wrote to the Quartermaster General. The reply came on February 27, 1945, and contained the following information:

The name of the Italian with whom your son was living prior to his death is not available to this office.

His companion who was also shot was a corporal by the name of Edward M. Majeski of Anderson, South Carolina.

I regret that I have no further particulars concerning your son's death have been received since the letter was written to you on 8 November 1944. Unfortunately, conditions of warfare do not always permit furnishing of full details at the time reports of this nature are made.

The full details were never furnished, during war time or afterward. At this point in time, my grandmother knew nothing other than that her son had been killed in Italy, supposedly at the hands of the Fascists and had been living with an Italian family at that time. The government did not tell her where he had been killed in Italy, or where he may have been buried. But the army was not idle regarding this issue. The following abstract dated October 31, 1944, addressed to the Adjutant General, Casualty Branch, appears in the war crimes files:

> An investigation conducted by this headquarters resulted in the finding, identification and reburial of Cpl's Robert A. Newton, 3516607 and Edwin M. Majeski, 14037579. It is determined that they were killed 9 March 1944, casualty cards reflecting this information will arrive in card shipment 271.

Included in the war crimes files was a Report of Reburial, dated October 7, 1944, and marked RESTRICTED. This document provides a number of details about the location and reburial of Matt and Alvey. It actually provides a sketch of the community cemetery in Santa Vittoria in Matenano and shows the delineation of their original graves. Matt was buried in the row just below

Alvey's feet. Also stated is the fact that they were exhumed in the presence of Antonio Viozzi, at whose house they stayed, and Ugo Tentoni, who buried them. Note that the British archives state that they were buried by Giuseppe Squarcia, the Santa Vittoria gravedigger.

The bodies of Matt and Alvey were transported to the US military cemetery in Bari, Italy, and reburied in coffins with sealed glass bottles containing identification information. Alvey was assigned grave No. 1275 and Matt was given grave No. 1277, right beside each other. For some time, I believed that Matt was still lying at rest in Italy, due to the fact that the Sicily-Rome American Cemetery at Nettuno, Italy, even now shows him buried in Plot E, Row 15, Grave 18. However, I recently became aware of a headstone in the New Silverbrook Cemetery in Anderson, South Carolina, that includes an engraving of his full name, date of birth (December 19, 1914) and death (March 9, 1944), beside the names of his mother and father on the same stone.

The single headstone bears witness that Matt's father, A.D. Majeski, died January 19, 1976, and his mother, Katie, died the same year on August 4, 1976. This was at least fourteen years before I began my quest for the truth in earnest. It would also explain why I received no response to my efforts to contact Matt's family members. One thing is for certain, neither Matt's, nor Alvey's families were ever in contact with each other. Yet, based on what we know about her, it seems improbable that Susie would not have reached out to the Majeskis in some fashion, since the Quartermaster had advised her of the name and hometown of the soldier killed with her son.

It is possible that Matt is still in Italy, and that his name was simply added to the headstone of his mother and father. But it cannot be ruled out that his remains were repatriated to his hometown sometime after he was taken from the temporary cemetery at Bari, to the permanent facility at Nettuno.

On April 28, 1947, the Quartermaster General wrote to my grandfather and provided him with a photograph of the US military cemetery in Bari, Italy, where Alvey was then buried. Among other things, the letter stated that the cemetery would be maintained as a temporary resting place until in accordance with the wishes of the next of kin, all remains were either placed in permanent American cemeteries overseas "or returned to the Homeland for final burial."

My grandmother wanted Robert Alvey brought back to America for reburial in Kentucky. She so instructed the army regarding her wishes in 1947, or 1948, and upon being advised that his remains were at the Columbus, Ohio, army depot, requested that Captain Joseph Kienly be allowed to escort Alvey's body to Kentucky for final burial.

A Logansport, Indiana, newspaper announcement regarding Alvey's impending funeral on a Saturday morning at 9:00 a.m. confirms this fact.

> Requiem High Mass will be read by the Rt. Rev. Louis Berriato. The body is scheduled to arrive at Litchfield, Ky. at midnight Wednesday escorted by Captain Joseph Kienly, a close friend who is stationed at Ft. Sheridan, Ill.

It is extremely astonishing that the same funeral notice makes the following statement:

> Cpl. Newton was killed on March 9, 1944 by the Germans after he had been freed by the Italians from a concentration camp following the surrender of Italy.

Killed by the Germans? I do not know the derivation of this information, but as far as I and anyone else in the family is aware, at the time of Alvey's funeral, the family believed that Italian

Fascists had killed him. Perhaps Robert Linker told my grandmother that Germans had done it. That will never be known. But it is unlikely that in 1964, Doc would have tried to tell my grandmother to dispel any concerns she may have had about the Italian people if she was already aware a few years after his murder that the Italian people were innocent of the crime. My family could not have been made aware at that time of the information in the war crimes files as they were still classified, even if the investigation had been concluded by 1947.

Another clipping, presumably from a local newspaper in Kentucky advises that:

> The body of Cpl. Robert Alvey Newton, who was killed March 9, 1944, in Italy, arrived Wednesday night of this week and is at the W.C. Alvey home in Clarkson.

My father once told me that his brother's funeral was both a happy and a sad occasion. Happy in the sense that it was wonderful to see all of the friends and family again. They had not been together since the end of the war. Doc Frie and Joe Kienly were there, as were Dick Alvey, Nell Loraine, and Katharine, and other friends and family members. Then too, it was an unbearably sad set of circumstances that brought about their reunion. Dad also told me that he and Doc and Joe Kienly went out for a few drinks to reminisce about Alvey and relieve some of the tension of the impending funeral, but when he returned to the Alvey farmhouse my grandmother took him aside and asked, "Did you have to do that?"

For several days, Alvey's body rested in the parlor of his aunt and uncle's farmhouse in Clarkson, Kentucky. His casket was draped with the American flag. The funeral service took place in Leitchfield, (not "Litchfield") Kentucky, on September 25, 1948. He was then buried in a plot of his own at the family gravesite in

St. Elizabeth Cemetery in Clarkson, Kentucky. Alvey is now at rest beside his "older" sister Mary Anderson Newton and his mother and father, among other family members. His grave is within viewing distance of the farm and people he dearly loved.

During a telephone conversation with Camp 59 survivor Robert J. Noah in 1992, he told me about a World War II cemetery in Italy where the soldiers of several nations had been buried together, including British, German, and Polish troops. He thought it was ironic that men had fought each other tooth and nail on separate sides, only to be gathered together and united in death. Robert Noah may have been referring to the military cemeteries at Monte Casino, where those fallen in the war are gathered under the flags of thirty-two nations. The essence of what he was trying to tell me is that this common ground in death was mute testimony to the tragedy and futility of war.

22

Inseperable Be My Thumb and Nose

The abstract in the war crimes files dated October 31, 1944, which is directed to the Adjutant General, Casualty Branch, also contains the following statement:

> 2. A jack knife and pipe bearing carved serial number 35166007 are the only personal effects to have reached this headquarters. Since these items have a definite bearing upon this investigation, they are forwarded for information and/or appropriate disposition.

Another abstract in the same file is dated August 26, 1944, and refers to the same personal effects and includes the statement that the two soldiers buried in the Santa Vittoria cemetery were "victims of what appears to be cold blooded murder." That conclusion was followed by the prediction, "It is unfortunate that the murderers will probably never be identified."

The pipe was the Kaywoodie sent by my grandmother to Alvey while he was overseas. Apparently, because his service number was carved into the pipe, it somehow made its way out of the war zone and into my grandmother's hands. At that point, friends and family discovered that he had not only carved his service number into the pipe, but also an incredible number of other iconic engravings. The artwork around the bowl included a map of the state of Indiana, with a star marking his hometown of Logansport; the triangular patch and emblem of the First Armored Division; and a list of places he had visited overseas: Northern Ireland, England, Tunisia, Italy, and then a "?"

Alvey also carved the initials RJF, in tribute to his best friend, Robert James Frie. He also worked into the pipe the following enigmatic initials in capital letters: L N C S A N A M K J. This is either some type of code forever lost to history, or a mnemonic, which is a simple device for aiding the memory. While it is purely speculation, the initials could have been etched into the pipe to help him remember the last names of some of his hut mates from Camp 59, so that he could give an accurate report to the authorities once he was repatriated. This is an educated guess based on the fact that many of the escapees kept diaries and note pads with the names and addresses of their fellow prisoners.

Again, it is pure speculation, but many of the initials match the first letters of the last names of some men known to be in the camp with him. Specifically, "L" could be Robert Linker, Bernard Lynch, who was in his hut, Charlie Lum, or even Ken Lightbody. "N" could be Herman Noble, who was in D Company with him. "M" could represent Dan McAnally, who was also in the same hut. The "K" could be James Kavana, another tanker he frequently chatted with. "S" could stand for Ray Skinner, who was also in Alvey's company. Alvey stated in a letter home from the prison camp that "some of my friends are here with me," so it is likely that at least some of the initials belong to those friends.

Alvey could have done the carvings while in the various prison camps, but it is more likely that his captors would not have let him keep the long pocketknife that was returned to my grandmother along with the Kaywoodie. More than likely, the knife was given to him by one of the Viozzi brothers, after his escape from Camp 59, due to the fact that the Viozzis remember that to be the case. Plus, he had about five months with the Viozzi family to work on the elaborate etchings.

One interesting fact about Kaywoodie pipes I have recently learned is that they were a particular favorite of MIS-X for hiding paper clip compasses in the stems. A prisoner of war behind the lines would be sent a pipe in a loaded care package that MIS-X assembled and had shipped, supposedly sent by a family member or friend. MIS-X also secreted radio components in baseballs, among other subterfuges. I have never had his Kaywoodie briar x-rayed, but due to the fact that Susie sent it to him long before he was captured, it is doubtful that his pipe was preloaded by MIS-X.

But the most amazing feature of the artifact is the legend Alvey carved into the stem: "INSEPARABLE BE MY THUMB AND NOSE." That inscription would probably not make any sense whatsoever to the average American born since World War II. But it had a great deal of import to the people who grew up during the Great Depression and struggled through the war.

Although the meaning of the gesture may now be obscure to modern America, or possibly even confused with a gang sign, thumbing the nose is still a prominent signal of derision, scorn, or contempt in England. It is made by putting your thumb on your nose and then wiggling your other four fingers. The precise etymology of the term and its corresponding gesture is thought to derive from the 1640s in Vienna. But it steadily gained popularity in the first half of the twentieth century United States, where it enjoyed equivalency with the "raspberry."

The gesture enjoyed widespread use during World War II. For example, there was a B-17 named "Nine O Nine" that featured a nose art cartoon of George Washington riding a bomb and thumbing his nose at a swastika. My heart was recently cheered to see a modern reference to the sacrosanct gesture in connection with World War II veterans. After the National Park Service attempted to close the World War II memorial ostensibly because of budgetary considerations, a group of World War II veterans involved in the Honor Flight Program knocked down the barricades so that they could see their memorial. Many had traveled long distances and suffered from various ailments. Yet, for many, this would have been their last chance to visit the memorial in Washington, DC, and it was a disgraceful political stunt that threatened their final opportunity. Anyhow, a reporter named Linda Torkelson with the Las Vegas *Guardian Express* wrote a column on October 2, 2013, with the headline, "WWII Vets: Nose Thumbing at Its Finest." She ended her story with the following sentence:

> As for defending our freedom, embracing democracy and realizing that sometimes in order to go forward we must compromise, I'm sticking with WWII vets and their nose thumbing at its finest.

My uncle would have wholeheartedly affirmed that sentiment. He was probably not expressing contempt or scorn for any particular agency, country, group, or circumstance, but for the human condition in general. He had left behind the impossibly disgusting and degrading fate of a prisoner of war, and upon detached reflection simply gave life in general an appropriate salute, which is now forever memorialized on a Kaywoodie briar. Then too, he could have simply been exercising the irreverent streak that is even today so prevalent in the family. I am speaking about myself here and most certainly about my own brother, Jim.

Grandma Susie gave the pipe and knife to Doc Frie. My father spoke about it from time to time and marveled at the telling legend "INSEPARABLE BE MY THUMB AND NOSE." But none of us with the exception of my dad had ever seen it. Then, in November of 1978, I took my mom and dad to Theresa Frie's wedding. After the reception, I was sitting at the kitchen table with Doc, Joe

Kienly and my dad. We were just visiting amongst ourselves when Doc rose from his chair and left the room.

He returned a few moments later with a battered and torn leather case, lined with a plastic material. Out of one of the compartments of the case, he gingerly lifted the Kaywoodie from its resting place. Then he did something completely unexpected. Doc loaded the pipe with tobacco, lit it up and passed it around. We all took a puff. Nobody said anything for a long while. After the tobacco had been consumed, Doc tapped out the residue from the Kaywoodie and returned it to the case.

I had previously been to summer parties with my parents at the Frie's house in Miraleste which Joe and Nellie Kienly also attended and there were always kind words spoken about Alvey as they reminisced about growing up in Logansport. They all wished that their own children could have had the same experiences. Then, Doc, my dad and Joe Kienly would get faraway, wistful looks in their eyes and must have all had allergies suddenly affect them as they once again toasted "the swellest guy" they had ever known.

Many more years would pass before I saw the pipe again. In August of 1983, I was at their dining table with Doc and Edie, when he again left the room. Once again, he came back with the pipe case, but this time he wordlessly handed it to me. There was no mistaking the tears in his eyes as he did so. I asked him if he was sure he wanted me to keep it and he simply said, "Yes." He died just three years after that most gracious gift to me. Doc's funeral in San Pedro, California was attended by more than 1,000 people. Many of those who paid their respects had been babies he delivered over the course of 37 years of practicing medicine, or perhaps the multitudes of indigents he treated on the nearby docks and at community clinics for free.

23

Famiglia Viozzi

The Viozzi family has been in the Le Marche region of Italy for more than 1,000 years. In fact, they received a medal from Mussolini due to their longevity in the area. The family originally hailed from Gaeta a coastal town about 75 miles south of Rome. Apparently, they derive from the *Nobili-Cavaliere*, which means "Noble Knight." According to one source, the Viozzis are an "Ancient and illustrious family of proven nobility." To that, I would simply add, "Amen!"

There are today, more than 114 people with the surname Viozzi in the Marches region. That of course does not include women of the family who married and took their spouses surnames. Most members of the family are concentrated in Santa Vittoria in Matenano, Servigliano and Fermo. Two are still listed in Montelparo.

Following the topographic map given to him by Joe Kienly, in 1964 Doc found the Viozzi family somewhere between Montelparo and Santa Vittoria in Matenano. But he returned to the United States shortly after that and did not write down the name of the family, or their address. Thus, when I started my own search several years after his death, all I had to go on were the slides that Edie had given me, showing pictures of the Italian family who risked their lives to shelter and feed my uncle, in addition to the surname Viozzi appearing on the witness list in the US war crimes files.

It was not until 1993 that I received copies of the war crimes files containing several entries that indicated Alvey and Matt had stayed at the home of a family named Viozzi. Several Viozzis were listed as witnesses. Among them were Primo Viozzi, Sesto Viozzi, and Antonio Viozzi. I later discovered that Primo and Antonio were the older sons of the family patriarch, Pietro Viozzi, and Sesto was his brother. Doc had mentioned a Papa Pietro, as well as the waitress named Maria he had first encountered, but again, he did not jot down any family surname.

In July 1999, my wife, Shannon, and I flew to Italy in an effort to find the Viozzi family and thank them for all they had done for "Roberto." I had with me prints of the photos taken by Doc's friend, Tony Cruciani, the name Viozzi and Joe Kienly's topographic map. We took the train from Rome to Ascoli-Piceno. Just outside the Ascoli-Piceno train station, we noticed some old men sitting on a bench, talking to one another. I stopped and asked one of them in my broken Italian for directions to our hotel, the Albergo Joli. He pointed in a general direction and we set out on foot for the main part of town.

We came to a bridge, which I believe was over the River Tronto, and stopped to take in the view. Out of the corner of my eye, I noticed that the old man had followed us. He was friendly and asked where we were from, I told him "Estati Uniti," ("United States"). He looked a little puzzled for a moment and then asked, "Americano?" I said, "Si." At this, he started pumping my hand, and asked why we were visiting. I told him that my uncle had been a prisoner of war in Servigliano. The old man then told me that he himself had been a prisoner of war in England for five years! He then pointed us in the right direction again, and we located our hotel about five minutes after that.

That afternoon we did some sightseeing and shopping in town, followed by dinner, which featured the local favorite of stuffed, fried olives. The next morning, we caught the Mazzucca bus and headed into the mountains toward Santa Vittoria in Matenano.

The driver dropped us on the road just below the town, and we walked up a rise and checked into the Albergo Farfense. The accommodations were first class. The balcony in particular, was amazing. We were given a room facing south toward Servigliano! As I marveled at the rolling green hills unfolding into the distance, I wondered if Alvey had taken this very route to the area the night of September 14, 1943.

I heard some rustling in the hall and looked out the door to see what was causing it. There was an elderly woman, about seventy-five years of age, sweeping the floor. Believing that she had been in the vicinity for many years, I showed her the pictures of the Viozzi family and mentioned the family name. She studied the group shots for a few moments and then said *"nella compagna,"* ie, "in the countryside."

A short while later, we were having lunch in the hotel restaurant, which was down a short staircase from the main lobby. A gentleman approached and introduced himself as the hotel proprietor. Evidently, the woman I spoke to was his mother and she told him that we were looking for a family named Viozzi. I showed him the pictures, explained that they had protected my uncle who was an escaped prisoner of war, and told him the family name was Viozzi. The proprietor left and returned a short while later. He was very excited as he told me that he had made a telephone call to a town called Fermo and in a burst of enthusiasm said, "a woman from the family is coming to see you at five o'clock tonight." I profusely thanked him for his effort, and that afternoon, we toured the town and visited the church that holds the remains and relics of Saint Victoria.

We were in our room about 5:00 p.m. when there was a knock at the door. The proprietor told us that the family was there to see us. We came down a winding staircase, and when we reached the final flight down, we could see about ten people there waiting for us! Basically, the whole family had come to greet the Americani.

I told them my uncle "Roberto Newtoni" had stayed with them during the war and that I was also named "Roberto Newtoni." Then I showed them the photographs that they had never seen before. They said *"Molto bene, Roberto,"* and seemed to really enjoy the photos that were taken thirty-five years before. We then met the three surviving brothers who were there when Alvey stayed with them. They were all younger than he was at the time. They are Giuseppe Viozzi, Gino Viozzi, and Dino Viozzi. That night, we also met their spouses, children, and many other family members, including their sister, Maria, who had been two years old when Alvey stayed there and had rocked her on his knee. They told me that their father Pietro had always regarded Roberto as one of his own sons. Then Gino added, and "Martino too." Pietro and Sesto had passed away years before, as had his wife and sons, Primo and Antonio.

That night, they drove us to the home of Ennio, Fabrizia, and Bianchmina Fabiani near Santa Vittoria in Matenano for dinner. We enjoyed many delicacies, together with the local rosso and blanco wines, and *acqua* (water), both gas and no gas, (ie with or without carbonation.) As we discovered, some Italians prefer to dilute the strength of their wine. They all laughed when I emphatically held my hand over the wine glass and said, "No *acqua!*"

The Viozzis told me that Alvey spoke Italian like a native and that he and "Martino" did chores around the farm to earn their keep. They also said that Alvey and Matt had made wooden toys for the children. The toys were possibly for Christmas because both of them were there at the time, and Cesare Viozzi later stated in an interview that "we had Christmas together." This was confirmed by Dino, who said that Alvey and Matt were with the family for five months, which was most of the time they were hidden behind the lines. Alvey occupied the place of honor at the head of their table, with Papa Pietro at the other end, at first as a guest of honor and later from habit. He taught them to play pinochle and spoke about his home in Indiana and his plan to go to medical school. Then, he told the Viozzis that after the war was over, he would return with his family to visit them.

The Viozzis drove us back to the hotel Farfense. But the next morning, they returned and essentially made us check out and insisted that we stay with them. Dino Viozzi and Giampietro Viozzi had come to the hotel very early to fetch us. As we left the hotel, I asked about the place where Alvey had been killed. Dino said something to Giampietro, who was driving, and Giampietro turned off the main road. The car came to stop beside what looked to me like a creek or irrigation canal. We exited the car, and I asked Dino, *"Roberto e satto uccissi qui?"* ("Was Roberto killed here?") He simply pointed to a spot beside the water and said, *"Si."* I took some pictures, including one of Dino Viozzi pointing to the exact spot where the two had been murdered.

We also stopped at the site of the Viozzi farmhouse where Alvey and Matt had stayed and been recaptured. The main structure has now been modified into an elegant villa. From the yard, we could see the town of Santa Vittoria in Matenano, high on a hill about three miles away. The stable, or shed, was still there but appeared to be dilapidated and about to collapse. The current owners of the house invited us in and produced a bottle of what I later learned was grappa, a potent, grape-based brandy, which varies between thirty-five percent and sixty percent alcohol. They poured some in a liqueur glass, which I quickly tossed down my throat. The Italians all then howled in laughter when I coughed sputtered and turned crimson red. I must have imbibed the sixty percent variety.

After thanking the current owners of the villa, we were off toward Servigliano. Along the way, Giampietro asked me about my father and what his occupation was. I did the best I could to convey that he had been an engineer and had worked in the space program. I made some gestures and sounds vaguely resembling a rocket being shot into space. Nevertheless, Giampietro seemed to get the idea.

We arrived in Servigliano a short time after that and came to the site of the former PG 59. It is now a recreation field, but the old camp walls still enclose the area. We walked around the walls for a bit and saw the railway station and front gate, among other sites. We returned to the car and headed to downtown Servigliano. Giampietro parked the car and went into an older building alone. When he returned, he beckoned us to come with him.

The four of us were ushered into the office of the mayor of Servigliano and seated at a conference table, like we were some kind of dignitaries. The mayor came in to greet us. Then, they offered us coffee and tea. Next, the vice mayor, Guido Colletti, advised us that if we would return at 3:00 p.m. that afternoon, a very important local historian, Angelo Paci, would give us a personal tour of the grounds. We thanked him and left.

Giampietro drove us to the main house in Fermo where most of the immediate family lived on three levels. We met some additional family members who had not come to the hotel, including Romeo and Irena, Dino's son and daughter; Giampietro's wife and son, Marco; and cousin Matteo, among many others. But the Viozzis thought we would be more comfortable at the home of Gino and his wife, Adele, in the neighboring area of Campiglione di Fermo. So we were based there for the duration of our visit.

We returned to Servigliano for our tour of the grounds of the former PG 59. There we met with Angelo Paci, who had the foresight to bring an interpreter. She was a very kind young woman and was expecting a baby. Angelo took us around the grounds and told us what he knew about the camp as his assistant translated. We spent an extended time marveling at the repaired hole in the wall through which perhaps more than a thousand men had escaped that fateful night.

Angelo next took us to his office, where he showed me the original plans, or blueprints for the camp. I then gave the interpreter a tip and told her it was for the *bambino*, and asked Angelo if there was anything I could do for him. He would not take any money, but he asked through the interpreter if once I returned home would I please send him a photograph of me with my father, the famous American astronaut! Apparently, Giampietro did not completely understand my impromptu explanation of what my father's occupation was.

Vice Mayor Colletti asked for my street and e-mail addresses and handed me two books about the history of Servigliano. Months later, on New Year's Day, I checked my e-mail and found that Guido had sent me New Year's greetings. His message simply said, "Good Year," in English, and he had attached a photograph of Camp 59 as it looked during World War II.

The Viozzis also drove us to the cemetery just outside Santa Vittoria in Matenano where Alvey and Matt were originally buried by Giuseppe Squarcia. The spot where the two soldiers were interred fifty-five years before that visit was covered in a type of pea gravel. But the outlines of a gravesite could still be seen. We saw the graves of some of the Viozzi family members also buried there.

While in Fermo, near dusk, we were treated to the venerated Italian custom of *la passeggiata*, which means to "stroll," or "take a slow walk." The Viozzis took us to the piazza, or town square in Fermo, where hundreds of townspeople were walking around and visiting, shopping and enjoying a meal or glass of wine as the sun was fading over the Apennine mountains to the west. We visited the shops and stands lining the piazza, bought some postcards and enjoyed the ambience of the real Italy.

Giampietro, the son of Giuseppe, took us to the gravesite of his grandfather *(nonno)*, Pietro, who had a marble crypt inside a mausoleum in Fermo. We paid our respects, and I pressed my palm against the marble and thanked Pietro for his sacrificial courage and for treating Alvey like a member of his own family.

Romeo Viozzi, who is Dino's son, is the civil engineer for the city of Fermo. He was then in his early thirties, a bachelor and motorcycle enthusiast. Romeo was very anxious for us to see his office and the old part of town, so he took us sightseeing. We saw the opera house, the Duomo di Fermo, high on a mount above the town, and the famous doors of Fermo. Romeo made sure that we had several posters of *"i portal di Fermo"* before leaving.

On Sunday, and throughout the day, the Viozzis dazzled us with a four-part feast *(feste)*, in honor of our visit. I was immersed in translated conversation with Giampietro when I noticed Gino drawing his finger across his throat in a cutting motion. He was telling me to break off the discussion. He was hungry and wanted to eat. Although I protested, the Viozzis insisted that I sit at the head of the table, the place of honor. It was hard not to think of Alvey enjoying the same honor at their table fifty-five years before.

The grand meal started about noon, and concluded in the early evening. There were several courses and dishes of beef, fish, rabbit, pizza, pasta, vegetables, and other delicacies. We finished with a very flavorful salad. Then too, there was a plentiful supply of vino rosso and blanco, and of course, *acqua*, "gas, or no gas."

During the meal, I told them that my father had died twenty years earlier, but that I had come in his place to thank them for all they had done for his brother. Then I toasted them. The next course arrived. I asked Matteo, one of the nephews who spoke some English, to identify an unusual but delicious meat on our plates. He replied, *"coniglio."* I looked puzzled, so he put his hands next to his ears and wiggled them, saying, "Bugs Bunny." Finally, when all of the courses were over, they outdid themselves when they unveiled a special cream cake they had made for us, topped with various fresh fruits with the words, "Benvenuti in Italia" (Welcome to Italy). They actually apologized to us for not having something more elaborate but explained that we did not give them much time to prepare. They could not have understood that we did not know where they were when we arrived in Italy and had no means to provide them with any advance notice.

I enjoyed talking with Maria and her husband, Pasquale. Maria had been about two years of age when Alvey stayed with her family and had bounced her on his knee. I told Maria that I had heard she had five cats. She smiled sheepishly and said, *"sei gatti"* (six cats).

We already had rail passes and reservations in other areas of Italy and had to very reluctantly leave them the next morning. We said goodbye to most of the Viozzis that night. I made a joke about how we have a saying in America that "Guests and fish start to stink after three days," and they laughed. They also thought it was hilarious when as we were all taking group pictures I said, *"formaggio."* They looked puzzled until someone interpreted that in America we say "cheese" when taking pictures so that people will make a smile for the camera. But, as my wife will testify, my particular style of humor has been known at times to completely backfire.

The next morning, the Viozzis had obtained a present for me. It was a quart bottle of grappa! We said our last goodbyes, and Romeo drove us to the train station. When we got there, he kept fidgeting with the rail pass around my neck. Apparently, he had not seen one just like it before and was worried that I did not really have a train ticket. But as the train arrived, we boarded it. When we reached our seats, I stuck my head out the window to say goodbye to Romeo, he reached up, pulled me toward him, grabbed my face and kissed me on both cheeks.

Since that time, I have kept in regular touch with the Viozzis, and we exchange Christmas and Easter greetings each year. Although the Viozzis were all farmers when my uncle stayed with them, many of them are now engaged in shoemaking. A few years after our visit, they sent a note asking what our European shoe sizes are. I was surprised to learn that I am a 44! We told them the sizes and a few weeks later, they sent me and my wife some custom-made shoes. They are of the finest leather. The wing-tips they sent me will without doubt outlive their owner by many decades.

A few months after we returned to the United States, we received a letter from Giampietro Viozzi with some documents they had just found. While I was in Italy, I had asked them if the American government had compensated the family after the war for taking care of Roberto and "Martino" as well as the damages to their property. They had originally answered no. Nevertheless, they looked and found some documents at the home of Gabriela, the daughter of Sesto Viozzi. They were unaware of the existence of these records because Sesto Viozzi had died prematurely in 1954, the documents were kept in a box, and his widow did not know what they were. After her mother's death, Gabriela had possession of the box at her home in Ascoli-Piceno.

The documents they sent me consisted of payment records for war and agricultural damage, a list of expenses prepared by Sesto Viozzi, and a certificate from the American government thanking them for the help they had given to the two soldiers. Allied planes had dropped leaflets to the *contadini* promising them compensation if they helped escaped prisoners of war. This was to counter the rewards offered by the Fascists and Nazis if they turned the prisoners in, or told the enemy where they were hiding.

There was also a scrap of paper with the printed names and addresses for Robert Newton and Martin Majeski. Due to the fact that the printing precisely matches the printing on a postcard that Alvey sent home from Camp 59, the note was undoubtedly written by him. This could also possibly be the handwritten note that a woman from the Viozzi family showed to Herman Noble, which he references in his war crimes statement.

It was not until March 11, 1948, that the Viozzis received the first payment from the American government. Based on the conversion rate at the time, it amounted to just $73.71. The next payment for agricultural damage was not made until August 9, 1969, twenty-four years after the war in the converted amount of $41.08!

The certificate given to the family by the US government consists of a preprinted form in script with the American eagle seal at the top. The name of the recipient was then inserted and written in calligraphy. It reads as follows:

> This certificate is awarded to
>   Viozzi Sesto di Vincenzo
>   As a token of gratitude for and in appreciation of help given to the Soldiers and Sailors of the United States, which enabled them to escape from, or evade capture by the enemy.

It was signed by Joseph T. McNarney, United States Army, Commanding General, Mediterranean Theater of Operations. The citation was well deserved. As Cesare Viozzi said at the end of his account:

> Our family suffered the most in the vicinity, but no one ever regretted having given hospitality to those poor boys.

Sacrificial acts of mercy epitomized the Viozzi family as well as countless other *contadini* households throughout Italy. They courageously rose to the occasion, even to the point of paying the ultimate price. One particularly heartrending example of this resolute, heroic attitude of the *contadini* was recounted by South African author Uys Krige in *The Way Out*.

> An escaper met a family whose five sons had all been shot by the Germans for helping prisoners of war, but they still gave them their help: "They have taken

everything from me. What more can they take? I started with my sons on this road, I shall continue along it . . . "

My Indiana cousins Sue Ann and Marilyn have also visited the Viozzis in the past few years and agree with me that they are the finest people you will ever want to meet. Even though I was only with them for three days, I can now genuinely understand why Alvey did not want to leave this loving family and their most gracious hospitality. I am also sure that he thoroughly enjoyed the opportunity to live and work on their farm after having seen far too much of war.

Not long before her own death, my aunt Carmen, among the last few alive to have actually known Robert Alvey, found some consolation in the fact that at the end of his life, he was with people who genuinely loved him. He had promised the Viozzis that one day he would bring his family to meet them. In a very real sense, he kept that promise. There is now an indelible bond between our two families and in remembering the Famiglia Vizzoi, we must always simply say, "*Grazie.*"

Acknowledgments

Camp 59 Survivors & Family Members

Zulah Dawson Ray, the very first Camp 59 survivor I met, who was nearby and witnessed Alvey and Matt Majeski being led away from the house by the German SS troops. Zulah also graciously provided me with a copy of his own manuscript, *Zulah Dawson Ray: His Stories*, by Evalynn Morgan Quisenberry.

Armie Hill, who escaped from Camp 59, and his wife, Eini Hill, for their kind assistance during my earliest phase of research and for providing me with the *Yank* magazine article about one of the more dynamic escapees from PG 59, Manuel Serrano, titled *Partisan from Brooklyn*.

Dennis Hill, of Indiana University, the son of Armie Hill and Eini Hill, who has the most comprehensive blog on the Internet, an organic tribute to the survivors of Camp 59. This is an incredible interactive resource for family members simply seeking information about their former prisoners of war, or serious researchers of these events in world history. I am indebted to Dennis as a fellow journeyman and colleague for the countless contributions he has made to my own understanding of the prisoner of war experience.

Anne Bewicke-Copley, UK attorney, for translating and forwarding a copy of the 2001 interview of Cesare Viozzi, by Filippo Ierano, and for her tireless pursuit of the stories of the Camp 59 survivors.

Ila F. Van Arsdale (Harry Van Arsdale), for providing me with a copy of a page from her husband Harry's notebook that listed

Robert Newton and Martin Majeski as being among the men in his hut at Camp 59.

Raymond Cox, for his detailed descriptions regarding life behind the lines, and who was just a few hundred yards away when he heard the gunshots that killed Alvey and Martin.

Robert J. Noah Sr., for his accounts of life in Camp 59, his time outside the wire at Monte San Martino, and the difficulty of obtaining effective medical care for serious ailments. Robert also confirmed the names of others who had escaped and offered me a place to stay if I ever visited Greensboro, North Carolina.

W. T. Miller, for his continuation of the fight among the *partigiani* and his effort to hunt down and rid the world of the infamous murderer and war criminal, Septimius "Settimio" Roscioli.

Warren Decker, a paratrooper from the 509th Parachute Regiment, who escaped from Camp 59 with Keith Argraves, and confirmed details about Keith's lasting impact on other prisoners.

Kenneth Lightbody, for sharing important details about the escape, life behind the lines and providing firsthand information regarding the execution of many other Allied soldiers by the Germans while he was in Comunanza.

Vern Linker, whose brother Robert Linker was in the Second Battalion of the First Armored Regiment with my uncle and also detained at Camp 59. After the war, Linker was the first person who knew Alvey to tell friends and family members what had happened to him, when he encountered Jack Hunter while mustering out at Camp Atterbury, Indiana. It is believed that my grandmother, acting on Jack Hunter's information, went to Fort Wayne to talk to Robert Linker. Sadly, Robert Linker passed away prematurely in 1966. I am indebted to Vern Linker for sharing with me what information he had.

Charles Lum, for providing me with the details of his escape and recapture and letting me know about his encounter with Everett Gregg in a German POW camp and what became of Gregg after the war.

Gerald W. "Tex" Rowland, who escaped from Camp 59, stayed with a family in Rotella and returned safely to Allied control. He called me by telephone from his sickbed to share what he knew although he could hardly even breathe. Tex said he did not remember Alvey, but my uncle had mentioned Tex in a letter home from PG 59 in 1943. Alvey said, "Tell George that Tex Rowland is here with me." Rowland and Alvey's boyhood friend George Kienly were both in the Thirteenth Armored Regiment.

Joe A. Rowland, Tex's son, who provided me with copies of his dad's papers, some of which Joe had never seen before, including intimate letters received from the Italians who sheltered and provided for Tex after his escape.

Mary McAnally (Dan McAnally), for providing details about how her husband, Dan, escaped from Camp 59 and made it back to Allied control, as well about his life after the war.

Ferree Grossman, for recalling for me his visit with my uncle at the Viozzi farmhouse near Santa Vittoria, and his description of the fear that gripped the other escaped prisoners of war after Alvey and Martin were executed.

Elmer Reece, for his kind comments and narrative of the major earthquake in nearby Offida, Italy, on October 3, 1943, which occurred shortly after the escape from PG 59, and resulted in the death of a baby girl. Reece vividly described for me in poignant detail the baby's funeral procession.

James Edward Kavana, for recalling how he and my uncle, both tankers, talked about how to escape from the camp, for his detailed description of life in Camp 59, and for escaping again after being recaptured, executing his SS guards in the process.

And to each of the following people who shared important details and advanced the composite view of life in PG 59, the escape, and beyond: Bernie Abrams; Howard "Sid" Delanoy; Clarence Dust; Homer Lewis; Paul Alsin; Henry Kane; John Garone; Mary Drazkowski (Theodore Drazkowski); Alvin Froelich; William Heslep; Dickson Parsons (Norman Parsons); Michael R. Kreisch; Edward

R. Herman; William L. Davidson; Alfred Nastasi; John Procko; Clovis G. Amos; Leo E. Keating; R.J. Downes; Henry Kane; Ralph De Salvo; Joseph C. Ainsworth; Walter Letter; Clair A. Baum; James Sanders; Russ Merritt; Charles W. Smith; Charles L. Holtzman; Shelby Blackman; Mario Barone; Jesse D. Lipscomb; Stanley Line; Tevis T. Skinner; Charles "Red" Simmons; Joseph P. Meredith; William J. "Kivvy" Kivlehan, Steve Schwietz; and Dorothy Whitaker (Leslie Parker).

Soldiers of the First Armored Division, Affiliated Units in North Africa & Italy & Family Members

C. Peter Fix and June Fix, for placing the ad that launched my journey, and their ongoing gracious hospitality, in their home as well as during the many memorable picnics we had with the former soldiers of Old Ironsides and their families.

A. Robert Moore, former President of the First Armored Division Association, for his detailed assessment of the virtues and deficiencies of the M-4 Sherman tank and the copies of the Sidi Bou Zid after-action memoranda and reports assembled by Lieutenant Colonel (later General) James D. Alger.

W. S. "Bill" Beasley, former secretary of the First Armored Division, for the numerous addresses provided and informational contacts he suggested to me.

Clifford Larkin, for his confirmation of the details of the prelude to Sidi Bou Zid and its aftermath.

Charles Doyle (509th Parachute Association), for the copy of the 1947 book written by his fellow paratrooper, Keith Argraves, titled *Keith Argraves: Paratrooper*, and for directing me to Warren Decker, another paratrooper who escaped from PG 59 with Keith Argraves.

Eric Holm and Mary Holm, for their kind efforts to help.

Clyde Fitz, who said to just call him "Fitzie," and told me about his battle experiences as a soldier in North Africa.

Hubert ("Herb") Olson and his wife, Ida Olson, for the many invaluable leads they jump-started and their genuine interest in my research. Herb was the first to tell me about Ferree Grossman, who, it turns out, actually knew my uncle, and about Charlie Lum, whom Herb said "had been running loose in Italy for a while."

Mrs. Mary Kaser (Mother of Lee C. Kaser Jr.), who lived to be more than 100 years of age, for her cheerful, generous spirit and the photo of her "gentle boy," Lee Cole Kaser Jr., the radio operator and gun loader in my uncle's tank. Although I was able to definitively tell her what happened to Lee at Sidi Bou Zid, to my profound regret, no living source had any information about what happened to Lee's body. He was simply carried on the rolls as missing in action, and I still hold out hope that he might someday be found.

Tim Bosanoz, (nephew of Lee Kaser), Robert Kaser (nephew of Lee Kaser), and William Kaser (brother of Lee Kaser), for their encouragement and support.

Joseph Frelinghuysen, for his acute exposition of escape from the officers' prisoner of war camp at nearby Chieti, Italy, and his profound knowledge of life behind the lines. I am also indebted to him for the copy of his own book, *Passages to Freedom*, and the gracious inscription he provided.

Alphonse L. Urbanovsky, assistant driver of my uncle's tank, for his frank summary assessment of the Battle of Sidi Bou Zid: "We never had a chance. It was five to one against us."

Philip Caldwell, the regular driver of my uncle's tank, who gave up his seat to Everett Gregg, the tank commander, because Captain Winkler took command of the tank at the Battle of Sidi Bou Zid. Phil followed behind in a tank destroyer and made it back to American lines. He was later wounded after being bombed by our own planes.

Province M. ("Perry") Winkler, Commander of D Company, First Armored Regiment, who provided me with important details about the Battle of Sidi Bou Zid, even though he was not anxious to talk about his combat experiences or his time in the army.

Jack Hunter, another friend of my uncle's from Logansport, Indiana, for his anecdotes and insights about his experiences in North Africa during the Oran invasion, and how he met up with my uncle just before the Battle of Sidi Bou Zid. Jack served in the Thirteenth Armored Regiment, as did George Kienly and Tex Rowland.

Harris O. Machus, for his keen review of the Battle of Sidi Bou Zid from a commanding officer's perspective and the copy of his book based on his own experiences as a captive in Germany and subsequent escape through Poland to Odessa as related in *Turmoil to Triumph*, by Angus Duncan McKeller. Interestingly, Mr. Machus owned the restaurant in Michigan where Jimmy Hoffa had his last meal.

Erly Paul Gallo, MD, (son of Francis "Frank" Gallo, MD) who confirmed that his father, "Frank" Gallo allowed himself to be taken prisoner in North Africa so that he could continue to treat wounded American soldiers. He also related to me that his father had jumped from a train in Italy carrying Allied prisoners north to Germany after the armistice.

And to Kelly Six, Paul S. Williams, William Sweeten, and Shelby Blackman for all the significant information they shared with me.

Italy

Famiglia Viozzi & Friends who represent, in my view, the most generous and courageous people on the face of the earth. The surviving family and friends of the *corragiosi* include: Gino Viozzi, Dino Viozzi, Giuseppe Viozzi, Cesare Viozzi, Maria Viozzi, Giampietro Viozzi, Romeo Viozzi, Pasquale Pazzaglia, Matteo Pomili, Biancmina Fabiani, Rachele Santini, Anna-Maria Viozzi, Erina Viozzi, Nella Viozzi, Ada Massimi, Ennio Fabiani, Adele

Vittori, Giordano Pomili, Cristina Fortuna (translator), and Veirella Paoloni.

Guido Colletti, vice mayor, Comune di Servigliano, who graciously welcomed us to his city and provided copies of historic documents and photographs of PG 59.

Angelo Paci, historian, Comune di Servigliano, who provided us with a guided tour of the Camp 59 grounds and explained the mechanics of the fateful escape.

Friends & Family

Robert J. Frie, MD, for lovingly preserving Alvey's pipe, artifacts, and letters for more than forty years, and for the critical discoveries he made during his 1964 trip to Italy. Most especially, he found the Viozzi family, which facilitated my own efforts when I followed in his footsteps thirty-five years later.

Edith P. Frie, for having the faith to entrust me with "Doc" Frie's treasure trove of photographs, intimate letters, and anecdotal details so that I could tell Alvey's story as it should be told.

Joe Kienly Sr., for his driven efforts to uncover very early on what happened to his friend Alvey, despite overwhelming obstacles, including obstructive red tape and a total blockade of official information.

Sue Ann Jargstorf and Marilyn Newton Williams, my cousins in Indiana, for critical background details, documents, photos, and insights regarding Alvey's Renaissance personality and the rich potential of a life so tragically cut short and for their enthusiasm and support over the years.

Researchers & Archivists

Ken Schlesinger, military archivist, National Archives, Military Reference Branch, for his efforts far above and beyond the call of duty to locate records and survivors of PG 59 as well as the war crimes files.

Brian Sims, UK researcher extraordinaire, who discovered files maintained in the British archives for seventy years and generously provided me with copies of papers that finally provided amazingly thorough and accurate details regarding the murders of Alvey and Matt Majeski at the hands of the Nazis.

Giuseppe Millozzi for his comprehensive dissertation titled "Allied Prisoners of War in the Region of the Marche and Prison Camp at Servigliano," and his kindness in sending me a copy of Dr. Derek Millar's *Memoirs* regarding the doctor's sacrificial efforts to help his fellow prisoners of war escape from Camp 59 unscathed.

Filippo Ierano for graciously granting me permission to quote extensively from his interview of Cesare Viozzi in *Antigone nella Valle del Tenna*, "Avevano Appiccato Il Fuoco" ("They set it on fire").

Notes

PART I: BONDS

Chapter 1: The Pirate Gang

1   *In 1901 alone, 216 trains:* Cass County Historical Society, www.casshistory.com

2   *The "Pennsy" was:* Pennsylvania Railroad Company, "Inspection of Physical Property by Board of Directors," November 10-11-12, 1948.

3   *Alvey's express homage:* Henry David Thoreau, *Walden.*

4   *Since 1919, Logansport:* Cass County Carousel, Inc., www.casscountycarousel.com/carousel-history/.

5   *Over 250,000 left home:* Scottish Rite Masonic Museum & Library, Inc., National Heritage Museum (Ulys Family Collection, www.nationalheritagemuseum.org

6   *In his 1935 yearbook: Tattler, 1935,* Logansport High School yearbook, p. 19.

7   *Joe Kienly was no stranger:* Hank Jewett, "Kienly Shares Colorful Military Career," *Five Cities Times-Press (Arroyo Grande, CA),* January 11, 1995.

Chapter 2: The Farm

8   *After being invited:* Brian Farmer, *American Conservatism: History, Theory and Practice* (Newcastle, UK: Cambridge Scholars Publishing, 2005), p. 116.

9   *The year 1785 saw:* Maryland to Kentucky, mdtoky.com.

10   *James Irvin Newton:* Transcribed remarks of Marcus E. Newton at Newton-Rhodes family reunion, Flaherty, KY, October 2, 1994; John A. Whitfield, "Newtons Recall Their Past," *Meade County (KY) Messenger,* October 12, 1994.

11   *He was widely recognized:* Affidavit of Albert Jacob Thompson, Flaherty, KY, November 27, 1929.

12   *I'm telling you, Bob:* Robert J. Frie Collection, letter, September 28, 1942.

13   *When President Franklin Delano Roosevelt:* FDR Fireside Chat No. 2, May 7, 1933, Franklin Delano Roosevelt Presidential Library.

14   *Six more days:* Robert Alvey Newton, Indiana University Papers.

15   *Just before he was drafted:* Robert Alvey Newton, letter to Eva Jane Blair.

PART II: WARBOUND

Chapter 3: Outbreak

16   *As of 1939, the United States:* Rick Atkinson, *An Army at Dawn* (New York: Henry Holt & Co., 2002), P. 8

17   *While German U-boats:* www.rafbombercommand.com

18   *On September 16, 1940:* www.history.com.

19   *In the United States:* George Flynn, *The Draft, 1940–1973* (Lawrence, KS: University of Kansas Press, 1993); "Conscription, World War II," *Americans at War,* John Resch, ed. (Detroit: Macmillan, 2005).

20   *They felt that they:* Heber Holbrook, "The Crisis Years: 1940 and 1941," *Pacific Ship Shore Historical Review,* July 4, 2001; Philip Gerard, "When the Cry Was Over the Hill in October," History News Service, April 30, 2004.

Chapter 4: Fort Knox

21 *Alvey wrote:* Frie Collection, letter, November 7, 1941.

22 *The First Armored Division:* Greg Worth, *1st Armored Division: World War II & Beyond* (Kentucky: Turner Publishing, 2005), p. 10.

23 *This "pyramid of power":* Carlo D'Este, *Patton: A Genius for War* (New York: HarperCollins, 1995).

24 *It initially consisted:* James Klotter, *Kentucky: Portrait in Paradox, 1900–1950* (Frankfurt, KY: Kentucky Historical Society, 2006).

25 *Alvey also frequented the post bowling alley:* Newton Family Collection, letter, February 5, 1942.

26 *In one letter to Robert Frie:* Frie Collection, letter, October 1, 1941.

27 *Still Alvey acknowledged:* Frie Collection, letter, October 1, 1941.

28 *Alvey also commented:* Frie Collection, letter, October 1, 1941.

29 *He related another episode:* Frie Collection, letter, October 1, 1941.

30 *The recruits practiced:* Frie Collection, letter, November 1, 1941.

31 *They were also:* Frie Collection, letter, November 7, 1941.

32 *He chided Robert Frie:* Frie Collection, letter, November 7, 1941.

33 *Alvey told his mom and dad:* Newton Family Collection, letter, January 8, 1942.

34 *A staff sergeant:* Frie Collection, letter, January 19, 1942.

35 *In fact, he said:* Frie Collection, letter, January 28, 1942.

36 *Alvey wrote home:* Newton Family Collection, letter, April 1, 1942.

Chapter 5: Transit

37 *Two Days Later:* Newton Family Collection, letter, April 10, 1942.

38 *He really enjoyed live firing:* Newton Family Collection, letter, April 27, 1942.

39 *In a letter to Robert Frie:* Frie Collection, letter, May 3, 1942.

40 *He remarked that he had seen:* Frie Collection, letter, May 23, 1942.

41 *Alvey went into New York City:* Frie Collection, letter, June 2, 1942.

42 *He also visited Philadelphia:* Frie Collection, letter, May 23, 1942.

43 *On May 28, 1942:* Newton Family Collection, letter, May 28, 1942.

44 *The next letter:* Newton Family Collection, letter, USO letterhead, undated.

45 *On July 3, 1942:* Newton Family Collection, letter, July 3, 1942.

Chapter 6: Mount Panther — Northern Ireland

46 *For weeks Alvey kept writing:* Newton Family Collection, letter, June 6, 1942.

47 *However, in 1990:* Author interview of Hubert Olson.

48 *The Thomas H. Barry:* David Grover, *US Army Ships and Watercraft of World War II* (Annapolis, MD: Naval Institute Press, 1987); Joseph Byofsky, *The Technical Services – The Transportation Corps: Operations Overseas* (Washington, DC: Center of Military History, US Army, 1996), p. 74; George Howe, *The Battle History of the 1st Armored Division* (Washington, DC: Association of the US Army, 1954), p. 16.

49 *But its men and tanks:* "United States Army in World War II: United States Army Forces in Northern Ireland Stations of Units," www.history.army.mil/reference/Ireland/nistat.htm.

50 *In a letter to Robert Frie:* Frie Collection, letter, August 7, 1942.

51 *With the bravado of an American youth:* Frie Collection, letter, October 18, 1942.

52 *For the first time:* Frie Collection, letter, August 7, 1942.

53 *On August 21, 1942:* Frie Collection, letter, August 21, 1942.

54 *A trooper named Fuentes:* Frie Collection, letter, October 18, 1942.

55 *On another occasion:* Frie Collection, letter, September 2, 1942.

56 *He spoke frequently:* Frie Collection, letter, September 28, 1942.

57 *They also had opportunities:* Frie Collection, letter, November 26, 1942.

58 *The men had spent:* Howe, pp. 22–23.

59 *But the vessels:* Atkinson, *An Army at Dawn*, p. 53.

Part III: THE MOUNTAINS OF THE MOON

Chapter 7: Operation Torch

60 *In his memoir:* Hamilton Howze, *A Cavalryman's Story* (Washington, DC: Smithsonian Institution, 1996), p. 43.

61 *In fact, he later lamented:* Atkinson, *An Army at Dawn*, p. 53.

62 *The code name:* Howe, p. 17.

63 *He kept repeating:* Atkinson, *An Army at Dawn*, p. 318.

64 *Even Herr Hitler:* Albert Speer, *Inside the Third Reich* (New York: Macmillan, 1970), p. 246.

65 *One such incident:* Frie Collection, letter, January 29, 1943.

66 *Indeed, the commander:* Atkinson, *An Army at Dawn*, p. 374.

Chapter 8: Algeria — The Mountain of the Lions

67 *Il Duce was doubly:* Colin Baxter, *The War in North Africa, 1940–1943* (Westport, Conn: Greenwood, 1996), p. 43.

68 *Over 15,000 German troops:* Atkinson, *An Army at Dawn*, pp. 319–320; www.history.army.mil

69   *Alvey wrote his first letters:* Newton Family Collection, and Frie Collection, December 23, 1942.

70   *The name "Oran" derives:* www.visitoran.com

71   *Alvey said that he wished:* Frie Collection, letter, December 23, 1942.

72   *Each US soldier was given: A Pocket Guide to North Africa* (Washington, DC: US War and Navy Departments, Government Printing Office, 1942).

73   *Alvey said that he and (Everett) Gregg:* Frie Collection, letter, December 23, 1942.

Chapter 9: Tunisia — Prelude

74   *Hence, Operation Satin:* Atkinson, *An Army at Dawn*, p. 303.

75   *Of his 96,000:* Earle Rice, *Erwin J. E. Rommel* (New York: Chelsea House, 2004), pp. 68–69; William Shirer, *The Rise and Fall of the Third Reich* (New York: Simon & Schuster, 1960), p. 76.

76   *Alvey's next letter:* Frie Collection, letter, January 19, 1943.

77   *Alvey again wrote Robert Frie:* Frie Collection, letter, January 29, 1943.

78   *While in Africa:* Frie Collection, letter fragment, undated.

79   *On February 8, 1943:* Frie Collection, letter, February 8, 1943.

80   *His last letter:* Newton Family Collection, letter, February 13, 1943.

81   *It is unfortunate:* Howe, p. 143.

PART IV: THE CHARGE OF THE LIGHT BRIGADE WITH TANKS

Chapter 10: Sidi Bou Zid — The Killing Zone

82   *The return trip was delayed by sporadic gunfire:* Dwight D. Eisenhower, *Crusade in Europe* (New York: Doubleday, 1948), pp. 142–143.

83 *Upon reaching Fredendall's compound:* Charles Whiting, *Kasserine: The Battlefield Slaughter of American Troops by Rommel's Afrika Korps* (New York, Stein and Day, 1984), p. 170; Note that Kay Summersby Morgan has a slightly different account: "The next thing I knew, he was in the tent, spreading out his sleeping bag on another cot. In minutes he was snoring like a one-man artillery bombardment," Kay Summersby Morgan, *Past Forgetting: My Love Affair with Dwight D. Eisenhower* (New York: Simon & Schuster, 1976), p. 128.

84 *Eisenhower asked a staffer:* Atkinson, *An Army at Dawn*, p. 331.

85 *American General Lucian Truscott:* Steven L. Ossad, "Command Failures: Lessons Learned from Lloyd R. Fredendall," *Army Magazine,* November 20, 2008.

86 *Eisenhower was seemingly:* Atkinson, *An Army at Dawn*, p. 332.

87 *Robinett was the most:* Atkinson, *An Army at Dawn*, pp. 333–334; Paul Robinett, *Armor Command* (Washington, DC: McGregor & Werner, 1958), pp. 161–162.

88 *Many have acknowledged that:* Charles Messenger, *Rommel: Leadership Lessons from the Desert Fox* (New York: Palgrave Macmillan, 2009), p. 181; Robert Greene, *The 33 Strategies of War* (New York: Penguin, 2007); Ronald Lewin, *Rommel as Military Commander,* synopsis (New York: Ballantine, 1972).

89 *At 1500 hours Alger: The Attack on Sidi Bou Zid,* narrative composed by officers of Second Battalion, First Armored Regiment while prisoners of war, undated, James D. Alger Collection, US Military Academy Archives; Angus McKellar, *From Turmoil to Triumph* (Birmingham, MI: Brookside Publications, 1987), p. 9.

90 *At 0400 hours: The Attack on Sidi Bou Zid,* narrative; McKellar, p. 9.

91 *This conclusion is due:* Frie Collection, undated letter from PG 204, Altamura, Italy.

92 *Also, Winkler told me in 1991:* Letter from Province M. Winkler to author, February 26, 1991.

93 *In 1992, I located Al Urbanovsky:* Author telephone interview, 1992.

94 *Winkler recalled:* Letter from Province M. Winkler to author, February 26, 1991.

95 *She told me that Lee:* Letter from Mary Kaser to author, December 2, 1990.

96 *Captain Machus, who:* McKellar, pp. 33, 35.

97 *Not long after this: The Attack on Sidi Bou Zid,* narrative composed by officers, Second Battalion, First Armored Regiment while prisoners of war, undated, James D. Alger Collection, US Military Academy Archives; McKellar, p. 31.

98 *The conclusion made:* W.G.E. Jackson, *The War in North Africa* (New York: Mason/Charter, 1975), p. 423.

99 *Alger fully concurred: The Attack on Sidi Bou Zid,* narrative; McKellar, p. xii, foreword by James D. Alger.

100 *After the war: The Attack on Sidi Bou Zid,* narrative.

101 *The Germans grilled the prisoners: The Attack on Sidi Bou Zid,* narrative.

102 *During the apex of the campaign:* Atkinson, *An Army at Dawn,* p. 374.

Chapter 11: The Aftermath

103 *But as LTC Alger: The Attack on Sidi Bou Zid,* narrative.

104 *In a battlefield survey:* Howe, p. 164 (map).

105 *During the morning of February 17, 1943:* McKellar, pp. 44–45.

106 *Many were suffering:* Evalynn Quisenberry, *Zulah Dawson Ray: His Stories* (Los Angeles: self-published, 1988), p. 42.

107 *While Ray and Alvey:* Quisenberry, p. 36.

108 *But Zulah Ray told me:* Author personal interview with Zulah Ray.

109 *Meanwhile, Alvey had written:* Newton Family Collection, postcard, February 28, 1943.

110 *The most compelling example:* "Prigionieri Americani Feriti Sbarcati in Italia," list of wounded American prisoners of war held in Italy, Vatican Secretary of State; Obituary, Stanley A. Macieiski, *Belleville (IL) News-Democrat,* December 18, 2001.

111 *Alvey sent an Italian form postcard:* Newton Family Collection, postcard, March 4, 1943.

112 *While at PG 204:* Frie Collection, undated letter.

113 *His next letter:* Newton Family Collection, undated letter from PG 75, transit camp near Bari, Italy.

114 *Alvey also wrote:* Frie Collection, undated letter from PG 75, transit camp near Bari, Italy.

115 *It is unlikely:* Newton Family Collection, undated letter, presumably from PG 59, Servigliano, Italy.

PART V: CAPTIVITY AND ESCAPE

Chapter 12: Servigliano — Camp 59

116 *The prisoners slept on wooden beds:* Dispatches from American Legation in Bern, Switzerland, to US State Department, reports on Camp 59, Italy.

117 *Francis Cecil "Dick" George of the Royal Navy:* www.bbc.co.uk/ history

118 *Although the Swiss Legation:* Harry Brundidge, "He Lived through Hell," *Cosmopolitan,* July/August 1944; author personal interview with Zulah Ray.

119 *Keith Argraves reported:* George Chambers, *Keith Argraves Paratrooper* (Nashville: Southern Publishing Association, 1946), p. 69.

120 *The Swiss Legation:* Dispatches from American Legation in Bern, Switzerland, to US State Department, reports on Camp 59, Italy.

121 *Alvey wrote a postcard:* Newton Family Collection, postcard, May 14, 1943; Frie Collection, postcard, May 14, 1943.

122 *He followed with a letter:* Newton Family Collection, letter, May 21, 1943.

123 *On June 23, 1943:* Newton Family Collection, letter, June 23, 1943.

124 *Alvey wrote to his mom and dad:* Newton Family Collection, letter, July 1943.

125 *He sent his mother a postcard:* Newton Family Collection, postcard, July 28, 1943.

126 *The final full length letter:* Frie Collection, letter, August 18, 1943.

Chapter 13: Through The Wall

127 *That night, Allied radio:* Atkinson, *The Day of Battle* (New York: Henry Holt, 2008), p. 195; Philip Morgan, *The Fall of Mussolini: Italy, the Italians and the Second World War* (New York: Oxford University Press, 2008).

128 *That same night, President Roosevelt:* FDR Fireside Chat No. 26, September 8, 1943, Franklin D. Roosevelt Presidential Library.

129 *One of the escapees:* Harry Brundidge, "He Lived through Hell," *Cosmopolitan*, July/Aug 1944.

130 *Zulah Ray knew Huddleston:* Author personal interview with Zulah Ray.

131 *Zulah Ray believed:* Quisenberry, pp. 50–51.

132 *Brundidge and another reporter:* Frederick Close, *Tokyo Rose: An American Patriot* (Lanham, MD: Scarecrow Press, 2009); "Investigation — Tokyo Rose," *History Detectives*, 2009, pbs. org; Glenn Beck, *Miracles and Massacres* (New York: Threshold Editions, 2013), chapter 9.

133 *Thus, according to popular:* Tom Carver, *Where the Hell Have You Been?* (London: Short Books, 2009); www.tomcarver.net

134 *An account by historian Dr. Giuseppe Millozzi:* Giuseppe Millozzi, "Allied Prisoners of War in the Region of the Marche and Prison Camp at Servigliano."

135   *First, Keith Argraves:* Chambers, pp. 74–76.

136   *Agraves tells the story:* Chambers, pp. 74–76.

137   *Second, Zulah Ray:* Quisenberry, pp. 49–54.

138   *A British SAS soldier:* Richard Dorney, *An Active Service* (Solihull, West Midlands, UK: 2006), p. 129.

139   *Charlie Smith confirms:* Ruby Smith, *Wine, Cheese & Bread* (Austin, TX: Woodburner Publishing, 1998), p. 70.

140   *At the time of the escape:* Letters from Ila Van Arsdale to author, April 15, 1992, and May 1, 1992.

141   *Zulah Ray said that when the shower door:* Quisenberry, p. 54.

142   *Kenneth Lightbody told me:* Author personal interview with Kenneth Lightbody.

143   *Zulah Ray told me:* Author personal interview with Zulah Ray.

Chapter 14: Brave Men

144   *Shortly after the escape:* Quisenberry, pp. 61–72.

145   *Soon, near Montefalcone:* Quisenberry, p. 74.

146   *What follows is Zulah's account:* Quisenberry, pp. 90–91.

147   *He called me:* Author telephone interview with Raymond Cox.

148   *I also met Hubert:* Author personal interview with Hubert Olson.

149   *I spoke with Charlie:* Author telephone interview with Charles Lum; letter from Charles Lum to author, January 10, 1992.

150   *He was nicknamed Trapper:* Quisenberry, p. 35.

151   *Zulah Ray recounted:* Quisenberry, p. 68.

152   *One day, living up to his reputation:* Quisenberry, pp. 96–97.

153   *Ken told me:* Author personal interview with Kenneth Lightbody.

154   *Grossman sent me:* Letters from Ferree Grossman to author, October 22, 1991, and January 31, 1992.

155   *Robert told me:* Author telephone interview with Robert J. Noah.

156   *He was treating our wounded:* Author telephone interview with Dr. Erly J. Gallo.

157   *I first learned about "Doc" Gallo:* Joseph Frelinghuysen, *Passages to Freedom* (Manhattan, KS: Sunflower University Press, 1990), p. 64.

158   *"Doc" Gallo and some others:* Author telephone interview with Dr. Erly J. Gallo.

159   *I later heard from:* Author telephone interview with Dr. Erly J. Gallo.

160   *After the war:* Letters from Jack Hunter to author, January 25, 1991; April 26, 1991; and December 19, 1991.

161   *Vern Linker called me:* Author telephone interview with Vern Linker.

162   *Serrano was a paratrooper:* Harry Sions, "The Partisan from Brooklyn," *Yank,* September 1, 1944.

163   *The local historian, Angelo Paci:* Author personal interview with Angelo Paci, at Servigliano, Italy, July 1999.

164   *Dan McAnally was:* Letter to author from Mary McAnally, June 26, 1992; undated Bucks County Community College Campus Notes article; letters to author from Ila Van Arsdale, April 15, 1992, and May 1, 1992.

165   *I found the details concerning Argraves:* Letters to author from Charles Doyle, November 2, 1992, and December 30, 1992; letter to author from Warren Decker, dated September 13, 1992; author telephone interviews with Charles Doyle and Warren Decker.

166   *In his own book:* Chambers, pp. 74–76.

167   *Decker told me:* Letter to author from Warren Decker, September 13, 1992; author telephone interview with Warren Decker.

168   *Argraves account recalls:* Chambers, p. 87.

169   *His band arrived:* Chambers, pp. 88–89.

170   *Keith related that five feet of snow:* Chambers, pp. 98–102.

171   *Those who had identification:* Chambers, pp. 102–109.

172 *Joe Meredith was:* Letter to author from Joseph Meredith, February 4, 1992.

173 *Elmer Reece escaped:* Letter to author from Elmer Reece, July 14, 1992.

174 *James Kavana was captured:* Letter to author from James Kavana, February 9, 1992.

175 *Red Simmons spoke:* Letter to author from Charles K. "Red" Simmons, February 6, 1992.

176 *Homer Lewis remembered:* Letter to author from Homer Lewis, February 7, 1992.

177 *Clarence Dust and a buddy:* Letter to author from Clarence Dust, February 8, 1992.

178 *Steve Schweitz was captured:* Letter to author from Steve Schweitz, February 15, 1992.

179 *Leo Keating was with:* Letter to author from Leo Keating, March 18, 1992.

180 *In one of his letters:* Frie Collection, letter, July 7, 1943.

181 *Joe took the time:* Letter to author from Joe Rowland, August 5, 1992.

PART VI: BESIDE THE RIVER ASO

Chapter 15: Beware the Ides of March

182 *In reply she received:* Newton Family Collection, letter from War Department, October 5, 1943.

183 *The family was also provided: Chicago Daily News,* interoffice memo from Elliott Crooks to Jim Puett, May 19, 1944.

184 *The most dreadful news:* Newton Family Collection, letter from First Armored Division chaplain, November 7, 1944; letter from War Department, November 8, 1944.

185 *It does appear:* US National Archives, Records Group 153, Judge Advocate General, War Crimes Case Files Nos. 16-34, 16-203, and 16-396.

186   *Corporal Herman I. Noble:* US War Crimes Files, sworn testimony of Herman I. Noble, July 1, 1944.

187   *On May 16, 1944:* US War Crimes Files, sworn testimony of Arthur S. Elliott, May 16, 1944.

188   *Curiously, there is also:* US War Crimes Files, recorded and indexed statement of Arthur S. Elliott.

189   *Francis A. Thomas was:* US War Crimes Files, sworn testimony of Francis A. Thomas, September 26, 1946.

190   *Walter Simon was also:* US War Crimes Files, sworn testimony of Walter John Simon, June 26, 1946.

191   *Neil Torssell was:* US War Crimes Files, sworn testimony of Neil Torssell, August 22, 1945.

192   *Pfc. Laurence Danich:* US War Crimes Files, sworn testimony of Laurence Danich, September 10, 1945.

193   *Bull Seldon was a corporal:* US War Crimes Files, sworn testimony of Kenneth G. Seldon, September 5, 1945.

194   *Staff Sergeant Worth Hampton:* US War Crimes Files, sworn testimony of Worth Columbus Hampton, August 8, 1944.

195   *Doc and Tony drove:* Author personal interviews with Robert J. Frie, MD.

196   *The following is an:* Frie Collection, letter to Susan Newton from Robert Frie, unsent, August 15, 1964.

197   *Here are excerpts:* Filippo Ierano, interview given by Cesare Viozzi, "Avevano Appiccato Il Fuoco" ("They Set It On Fire"), *Antigone nelle Valle del Tenna,* July 2001.

198   *According to the Viozzi family:* E-mail to author from Marco Viozzi, December 23, 2013.

Chapter 16: Crimini di Guerra

199   *On October 18, 1942:* Commando Order – Document 498-PS, *Nazi Conspiracy and Aggression,* vol. III (Washington, DC: US Government Printing Office, 1946).

200   *In the spirit of this barbarous:* German commander, Servigliano,

"Warning," September 22, 1943, Monte San Martino Trust; Millar, Derek memoirs.

201 *This was not an isolated incident:* US War Crimes Files, sworn testimony of Moses Melmed, May 2, 1944.

202 *Moe Melmed gave the following:* US War Crimes Files, sworn testimony of Moses Melmed, May 2, 1944.

203 *Leroy Thurman escaped:* US War Crimes Files, sworn testimony of Leroy Thurman, May 1, 1945.

204 *Manuel Serrano was with the partisans:* US War Crimes Files, sworn testimony of Manuel Serrano, September 18, 1945.

205 *Gus Teel was a private:* US War Crimes Files, sworn testimony of Gus Oliver Teel, August 26, 1946.

206 *Simon was at Comunanza:* US War Crimes Files, sworn testimony of Walter John Simon, June 26, 1946.

207 *Thomas was also at Comunanza:* US War Crimes Files, sworn testimony of Francis A. Thomas, September 26, 1946.

208 *One historian has estimated:* Hans-Jurgen Schlamp, interview of Carolo Gentile, University of Cologne, Der Spiegel Online, December 20, 2012.

209 *UK researcher Brian Sims provided me:* British National Archives, Records Group 310, War Crimes Files, Nos. WO 310/198, 310/51, 60 Section, Special Investigation Branch.

210 *Another war crime of particular moment:* Robert Katz, *Death in Rome* (New York: Macmillan, 1967); Klaus Wigriefe, "Unpunished Massacre in Italy: How Postwar Germany Let War Criminals Go Free." Spiegel Online International, January 19, 2012; law reports of the War Crimes Commission, 1947.

211 *Yet another war crime:* Proceedings of the International Military Tribunal, Nuremberg, Germany, vol. 4, H.M. Stationery, p.8; "German General Sentenced to Die For Slaying Yanks," *Pittsburgh Press,* October 12, 1945.

Chapter 17: Mad Roscioli

212 *As far as I have:* Central Register of War Criminals of the United Nations War Crimes Commission (CROWCASS); Consolidated Wanted List.

213 *In March 1992:* Letter to author from W. T. Miller, March 23, 1992.

214 *They sent him a newspaper article:* Undated article from *Voce Adriatica*, circa 1946.

215 *On January 3, 2014:* British National Archives, Records Group 310, War Crimes Files, Nos. WO 310/198, 310/51, 60 Section, Special Investigation Branch.

216 *As I understand it:* SS Scillin WW2 People's War – BBC; www.wrecksite.eu.

217 *Further research revealed:* *Toronto Daily Star,* May 21, 1945; *Ottawa Citizen,* May 21, 1945.

218 *As far as I:* "Euprazione e amnistia alla fine della II guerra mondiale" (Purge and amnesty at the end of World War II), note 21, Dissertation: Albertini, Federico, Universita di Bologna, 2002.

219 *The most telling:* US National Archives, Records Group 153, Judge Advocate General, War Crimes Case Files Nos. 16-34, 16-203, and 16-396.

220 *Then there is a document:* US National Archives, Records Group 153, Judge Advocate General, War Crimes Case Files Nos. 16-34, 16-203, and 16-396.

221 *The file materials provided by Brian Sims:* Alberto Orlandi Report, British National Archives, Records Group 310, War Crimes Files, Nos. WO 310/198, 310/51, 60 Section, Special Investigation Branch.

222 *Here is his report:* CSM Cohen Report, British National Archives, Records Group 310, War Crimes Files, Nos. WO 310/198, 310/51, 60 Section, Special Investigation Branch.

223 *One of the most striking:* Alberto Orlandi Report, British

National Archives, Records Group 310, War Crimes Files, Nos. WO 310/198, 310/51, 60 Section, Special Investigation Branch.

224 *The Americans did investigate:* US National Archives, Records Group 153, Judge Advocate General, War Crimes Case Files Nos. 16-34, 16-203, and 16-396.

225 *The Docket Sheet:* US National Archives, Records Group 153, Judge Advocate General, War Crimes Case Files Nos. 16-34, 16-203, and 16-396.

226 *There is also a document:* US National Archives, Records Group 153, Judge Advocate General, War Crimes Case Files Nos. 16-34, 16-203, and 16-396.

227 *A document prepared:* US National Archives, Records Group 153, Judge Advocate General, War Crimes Case Files Nos. 16-34, 16-203, and 16-396.

228 *One extreme example:* "Accused SS Major Says US Shielded Him," *Chicago Tribune,* January 20, 1997; Der Spiegel Online, January 20, 1997.

229 *Turning a blind eye became routine:* Angelo Iacovella, L'Orientalista Guerriero. Omaggio a Pio Filippani. Ronconi, Rimini, Il Cerchio, 2011; Piscitelli, Alfonso. Esoterismo e Fascismo: Suggestioni esoteriche nelle SS italiane. Rome. Edizioni Mediteranee, 2006.

230 *Another example of justice denied:* Richard Lamb, *War in Italy* (New York: Capo Press, 1996), pp. 35–36; British National Archives, Records Group 235, File No. 235/139

231 *Cabinet Minister Mirko Tremaglia:* "Italians Grow Nostalgic for the Days of Mussolini." *Guardian,* September 9, 2001.

Chapter 18: The Brandenburgers

232 *Prior to receiving:* Franz Kurowski, *The Brandenburgers – Global Mission* (Winnepeg, Canada; J.J. Federowicz Publishing, 2006); Eric Lefevre, *Brandenburg Division*

Commandos of the Reich (Paris: Histoire & Collections, 2000); Ian Westwell, *Brandenburgers: The Third Reich's Special Forces*, (Hersham Surrey, UK: Ian Allan Publishing, 2003); www. axishistory.com — Division Brandenburg.

233   *One of their most notorious missions:* Kurowski, p. 208.

234   *Yet, elements of the Third Brandenburg Regiment:* Hannes Heer, *War of Extermination: The German Military in World War II* (New York: Berghahn Books, 2004), p. 191.

235   *The US files said that:* US National Archives, Records Group 153, Judge Advocate General, War Crimes Case Files Nos. 16-34, 16-203, and 16-396.

236   *The previously referenced report:* Alberto Orlandi Report, British National Archives, Records Group 310, War Crimes Files, Nos. WO 310/198, 310/51, 60 Section, Special Investigation Branch.

237   *The British War Crimes file number W0310/198:* British National Archives, Records Group 310, War Crimes Files, Nos. WO 310/198, 60 Section, Special Investigation Branch.

238   *A composite picture of the documents in this file:* British National Archives, Records Group 310, War Crimes Files, Nos. WO 310/198, 60 Section, Special Investigation Branch.

239   *An interesting aside:* Chambers, 100.

240   *One clue that Argraves and Decker are mistaken:* Chambers, 103.

241   *According to Argraves:* Chambers, p. 105.

242   *It does bear mentioning here:* Robert Graham, S.J., "Foreign Intelligence and the Vatican," *Catholic World Report*, March 1992; David Alvarez and Robert Graham, S.J., *Nothing Sacred: Nazi Espionage Against the Vatican, 1935–1945* (New York: Routledge, 1998).

243   *In his report:* Alberto Orlandi Report, British National Archives, Records Group 310, War Crimes Files, Nos. WO 310/198, 310/51, 60 Section, Special Investigation Branch.

244 *I recently discovered a photograph:* "Rommel's Nephew Gets Ready for Christmas," *Leicester Mercury,* December 17, 1946 (posted online December 23, 2013).

245 *There is also an unrelated:* "Rommel's Nephew Linked to War Crime," *U.K. Guardian,* May 9, 2001.

246 *Padre Leight testified:* British National Archives, Records Group 310, War Crimes Files, Nos. WO 310/198, 310/51, 60 Section, Special Investigation Branch.

247 *Some surviving prisoners of war:* US War Crimes Files, sworn testimony of Laurence Danich, September 10, 1945; author personal interview with Zulah Ray.

248 *Third, there were two Waffen SS:* Christian Ortner, *Marzabotto: The Crimes of Walter Reder – SS Sturmbannfuhrer,* (Vienna: Dokumentationsarchiv der osterreichischen Widerstandes, 1986); Jack Olsen, *Silence on Monte Sole* (New York: Putnam, 1968); Gordon Williamson, *The Waffen SS* (New York: Osprey, 2012).

249 *Witness the following undated proclamation:* CSM Cohen Report, British National Archives, Records Group 310, War Crimes Files, Nos. WO 310/198, 310/51, 60 Section, Special Investigation Branch.

250 *Finally, the British records unearthed:* Alberto Orlandi Report, British National Archives, Records Group 310, War Crimes Files, Nos. WO 310/198, 310/51, 60 Section, Special Investigation Branch.

251 *In a letter to my grandmother:* Frie Collection, letter to Susan Newton, unsent, August 15, 1964.

252 *The US War Crimes files:* US National Archives, Records Group 153, Judge Advocate General, War Crimes Case Files Nos. 16-34, 16-203, and 16-396.

253 *When I read the foregoing account:* Letters to author from Ferree Grossman, October 22, 1991, and January 31, 1992.

254 *A very detailed account:* Camp 59 Survivors: Experiences of

Allied Servicemen Who Were Prisoners of War at Servigliano, Italy, http://www.camp59survivors.wordpress.com.

255   *The investigators reached the conclusion:* British National Archives, Records Group 310, War Crimes Files, Nos. WO 310/198, 310/51, 60 Section, Special Investigation Branch.

256   *Padre Leight had remarked that SS troops:* British National Archives, Records Group 310, War Crimes Files, Nos. WO 310/198, 310/51, 60 Section, Special Investigation Branch.

257   *Count Marcatilli also said:* British National Archives, Records Group 310, War Crimes Files, Nos. WO 310/198, 310/51, 60 Section, Special Investigation Branch.

258   *A-Force special agent Alberto Orlandi:* Alberto Orlandi Report, British National Archives, Records Group 310, War Crimes Files, Nos. WO 310/198, 310/51, 60 Section, Special Investigation Branch.

259   *In sentencing Amery:* "Amery Sentenced to Death: a Self-Confessed Traitor," *Times*, November 29, 1945.

PART VII: RESCUE EFFORTS

Chapter 19: Operations Begonia-Jonquil and Darlington II

260   *The most notable of these:* British National Archives, Records Group 218, No. WO218/181, summary of events; F. H. Fox, "The S.A.S. WWII POW Rescue," *Modern History, Political Science, and Science,* (blog), May 26, 2012, ffoxrt.blogspot.com.

261   *A few days after the announcement:* British National Archives, Records Group 218, No. WO218/181, summary of events; F. H. Fox, "The S.A.S. WWII POW Rescue," *Modern History, Political Science, and Science,* (blog), May 26, 2012, ffoxrt.blogspot.com.

262   *One particular incident:* Captain Power Report, British National Archives, Records Group 218, No. WO218/181, summary of vents; Fox, F.H. "The S.A.S. WWII POW

Rescue." Blog: "Modern History, Political Science and Science. (blog), May 26, 2012, ffoxrt.blogspot.com.

263 *A few men have mentioned to me:* Author telephone interview with Raymond Cox; author personal interviews with Zulah Ray and Kenneth Lightbody.

264 *On the night of May 25–26:* WW2 Escape Lines Memorial Society, www.ww2escapelines.co.uk.

265 *The US Navy Beach Jumpers:* US Navy Beach Jumpers Association, www.beachjumpers.com; Kenneth Macksey, *Commando Special Forces in World War II,* (Michigan: Scarborough House, 1990).

Chapter 20: MIS-X — MI9 — IS9

266 *Two years ago, I became aware:* Lloyd Shoemaker, *The Escape Factory* (New York: St. Martin's Press, 1990); M. R. D. Foot, *MI9 Escape and Evasion* (London: Biteback Publishing, 2011).

267 *It is now known:* Shoemaker, pp. 41, 48–49; Oflag 64 Association, www.oflag64.us.

268 *In Italy, the "ratline":* Foot, pp. 89–99; Wikipedia biography: Curtis Bill Pepper.

269 *Orlandi had this to say:* Alberto Orlandi Report, British National Archives, Records Group 310, War Crimes Files, Nos. WO 310/198, 310/51, 60 Section, Special Investigation Branch.

270 *Samples of these are now:* ww2talk.com; homepage.ntlworld.com

PART VIII: LEGACY

Chapter 21: The Last Full Measure

271 *My grandmother also wrote:* Newton Family Collection, letter from War Department, October 5, 1943.

272 *Somehow, my grandmother also came into possession:* Chicago

Daily News, interoffice memo from Eliott Crooks to Jim Puett, May 19, 1944.

273 *On Saturday, November 11, 1944:* Newton Family Collection, letter from War Department, Adjutant General, November 11, 1944.

274 *On November 13, 1944:* Newton Family Collection, letter to Joseph N. Newton, November 13, 1944.

275 *My father wrote back on November 27:* Newton Family Collection, letter to Susan Newton, November 27, 1944.

276 *He tried to express his deep feelings in a poem:* Newton Family Collection.

277 *Robert Frie wrote to my father overseas:* Newton Family Collection, letter to Joseph N. Newton, January 18, 1945.

278 *The reply came on February 27, 1945:* Newton Family Collection, letter from Provost Marshal, Quartermaster General, February 27, 1945.

279 *The following abstract:* Abstract, October 31, 1944, US National Archives, Records Group 153, Judge Advocate General, War Crimes Case Files Nos. 16-34, 16-203, and 16-396.

280 *On April 28, 1947:* Newton Family Collection, letter from Quartermaster General, April 28, 1947.

281 *A Logansport, Indiana, newspaper announcement:* Undated article, *Pharos-Tribune* (Logansport, IN).

282 *Another clipping:* Undated, unidentified funeral notice, presumably Grayson County, Kentucky.

Chapter 22: Inseparable Be My Thumb and Nose

283 *The abstract in the war crimes files:* Abstract, October 31, 1944, US National Archives, Records Group 153, Judge Advocate General, War Crimes Case Files Nos. 16-34, 16-203, and 16-396.

284   *Another abstract in the same file:* Abstract, August 26, 1944, US National Archives, Records Group 153, Judge Advocate General, War Crimes Case Files Nos. 16-34, 16-203, and 16-396.

285   *He did state in a letter home:* Newton Family Collection, undated letter from Camp 59, Servigliano, Italy.

286   *One interesting fact about Kaywoodie pipes:* Shoemaker, Chapter 14, photograph inserts.

287   *Although the meaning of the gesture:* David McNeill, *Hand and Mind: What Gestures Reveal about Thought* (Chicago: University of Chicago Press, 1992); Joseph Shipley, *The Origins of English Words* (Baltimore: JHU Press, 2001) p. 302; www. urbandictionary.com, "Thumb Your Nose."

288   *Anyhow, a reporter named Linda Torkelson:* "WWII Vets: Nose Thumbing at Its Finest," *Guardian Express* (Las Vegas, NV), Oct. 2, 2013.

Chapter 23: Famiglia Viozzi

289   *Apparently, they derive:* www.heraldryinstitute.com.

290   *One particularly heartrending:* Uys Krige, *The Way Out,* (New York: Collins, 1966), p. 307.

Resources

Books

Abbott, Harry P. *The Nazi "88" Made Believers.* Dayton, OH: Otterbein Press, 1946.

Alvarez, David, and Robert Graham, S.J. *Nothing Sacred: Nazi Espionage Against the Vatican, 1935–1945.* New York: Routledge, 1998.

Atkinson, Rick. *An Army at Dawn.* New York: Henry Holt and Company, 2002.

———. *The Day of Battle.* New York: Henry Holt and Company, 2008.

Ball, Don. *The Pennsylvania Railroad.* Chester, VT: Elm Tree Books, 1986.

Baxter, Collin. *The War in North Africa, 1940–1943.* Westport, CT: Greenwood, 1996.

Blood, Philip. *Hitler's Bandit Hunters.* Washington, DC: Potomac Books, 2006.

Blumenson, Martin. *Kasserine Pass.* New York: Cooper Square Press, 2000.

Brooks, Thomas. *The War North of Rome.* New York: Sarpedon Press, 1996.

Byoksky, Joseph. *The Technical Services – The Transportation Corps: Operations Overseas.* Washington, DC: Center for Military History, US Army, 1996.

Carver, Tom. *Where The Hell Have You Been?* London: Short Books, Ltd., 2009.

Chambers, George. *Keith Argraves Paratrooper.* Nashville: Southern Publishing Association, 1946.

Close, Frederick. *Tokyo Rose: An American Patriot.* Lanham, MD: Scarecrow Press, 2009.

Corso, Max. *The O.S.S. in Italy: 1942–1945, A Personal Memoir.* Westport, CT: Praeger Publishers, 1990.

Crisp, Robert. *Brazen Chariots.* New York: Bantam Press, 1978.

D'Alesio, Dominick. *The Worst Is Yet to Come.* New York: Vantage Press, 2001.

D'Este, Carlo. *Patton: A Genius for War.* New York: HarperCollins, 1995.

Domenico, Roy. *Italian Fascists on Trial 1943–1948.* Chapel Hill: University of North Carolina Press, 1991.

Dorney, Richard. *An Active Service.* Solihull, West Midlands, UK, 2006.

Farmer, Brian. *American Conservatism: History, Theory and Practice.* Newcastle, UK: Cambridge Scholars Publishing, 2005.

Eisenhower, Dwight. *Crusade in Europe.* New York: Doubleday, 1948.

Flynn, George. *The Draft 1940–1973.* Lawrence: The University of Kansas Press, 1993.

Foot, M. R. D., and J. M. Langley, *MI9 Escape and Evasion, 1939–1945.* London: Biteback Publishing, 2011.

Forty, George. *M4 Sherman.* UK: Blandford, 1987.

Frelinghuysen, Joseph. *Passages to Freedom.* Manhattan, KS: Sunflower University Press, 1990.

Greene, Robert. *The 33 Strategies of War.* New York: Penguin, 2007.

Grover, David. *US Army Ships and Watercraft of World War II.* Annapolis, MD: Naval Institute Press, 1987.

Heer, Hannes, and Heer Naumann. *War of Extermination: The German Military in World War II.* Oxford, NY: Berghan Books, 2004.

Howe, George. *The Battle History of the 1st Armored Division.* Washington, DC; Combat Forces Press, 1954.

————. *US Army in World War II: Mediterranean Theater of Operations – Northwest Africa: Seizing the Initiative in the West.* Washington, D.C: Department of the Army, 1957.

Howze, Hamilton. *A Cavalryman's Story.* Washington, DC: Smithsonian Institution Press, 1996.

Iacovella, Angelo. *L'Orientalists Guerriero. Omaggio a Pio Filippani-Ronconi.* Rimini, Italy: Il Cerchio, 2011.

Ierano, Filippo. *Antigone nella Valle del Tenna.* Interview given by Cesare Viozzi, "Avevano Appiccato Il Fuoco" ("They set it on fire.") Quaderni Consiglio Regionalle delle Marche, 2002.

Jackson, W.G.F. *The Battle for North Africa.* New York: Mason/Charter Publishers, 1975.

Katz, Robert. *Death in Rome.* New York: Macmillan, 1967.

Kelly, Orr. *Meeting the Fox.* New York: John Wiley & Sons; 2002.

Kilby, Keith. *In Combat, Unarmed.* Cornwall, UK: Monte San Martino Trust, 2013.

Klotter, James. *Kentucky: Portrait in Paradox, 1900–1950.* Frankfort, KY: Kentucky Historical Society, 2006.

Krige, Uys. *The Way Out.* New York: Collins, 1946.

Kurowski, Franz. *The Brandenburgers – Global Mission.* Winnepeg, Canada: J.J. Federowicz Publishing, 1997.

Lamb, Richard. *War in Italy, 1943–1945.* New York: De Capo Press, 1996.

Lefevre, Eric. *Brandenburg Division Commandos of the Reich.* Paris: Histoire & Collections, 2000.

Lewin, Ronald. *Rommel as Military Commander.* New York: Ballantine, 1972.

Lucas, James. *Panzer Army Africa.* San Rafael, CA: Presidio Press, 1978.

Macksey, Kenneth. *Commando.* Michigan: Scarborough House, 1990.

McKellar, Angus. *Turmoil to Triumph.* Birmingham, MI.: Brookside Publications, 1987.

McNeill, David. *Hand and Mind: What Gestures Reveal About Thought.* Chicago: University of Chicago Press, 1992.

Messenger, Charles. *Rommel: Leadership Lessons from the Desert Fox.* New York: Palgrave Macmillan, 2009.

Morgan, Kay Summersby. *Past Forgetting.* New York: Simon & Schuster, 1976.

Moorehead, Alan. *Desert War.* New York: Penguin Group, 2001.

Morgan, Philip. *The Fall of Mussolini: Italy, The Italians and The Second World War.* New York: Oxford University Press, 2008.

Olsen, Jack. *Silence on Monte Sole.* New York: Putnam, 1968.

Ortner, Christian. *Marzabotto: The Crimes of Walter Reder – SS Stormbannfuhrer.* Vienna: Dokumentationsarchiv der Osterreichischen Widerstandes, 1985.

Piscitelli, Alfonso. *Esoterismo e Fascismo: Suggestioni esoteriche nelle SS italiane.* Rome: Edizioni Mediterranee, 2006.

Pyle, Ernie. *Here Is Your War.* New York: Henry Holt, 1943.

———. *Brave Men.* Lincoln: University of Nebraska Press, 2001.

Quisenberry, Evalynn. *Zulah Dawson Ray: His Stories.* Los Angeles: self-published, 1988.

Rame, David. *Road to Tunis.* New York: Macmillan, 1944.

Resch, John, ed. *Conscription, World War II.* Detroit: Macmillan, 2005.

Rice, Earle. *Erwin J. E. Rommel.* New York: Chelsea House Publications, 2004.

Robinett, Paul. *Armor Command.* Washington, DC: McGregor & Werner, 1958.

Rutherford, Ward. *Kasserine Baptism of Fire.* New York: Ballantine, 1970.

Sexton, Winton. *Back Roads to Freedom.* Kansas City: Lowell Press, 1985.

Shaine, Frederick. *And No Quarter: An Italian Partisan in World War II.* Athens: Ohio University Press, 1972.

Shipley, Joseph. *The Origins of English Words.* Baltimore: JHU Press, 2001.

Shirer, William. *The Rise and Fall of the Third Reich.* New York: Simon & Schuster, 1960.

Shoemaker, Lloyd. *The Escape Factory.* New York: St. Martin's Press, 1990.

Smith, Ruby. *Wine, Cheese & Bread.* Austin, TX: Woodburner Press, 1998.

Speer, Albert. *Inside the Third Reich.* New York: Macmillan, 1970.

Strawson, John. *The Battle for North Africa.* New York: Bonanza Books, 1969.

Summersby, Kay. *Eisenhower Was My Boss.* New York: Prentice-Hall, 1948.

Taber, Graham. *History of Logansport and Cass County.* Pharos-Tribune, Logansport, IN. 1947.

Thoreau, Henry David. *Walden.* New Haven, CT: Yale University Press, 2004.

Tudor, Malcolm. *At War In Italy.* U.K.: Emilia Publishing, 2007.

————.*Escape From Italy 1943–45.* U.K.: Emilia Publishing, 2003.

Von Lingen, Kerstin. *Allen Dulles, the OSS and Nazi War Criminals: The Dynamics of Selective Prosecution.* Cambridge, U.K.: Cambridge University Press, 2013.

Watt, William. *The Pennsylvania Railroad in Indiana.* Bloomington, IN.: Indiana University Press, 2000.

Weckstein, Leon. *200,000 Heroes: Italian Partisans and the American OSS in WWII.* Ashland, OR: Hellgate Press, 2011.

Westwell, Ian. *Brandenburgers: The Third Reich's Special Forces.* Hersham Surrey, U.K.: Ian Allan Publishing, 2003.

Williamson, Gordon. *The Waffen SS.* New York: Osprey Publishing, 2012.

Whiting, Charles. *Kasserine The Battlefield Slaughter of American Troops By Rommel's Afrika Korps.* New York: Stein And Day, 1984.

Worth, Greg. *1st Armored Division: WWII & Beyond.* Kentucky: Turner Publishing, 2005.

Zaloga, Steven. *Kasserine Pass 1943.* New York: Osprey Publishing, 2008.

Zaloga, Steven. *US Armored Units In The North African and Italian Campaigns 1942–45.* New York: Osprey Publishing. 2006.

Periodicals

Brundidge, Harry and Sheehan, Earnest. "He Lived Through Hell." *Cosmopolitan,* Jul/Aug 1944.

DiPrimio, Pete. "What's In A Name?" *Indiana University, Alumni Magazine,* Winter/Spring 2012.

Graham, Robert, S.J. *"Foreign Intelligence and the Vatican."* Catholic World Report, March 1992.

Holbrook, Heber. "The Crisis Years 1940 and 1941." Dixon, CA: *The Pacific Ship and Shore Review,* July 4, 2001.

Newton, Robert. "Ambushed By the Afrika Korps." *World War II Magazine,* Sept. 2002.

Ossad, Steven L. "Command Failures: Lessons Learned From Lloyd R. Fredendall." *Army Magazine,* Nov. 20, 2008.

Schlamp, Hans-Jurgen. Interview of Carolo Gentile. University of Cologne. *Der Spiegel Online,* Dec. 20, 2012.

Sions, Harry. "The Partisan From Brooklyn." *Yank Magazine,* Sept. 1, 1944.

Torssell, Neil. "Italian POW Camp 59, Servigliano, Italy." *Ex-POW Bulletin.* Vol. 49, Oct. 1992.

Wigriefe, Klaus. "Unpunished Massacres In Italy: How Germany Let Criminals Go Free." *Spiegel Online International,* Jan. 19, 2012.

Wolff, Kurt., description of Battle of Sidi Bou Zid, in *Das Reich,* April 11, 1943, translated at the Command and General Staff School, Fort Leavenworth, KS, from Tactics Department, The Armored School, Fort Knox, KY, December 1943.

Newspapers

Alexander, Field Marshal the Viscount. "The African Campaign From El Alamein to Tunis. *Supplement to the London Gazette,* 5 February 1948.

Gerard, Philip. "When The Cry Was Over The Hill In October." *History News Service.* Apr. 30, 2004.

"Italians Grow Nostalgic For The Days of Mussolini." *The Guardian,* Sept. 9, 2001.

Jewett, Hank. "Kienly Shares Colorful Military Career." *Five Cities Times-Press*, Jan. 11, 1995.

"Rommel's Nephew Gets Ready For Christmas." *Leicester Mercury*, Dec. 17, 1946.(Photo Posted online Dec. 23, 2013)

Lichtblau, Eric. *Nazis Were Given 'Safe Haven' In US, Report Says.* The New York Times, Reprints, Nov. 13, 2010.

Ottawa Citizen, May 21, 1945. Capture of Settimio Roscioli in Rome. Pyle, Ernie. "Tank Battle at Sidi Bou Zid: The Tunisian Front. *Scripps-Howard*, Mar. 1, 1943.

"Amery Sentenced to Death: A Self-Confessed Traitor." The *Times*, Nov. 29, 1945.

Torkelson, Linda. "WWII Vets: Nose Thumbing At Its Finest." *Las Vegas Guardian Express*, Oct. 2, 2013.

Toronto Daily Star, May 21, 1945. Capture of Settimio Roscioli in Rome.

"Rommel's Nephew Linked to War Crime." U.K. Guardian, May 9, 2001.

"Roscioli, Criminale di Guerra." *Voce Adriatica*, ca. 1946.

Whitfield, John A. "Newtons Recall Their Past." *The Meade County Messenger*, Brandenburg, KY, Oct. 12, 1994.

Wilson, Jamie. "Rommel's Nephew Linked to War Crime." *The Guardian*, 9 May 2001.

Manuscripts

Albertini, Federico"Euprazione e amnistia alla fine della II guerra mondiale," (Purge and amnesty at the end of World War II), note 21. Dissertation. Universita di Bologna, 2002.

Millozzi, Giuseppe. "Allied Prisoners of War in the region of the Marche and Prison Camp at Servigliano." Dissertation.

Miscellany

"A Pocket Guide to North Africa." War and Navy Departments, Washington, D.C.

Affidavit of Albert Jacob Thompson, Flaherty, KY, Nov. 27, 1929.

Bedell, A.D., et., al. "Battle Analysis of the Battle of Sidi Bou Zid, Tunisia, North Africa, Defensive, Encircled Forces, 14 February 1943." Army Command and General Staff Combat Studies Institute, Fort Leavenworth, KS.

Bucks County Community College. Campus Notes article, "BCCC Security Guard Recalls Flight As POW Escapee." Undated.

Bulletin of the 1ˢᵗ Armored Division Association. "The Lessons of Defeat." Augusta, GA, Spring 1993.

Chicago Daily News. Interoffice Memo from Elliott Crooks to Jim Puett, May 19, 1944.

Hitler's Commando Order – Document 498-PS, "Nazi Conspiracy and Agression," Vol. III. Washington, D.C: United States Government Printing Office.

Kasserine Pass Battles, Maps and Sketches Appendix, US Army Center of Military History.

Newton Family History and Life Album and Biography of Robert Alvey Newton. Compiled by Sue Ann Jargstorf and Marilyn Williams.

Newton, Marcus. Transcribed remarks at Newton-Rhodes family reunion, Flaherty, KY, October 2, 1994.

Pennsylvania Railroad Company, "Inspection of Physical Property by Board of Directors," November 10-11-12, 1948.

Seaweeds Ship's History. *Oriente – USS Thomas H. Barry.*

"Tank, Medium, M4." War Department Technical Manual No. 9-731A, Washington, DC, November 14, 1942.

"Tattler, 1935." Logansport High School Yearbook.

"The Attack on Sidi Bou Zid." Narrative composed by officers, Second Battalion, First Armored Regiment while prisoners of war, undated, James D. Alger Collection, US Military Academy Archives.

"The War in North Africa, Part 1 (Operations in Egypt and Libya)." United States Military Academy, West Point, NY, 1945.

"The War in North Africa, Part 2 (The Allied Invasion)." United States Military Academy, West Point, NY, 1945.

Archival Documents

British National Archives, Records Group 310, War Crimes Files, Nos. WO 310/198, 310/51, 60 Section, Special Investigation Branch, (Courtesy of Researcher Brian Sims.); Records Group 218, File No. 218/181, (Reports on Operations Begonia-Jonquil).

Central Register of War Criminals of the United Nations War Crimes Commission (CROWCASS); Consolidated Wanted List.

Combat Studies Institute, Fort Leavenworth, KS. Combat Studies Institute Battlebook 4-D, "The Battle of Sidi Bou Zid," May 23, 1984.

Dispatches from American Legation in Bern, Switzerland, to US State Department, reports on Camp 59, Italy.

Headquarters, Combat Command B, reports on combat experience and battle lessons for training purposes.

Law reports of the War Crimes Commission, 1947.

"Prigionieri Americani Feriti, Sbarcati In Italia," (list of wounded American prisoners of war held in Italy). Vatican Secretary of State, 1943.

Proceedings of the International Military Tribunal, Nuremberg, Germany, vol. 4. H. M. Stationery, p.8.

Report of British War Crimes Section of Allied Force Headquarters on German Reprisals for Partisan Activities in Italy, Document UK-66, Source: Nazi Conspiracy and Agression, vol. VIII, US Government Printing Office, Washington, 1946, pp. 572–582.

The Trial of German Major War Criminals – Proceedings of the International Military Tribunal, Nuremberg, Germany, vol. 4, H. M. Stationery.

United Nations War Crimes Commission. Central Register for War Criminals (CROWCASS), Consolidated Wanted List.

US Army Military History Institute, Carlisle, PA: Headquarters First Armored Division and First Armored Regiment, records and reports on operations in North Africa; Headquarters First Armored Regiment, casualty lists and lists of awards and citations.

US National Archives, FBI Files Received By NARA – Nazi War Crimes Disclosure Act Alphabetized Chart.

US National Archives, Records Group 153, Judge Advocate General, War Crimes Case Files Nos. 16-34, 16-203 and 16-396 (Robert Alvey Newton, Edwin Martin Majeski and Comunanza).

Blogs and Websites

American Battle Monuments Commission. www.wwiimemorial.com

American Ex-Prisoners of War. www.axpow.com.

Cass County Historical Society: www.casscountyin.tripod.com/CCHSRailroad_History.html.

Cass County Carousel, Inc.: www.casscountycarousel.com/carousel-history/.

Curtis Bill Pepper. www.curtisbillpepper.com.

First Armored Division Association. www.1st-armored-div.com.

Fox, F. H. *Modern History, Political Science and Science.* "The SAS WWII POW Rescue." May 26, 2012. ffoxrt.blogspot.com.

Hill, Dennis. *Camp 59 Survivors: Experiences of the Allied Servicemen Who Were Prisoners of War at Servigliano Italy.* http://camp59survivors.wordpress.com.

Homepage.ntlworld.com.

Lone Sentry. www.lonesentry.com. "Interviews with Officers and Men of the 2nd Battalion, 1st Armored Regiment," April 11, 1943.

Maryland to Kentucky. mdtoky.com.

Monte San Martino Trust. www.msmtrust.org.uk.

Oflag 64 Association. www.oflag64.us.

Scottish Rite Masonic Museum & Library, Inc. National Heritage Museum (Ulys Family Collection). www.nationalheritagemuseum.org

US Navy Beach Jumpers Association. www.beachjumpers.com.

WW2 Escape Lines Memorial Society. www.ww2escapelines.co.uk.

www.heraldryinstitute.com.

ww2talk.com.

www.urbandictionary.com. "Thumb Your Nose."

www.wrecksite.eu. SS Scillin.

Correspondence

Abrams, Bernie. Letter to author, February 29, 1992.

Ainsworth, Joseph. Letter to author, February 4, 1992.

Amos, Clovis. Letter to author, April 3, 1992.

Barone, Mario. Letter to author, February 26, 1992

Baum, Clair. Letter to author, January 2, 1994.

Beasley, Bill. Letter to author, June 4, 1990.

Blackman, Shelby. Letter to author, December 21, 1993.

Caldwell, Philip. Letters to author, June 27, 1990, August 22, 1990, and November 1, 1990.

Davidson, William. Letter to author, March 25, 1992.

Decker, Warren. Letter to author, September 13, 1992.

Delanoy, Howard, S. Letter to author, September 17, 1992.

DeSalvo, Ralph. Letter to author, April 4, 1992.

Downes, R.J. Letter to author, October 23, 1992.

Doyle, Charles. Letters to author, November 2, 1992, and December 30, 1992.

Drazkowski, Mary. Letter to author, February 3, 1992.

Dust, Clarence M. Letter to author, February 8, 1992.

Fix, C. Peter and June. Letters to author, April 13, 1990, and July 18, 1991.

Frelinghuysen, Joseph. Letter to author, December 16, 1992.

Frie, Robert J. Collection of World War II Letters from Robert Alvey Newton, 1941–1943.

Froelich, Alvin. Letter to author, December 22, 1993.

Garone, John. Letter to author, February 3, 1992.

Grossman, Ferree. Letters to author, October 22, 1991, and January 31, 1992.

Herman, Edward. Letters to author, October 20, 1992, and February 1, 1993.

Heslep, William. Letter to author, September 19, 1990.

Hill, Armie and Eini. Letter to author, February 12, 1992.

Holm, Eric and Mary. Letters to author, January 2, 1991, and August 28, 1991.

Holtzman, Charles. Letter to author, February 29, 1992.

Hunter, Jack. Letters to author, January 25, 1991, April 26, 1991, and December 19, 1991.

Kane, Henry. Letter to author, March 1, 1992.

Kaser, Mary. Letters to author, May 20, 1991, December 2, 1990, June 10, 1991, and December 18, 1991.

Kaser, Robert. Letters to author, June 13, 1990, and August 2, 2002.

Kaser, William. Letter to author, May 16, 1990.

Kavana, James. Letter to author, February 9, 1992.

Keating, Leo. Letter to author, March 18, 1992.

Kreisch, Michael. Letter to author, July 31, 1992.

Lamb, William. Letter to author, July 25, 1992.

Lewis, Homer. Letter to author, February 7, 1992.

Letter, Walter. Letter to author, February 10, 1992.

Line, Stanley. Letter to author, January 7, 1991.

Lipscomb, Jesse. Letter to author, December 15, 1993.

Lum, Charles. Letter to author, January 10, 1992.

Machus, Harris O. Letter to author, October 27, 1992.

McAnally, Mary. Letter to author, June 26, 1992.

Meredith, Joseph. Letter to author, April 6, 1993.

Merritt, Russ. Letter to author, October 3, 1992.

Miller, W. T. Letters to author, February 17, 1992, and March 23, 1992.

Moore, A. Robert. Letters to author, September 18, 1990, and September 27, 1990.

Newton Family. Collection of World War II Letters from Robert Alvey Newton, as well as friends and family members, 1941–1944.

Noah, Robert J. Sr. Letter to author, May 21, 1992.

Parsons, Dickson. Letter to author, February 8, 1993.

Ray, Zulah D. Letter to author, June 26, 1991.

Reece, Elmer. Letter to author, July 14, 1992.

Rowland, Joe. Letter to author, August 5, 1992.

Sanders, James. Letter to author, February 8, 1992.

Schweitz, Steve. Letter to author, February 15, 1992.

Simmons, Charles. Letter to author, February 6, 1992.

Six, Kelly. Letter to author, February 22, 1991.

Skinner, Tevis. Letter to author, February 12,1992

Smith, Charles. Letter to author, March 18, 1992

Sweeten, William. Letter to author, November 30, 1992.

Van Arsdale, Ila. Letters to author, April 15, 1992, and May 1, 1992.

Whitaker, Dorothy. Letter to author, June 24, 1992.

Williams, Paul. Letter to author, January 6, 1993.

Winkler, Province M. Letters to author, February 26, 1991, March 12, 1991, April 4, 1991, and January 28, 1992.

Author Interviews

Paul Alsin; William "Bill" Beasley; Timothy Bosanoz; Warren Decker; Raymond Cox; Clyde Fitz; C. Peter Fix; Robert J. Frie, MD; Erly Paul Gallo, MD; Eric Holm; Robert Kaser; William Kaser; Joe Kienly; Clifford Larkin; Kenneth

Lightbody; Vern Linker; Charles Lum; A. Robert Moore; Robert J. Noah Sr.; Hubert Olson; Angelo Paci; John Procko; Zulah Ray; Gerald "Tex" Rowland; Alphonse Urbanovsky; Dino Viozzi; Gino Viozzi; Giuseppe Viozzi; and Maria Viozzi.

Index

Page locators in *italics* indicate photographs and maps.

war crimes (continued)
  repatriated POW
    questionnaires, 267–68
  Roscioli's arrest and trial,
    216–20
  tribunals, 216–22
War Department, 34, 44, 83,
    174–75, 221, 273–74, 275–76
Ward, Orlando "Pinky," 55, 73, 76
Werner, Frank, 220
White, David, 215
White, Thomas, 208
Williams, Marilyn Newton, *169*,
  302
Winchell, Walter, 113
Wine, Cheese, and Bread (Smith),
  130
Winkler, Province, 62–63, 66, 78,
  81, 82–83, 84, 90, 95
women
  Muslim women in North
    Africa, 60
  wartime dating and
    lovemaking, 32, 46, 48
  WAVEs and WACs, 60
World War II
  outbreak of, 25–28
  and Spanish Civil War, 25–26
  World War II memorial,
    287–88
Wormes, Eugene, 5
Wright, Ronald Selby, 114

X
X-2 OSS division, 256, 257

Z
Zulah Dawson Ray (Quisenberry),
  115, 124